FILM GENRE 2000

◻

New Critical Essays

Edited by

WHEELER WINSTON DIXON

STATE UNIVERSITY OF NEW YORK PRESS

Published by
State University of New York Press, Albany

Printed in the United States of America

For information, address State University of New York Press,
State University Plaza, Albany, N.Y., 12246

Production by Marilyn P. Semerad
Marketing by Dana Yanulavich

Library of Congress Cataloging-in-Publication Data

Film genre 2000 : new critical essays / edited by Wheeler Winston
    Dixon.
        p.   cm. — (The SUNY series, cultural studies in cinema/video)
    Includes bibliographical references and index.
    ISBN 0-7914-4513-5 (hardcover : alk. paper). — ISBN 0-7914-4514-3
(pbk. : alk. paper)
    1. Film genres—United States. I. Dixon, Wheeler W., 1950–
II. Title: Film genre two thousand. III. Series.
PN1995.F45787 2000
791.43´6—dc21
                                                            99-29901
                                                                CIP

10 9 8 7 6 5 4 3 2 1

FILM GENRE 2000

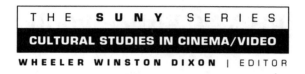

THE **SUNY** SERIES

CULTURAL STUDIES IN CINEMA/VIDEO

WHEELER WINSTON DIXON | EDITOR

CONTENTS

ILLUSTRATIONS

---◼---

CHAPTER ONE

◙

Introduction:
The New Genre Cinema

WHEELER WINSTON DIXON

One of the peculiar characteristics of American genre filmmaking in the 1990s is its apparent facelessness, its desire to subsume itself into the larger framework of genre cinema, and not to identify each film as a unique exemplar.

This is particularly true in the case of George Lucas's *The Phantom Menace* (1999), the "first" episode in the *Star Wars* series, a film that seeks to continue the concerns of the three earlier films in the *Star Wars* canon, while simultaneously ensuring audiences of a return to the generic "past" of cinema. Though laden with high-tech digital effects, *The Phantom Menace* is curiously devoid of an authentic human presence, and despite it's juggernaut performance at the box office, even its most ardent adherents must find the film a trifle lackluster. After all, the *Star Wars* films are directly indebted to the *Flash Gordon* series of the 1930s, from their opening crawl titles onward, and now, with *The Phantom Menace*, the series seems poised to replicate *itself* over two additional episodes (both to be shot entirely with digital technology) in the next few years. Yet as films, the *Star Wars* series run together in a curiously unsatisfying fashion: where do they truly begin or end?

This in direct contrast to the genre cinema of nearly every other decade in cinema history, where individual genre films, even in long-run-

1

ning series, typically strive to establish an individual identity while still retaining their grand name status. Looking at a film like Roger Corman's *The Trip* (1967), one is struck by the fact that the film, while ostensibly belonging to the "teen youth rebellion" market, is also very much a personal statement on the part of its actors and technicians. More ambitious genre films of that era, such as Dennis Hopper's *Easy Rider* (1969) and Michaelangelo Antonioni's *Zabriskie Point* (1970), also adhere to the "outlaw youth" genre yardstick, while simultaneously seeking to establish themselves as individual works of art. All of these films sought not only to entertain then-contemporary audiences they also hoped to add to the ongoing discussion on matters of race, sexual freedom, political rights, women's rights, and other social concerns of the day.

Similarly, many genre films of the 1920s, 1930s, and 1940s, while fulfilling the unspoken requirements for audience satisfaction of a genre musical, western, horror film or suspense thriller, often also sought to extend beyond the boundaries circumscribed by economic concerns, and thus serve as sites for discussion for audiences and critics alike. In this, they were often strikingly direct in their address to the audience; films such as Wesley E. Barry's *Creation of the Humanoids* (1962), Philip Ford's *The Mysterious Mr. Valentine* (1946), Howard Hawks's *To Have and Have Not* (1944), Charles Chaplin's *Shoulder Arms* (1918), Ernst Lubitsch's *So This Is Paris* (1926), Delbert Mann's *That Touch of Mink* (1962), Lubitsch's *To Be or Not to Be* (1942), Mervyn LeRoy's *Tugboat Annie* (1933), Harry Essex's *Mad at the World* (1955), William A. Seiter's *Make Haste to Live* (1954), John Frankenheimer's *The Manchurian Candidate* (1962), Herbert Ross's *Funny Lady* (1975), Normam Taurog's *G.I. Blues* (1960), Wallace Fox's *The Avenging Rider* (1928), Lew Landers's *Back in the Saddle* (1941) and numerous other films from a wide variety of genres, including film noir, horror, jungle, romance, western, science fiction, war, and romance films, often served up a message with their "stations of the cross" adherence to audience expectations. This was never allowed to impinge upon the central concern of the film: to provide escapist entertainment for mass audiences.

Horror films must, of course, have monsters, mad scientists, and Gothic castles; westerns need dusty towns, posses, and a climactic shoot-out; musicals need dance numbers, exotic locations, and lavish sets; and romance films require (for the most part) a heterotopic dance of the hours; this much we know, and collectively take for granted. But along with the exterior surface of the film, many genre films of previous decades contained a subtext that could be appreciated by those who cared to delve below the glossy surface of the work. *Creation of the Humanoids* deals convincingly with a post-apocalyptic nuclear future, and the resultant dehumanization of the surviving members of the human race, as do the *Mad Max* films, made between 1979 and 1985; *The Mysterious Mr. Valentine* considers the mutability of human experience in a postwar social landscape where nothing is reliably what it seems; *To Have and Have Not* concerns itself with issues of individual social responsibility during World War II in the fight against the Nazis; *To Be or Not To Be* also spoofs the Nazis, within the framework of a deliciously contrived knockabout farce. The list goes on and on.

By contrast, such recent films as Michael Bay's *Armageddon*, Bobby and Peter Farrelly's hugely successful *There's Something about Mary*, John Dahl's *Rounders*, Rob Bowman's *The X Files*, Mimi Leder's *Deep Impact*, Tsui Hark's *Knock Off*, Vincent Ward's *What Dreams May Come* (all 1998), and other contemporary films seem concerned exclusively with surface presentation, aided and abetted by the proliferation of digital special effects and postproduction doctoring that makes the impossible seem ordinary, and the everyday seem, paradoxically, airbrush perfect. *Armageddon* and *Deep Impact* suggest that it is a very bad thing for a meteor to threaten the destruction of the Earth, and that all possible means should be used to prevent the coming conflagration. But that seems about all that both films are willing to commit to. *Rounders* is a rather tame rehash of Martin Scorsese's *Mean Streets* (1973) and Robert Rossen's *The Hustler* (1961), lacking the resonance of John Dahl's earlier films, *Red Rock West* (1992) and *The Last Seduction* (1994), both of which were made at the margins of cinematic discourse, where the most interesting work continues to thrive, until the writers and directors of these phantom films are inevitably co-opted by Hollywood. *The X Files* thrives on rampant paranoia, but little else; *Knock Off* showcases Jean-Claude Van Damme's acrobatic skills, does nothing with its potential promising concept of counterfeit name-brand merchandise sold on an international scale; and *What Dreams May Come* is yet another reworking of Cocteau's *Orpheus* (1949), in which a profusion of digital special effects replace both poetry and imagination. But is this really the case?

Richard Donner, for example, crowds the visual backgrounds on his series of *Lethal Weapon* films (1987–1998) with posters advocating animal rights and an end to apartheid in South Africa (when this social doctrine was still in force), and Roland Emmerich's *Independence Day* (1996) mixes equal parts of Shakespeare's *Henry V*, Byron Haskin's *War of the Worlds* (1953), and Fred F. Sears's *Earth vs. The Flying Saucers* (1956) to serve up a contemporary morality tale that is one part science-fiction film, one part social criticism tract, one part political harangue, and one part sitcom, which seeks to give audiences a sense of hope against seemingly overwhelming odds. One could argue that contemporary genre films also have a stake in shaping current political and social discourse, in such films as Barry Levinson's *Wag The Dog* (1998) and Steven Spielberg's *Saving Private Ryan* (1998). That these are both genre films there can be no doubt (political satire and war film, respectively), and that in each case, the director sought to make an individuated statement can also be beyond question.

Yet compared to the political satires of another era (such as Theodore J. Flicker's *The President's Analyst* [1967], Norman Taurog's *The Phantom President* [1932], and Stanley Kubrick's *Dr. Strangelove, Or How I Learned to Stop Worrying and Love the Bomb* [1964], to name only a few of many possible candidates), *Wag the Dog* seems both timid and poorly constructed; similarly, *Saving Private Ryan* works best during the opening forty-minute action sequence, in which the soldiers storm the beach on D day despite nearly insurmountable odds. When the action dwindles, Spielberg falls back on war-film genre clichés so numerous as to almost defy enumeration. In the end, *Saving Private Ryan* is nothing so much as a deftly mounted and brutally graphic Jimmy Stewart war film, starring the 1990s version of Stewart, everyman Tom Hanks.

Both films wear their thematic concerns on their respective sleeves. *Wag the Dog* tells us that politics is merely a dog-and-pony-show; *Saving Private Ryan* informs us that war is hell. These are certainly reasonable assumptions, yet behind these surface statements, each film seeks to conform more to generic requirements than to create a singular impression. Because of this, most audiences will be content to contemplate the surface text presented in both films, while being momentarily thrown off guard by the lavish scale of execution, or the supposed freshness of the film's concept. What truly lurks beneath the surface of each genre entertainment remains more difficult to discern, when these films are stripped of pyrotechnics, stepped-up gore, or chic political cynicism.

In direct contrast to the economical style of their predecessors, the 1990s genre film is everywhere a creature of excess—excess running time, excess budgeting, excess spectacle. It is not enough that every frame of the 1990s genre film be absolutely perfect, "tweaked" through the magic of computer image generation or digital clean-up processes; the soundtrack of the film must resonate with appropriate volume and intensity so as to literally shake spectators from their seats. William Castle tried much the same thing with his minimally budgeted horror film *The Tingler* (1959); during key sequences of the film, Castle saw to it that certain, prewired audience seats received jolts of electricity on cue from the projection booth, to further hype audience participation for the film. Roland Emmerich's recent remake of *Godzilla* (1998) was, in much the same fashion, mostly a construct of noise and spectacle, presented in thunderous digital sound, in a desperate attempt to mask the lack of content in the film, which in no way matched the thematic resonance or pictorial authority of Inoshira Honda and Terry O. Morse's 1954 original.

Coupled with deafening soundtracks, there is also the issue of length; where genre films in the teens through the early seventies reliably clocked in at 70 to 80 minutes, by the late seventies, with the release of George Lucas's *Star Wars* (1977), genre films began their inexorable rise in running time. The 1998 *Godzilla*, for example, takes a full 140 minutes to unreel, in sharp contrast to the 81-minute running time of the Japanese/U.S. 1954 original. *Saving Private Ryan* lasts 170 minutes; *Independence Day* (1996) has a running time of 142 minutes. (All of these running times vary slightly from country to country; figures given are the U.S. running times in all cases). It seems that sheer, massive bulk is what is required more than any other consideration in today's genre filmmaking. The contemporary audience has succumbed to the dictum that "more is more," and seems to demand epic length as a requirement for generic satisfaction.

Although characterization has never been the strong point of the genre film, in which most characters are sketched in with a few "back story" details rather than fully rendered, today's genre protagonists are more "instant read" iconic glyphs than ever before, presented to the audience as a series of costumes, hairstyles, and lighting strategies. Similarly, filming locations are now rendered as caricatures of actual physical surroundings. When a film is shot on location, as with Mike Figgis's *Leaving Las Vegas* (1995), it attempts to hype the actual location with either unusual camera angles, or hand-held filming (*Leaving Las Vegas* was, in fact, shot in Super 16 mm, so that the cameras could be moved with a minimum of difficulty from setup to setup). This in itself echoes such films as Billy Wilder's *The Lost Weekend* (1945), another film about self-destructive alcoholism, which was also shot, for the most part, on location, in an attempt to anchor protagonist Don Birnam's struggle against the bottle to a specific time and place: New York in the 1940s. It can tangentially be argued that neither *Leaving Las Vegas* nor *The Lost Weekend* is a genre film, with some justification, but unless a contemporary film is manifestly a personal project, it will remain (for the most part, at the studio's behest) a back-lot construct.

In the late 1990s, gone is any attempt at even ersatz neorealism that marked such genre thrillers as *The House on 92nd Street* (1945) or *Naked City* (1945); now, all is done in the studio, for both safety and economy. There are exceptions, such as Mike Figgis's shot-on-location *Leaving Las Vegas* (1995), but these are aberrations, rather than the norm. A trench coat makes this person a tough guy; a kitchen window bursting with yellow sunlight becomes the hallmark of a happy home. Despite the length of the contemporary genre film, there is little attempt to develop any humanist connection with the audience. It is seemingly enough to present one chase after another, one explosion to follow yet another cataclysmic maelstrom of violence, and supposedly, the audience will be satisfied. Even if audiences find a film too formulaic, the sheer visual bombast of the piece will carry them along for a few hours, in which they may forget the exigencies of their everyday existence, and find vicarious escape through the medium of the cinema. Costumes, sets, and properties in the late-1990s genre cinema are always perfect, in direct contrast to the sometimes thrown-together look of such earlier genre films as *Attack of the 50 Foot Woman* (1958) or *The Baron of Arizona* (1950).

As with genre films as a general rule, remakes abound. But contemporary remakes of genre classics seek to obscure their humble, or perhaps more accurately, populist origins with a panoply of expensive sets and cameo performances by fleetingly popular television stars, all to justify the price of an increasingly expensive admission ticket. Hal Roach's series of two-reel comedies, *The Little Rascals*, went through its first modernization when MGM bought the rights to series. MGM immediately reduced the films to ten minutes apiece instead of the original twenty-minute length, while simultaneously smoothing off the rough edges of the original, often transcendantly anarchic films, and transforming the comedies into a series of brief instructional films, designed to inculcate dominant social values in their audiences, rather than encourage the spirit of free play and discourse. When the series returned to the big screen in Penelope Spheeris's *The Little Rascals* (1994), plots from the original two-reel films were recycled and stitched together to form an uneasy pastiche of sight gags and pratfalls, spiced up with cameo appearances by Donald Trump, Mel Brooks, Whoopi Goldberg, George Wendt, and Reba McEntire. While the feature film has a certain easy charm to its ramshackle construction, and a socially disruptive message that is director Spheeris's alone, it is nevertheless a spectacle rather than a series of intimate human interchanges that we are presented with, and that is what audiences in the 1990s have come to expect above all other considerations.

Similarly, when Vincente Minnelli's *Father of the Bride* (1950) was remade in 1991 by Charles Shyer, and its sequel, Minnelli's *Father's Little Dividend* (1951), was remade by Shyer as *Father of the Bride II* (1995), the new versions took place in locations so opulent as to be beyond the reach of all but the most affluent viewers; it is this conspicuous display of privilege that is the hallmark of the contemporary genre film in most of its manifestations. David Swift's 1961 *Parent Trap* was remade in 1998 by Nancy Meyers as a film that seemed more interested in the sets than in the characters that inhabited them. In contrast, the original film, though set in a distinctly upper-income household, did not inhabit the phantom zone of consumer culture so resolutely occupied by the 1990s remake. What is happening here is a return to the past, but with a new series of values imposed on source material that was once upon a time more in tune with average audience/consumer expectations. Thus, the new versions of these films are triumphs of style over substance, in which even the most minor physical detail is given all the weight of a major stylistic makeover.

This surface presence enthralls contemporary cinemagoers, and for the most part, late-1990s audiences fail to look beneath the surface of a given film's exterior narrative, and concern themselves solely with issues of star power, box-office grosses (the weekly, or even daily ranking of film revenues has now become a national spectator sport), and the pyrotechnics inherent in today's overproduced megaspectacles. What cost $1–3 million to produce in the 1960s and 1970s, for example, the *Planet of the Apes* films (1968–1973), now costs many millions to bring to the screen; even the most modest drama, requiring neither extensive sets nor special effects, still manages to cost between $50 and $60 million, due to a combination of rising star salaries, union wages, saturation distribution requirements, and other exigencies. (With a new *Planet of the Apes* film announced for production in 1999, we will have a chance to see how much these modest program films of a quarter century ago now cost to produce.) The day of the modestly budgeted genre film is a memory;

genre films are now beholden more to banks and stockholders than to any other entity, and even the slightest deviation from preconceived design is a matter of grave concern to a film's production entity. It has always been thus, but today, the stakes are considerably higher. Several poor marketing decisions may well put a studio in serious financial peril; why takes risks when you can play it safe, recycle the past, and reap presold rewards in the present-day marketplace?

What this book argues, among other things, is that the implicit message in contemporary genre films is rarely that which is signified by film's external or even internal narrative structure. What drives the thematic and structural concerns of genre filmmaking in the 1990s is the recovery of initial investment, made all the more pressing by the fact that each film released theatrically now represents an investment of many millions of dollars. Gone are the days when one could make a film for several hundred thousand dollars, open it nationally with a minimal campaign (no television ads necessary), and hope to have it compete with major studio fare.

Genre films today are no longer "B" films ("B," or bottom-half-of-the-double-bill films, vanished in the late 1960s to early 1970s), nor are they cheap knock-offs in a series of predictable entertainments, even if they sometimes look and sound that way. The *Andy Hardy* series, the *Whistler* series, and the *Bowery Boys* films have long since been replaced by regular television series programming. Shows such as *Everybody Loves Raymond* and *Frazier* have drained off the theatrical market for low-key domestic farce, while Fox brings forth a new crop of "racy" shows each season to keep teens glued to the television. Modestly produced films will no longer suffice to lure in the average theatrical film patron, and yet originality is not the issue here.

What audiences today desire more than ever before is "more of the same," and studios, scared to death by rising production and distribution costs, are equally loathe to strike out in new generic directions. Keep audiences satisfied, strive to maintain narrative closure at all costs, and keep within the bounds of heterotopic romance, no matter what genre one is ostensibly working in. Yet, at the same time, the studios must present these old fables in seductive new clothing, with huge budgets, major stars, lavish sets, and (if the genre demands it) unremitting action to disguise the secondhand nature of the contemporary genre film. These are just some of the unwritten rules that define and delimit American genre filmmaking in the 1990s, and some of the concerns we hope to explore in this work.

Another structural factor driving the creation of this text was to locate its cultural and critical concerns almost exclusively in American genre cinema of the 1990s. While there are numerous excellent film-genre texts available on the market today, most of these texts, while thoughtful and well-constructed, deal with classic genre films of the 1930s through the 1970s, with very little commentary on the genre films of the 1990s—precisely those films that contemporary audiences are most familiar with. To remedy this situation, I asked a group of colleagues to create a series of essays that examine the postmodern condition of film genre in the American cinema, examining, for the most part, recent examples of filmic genre enterprise. The approaches in this volume vary widely; some of the authors chose to create survey pieces, while others offer meditations on the nature of specific genres, demonstrating how these particular forms of filmic entertainment and expression have changed and developed over the past hundred years of cinema.

While American genre cinema in the 1990s seems, in many respects, more formulaic than ever, even if it is presented with a fine sheen thanks to digital special effects, there is nevertheless a core of meaning imbedded in even the most desultory entertainments. There is, indeed, "more than meets the eye" in such films as *The Rock* (1996), *Starship Troopers* (1997), *Pocahontas* (1995), and other commercial films. But often, the most interesting subtext in a contemporary genre film is not that which the filmmaker, or producer, may have intended. In addition to their avowed thematic concerns, *The Rock* implicitly posits a world where only violence serves because violence rules; *Starship Troopers* parodies Leni Riefenstahl's Nazi propaganda films to make a futuristic case for consenting fascism; and *Pocahontas* homogenizes racial difference in the name of celebrating individual social and racial identity. None of these films can be transparently *seen* to pursue these goals, but their structure, execution, and dissemination as part of the Hollywood movie machine leaves little doubt as to their true cultural signification. For better or worse, American genre cinema dominates the globe. The Hollywood genre film has become one of America's most prolific and profitable social exports. These contemporary genre films all seek to further the values of their nation of origin as they journey throughout the world on film, videotape, DVDs and on television; it is the pervasive influence, and the numerous subtexts, of these films that we seek to analyze here.

Thus, in this volume, I sought to bring together some of the most accessible and direct writing on these films, essays that can be appreciated by the scholar and the general reader alike. And yet, as the genre film in the 1990s remains much indebted to its predecessors of the previous decades, a fundamental shift in image production and reception is beginning to gain ground at cineplexes all over the world. It is entirely appropriate that this volume should be published during the final days of the twentieth century, for we may now be seeing a complete change in that which we traditionally call a film; in the future, films may well undergo a radical technical metamorphosis that plug viewers in more directly to the spectacle they are witnessing, either through the use of responsive "hand gear" (as in point-and-shoot video arcade games), or perhaps through the implementation of laser equipment that will present vast, three-dimensional holographic spectacles to an auditorium of rapt observers. No matter what changes the coming decades bring, it is important to remember that 1990s genre filmmaking draws on the genre filmmaking of the past for many of its plots and formulas, as well as for the basic thematic structures it so successfully employs again and again (as genres will).

In creating this volume, I wish to thank not only the individual contributors themselves, who worked so hard to create the essays contained within this text, but also my many students over the years, who have repeatedly expressed a desire for such a book. They required a text that would demonstrate to them, using films they were familiar with, exactly how the process of genre signification operated. They required a text that was accessible, dealing with films they were familiar with, and above all, a text that demonstrated the precedence of the classics; exactly *where* these films of the 1990s that they knew so well came from, and how the genre classics have shaped contemporary cinematic practice.

We have not attempted to deal with every possible genre, but rather to highlight those genres that are most active as the 1990s draw to a close. Thus the new Black cinema is represented here, as well as horror films, science-fiction films, films for children, romances, teen films, political films, westerns, musicals, and other dominant genres, all in discussions that ground themselves in contemporary texts with which even the most casual filmgoer should be familiar. This was not an easy task, and so to all the contributors who labored so hard and so diligently to create these texts, I again extend my sincere thanks and admiration. Despite the enormous amount of work involved, this text has been a pleasure to create.

If film genre in the late 1990s is in many ways an entirely new sort of construct, then it is vitally important that we understand just how it operates, in contrast to the generic films that satisfied audiences of an earlier era. The history of cinema is one of repetition, in which ideas and stories are constantly recycled and revamped with new sets, new costumes, and updated physical execution. There is nothing new in this process, which has informed the backbone of the Hollywood genre cinema since the inception of the studio system. What is different, however, is that now, so much depends upon the financial success of each individual film. The studios, no longer the factories they once were in their glory days, are now merely production and distribution facilities that traffic in essentially independent productions, in which stars, directors, producers, composers, and even some technical personnel are corporate entities that exist to be packaged by conglomerate agencies such as ICM, CAA, and William Morris.

With genre filmmaking, as always, constituting the bulk of film production, and with the pervasiveness of mainstream cinema at an all-time intensity (current releases are now opened routinely in from fifteen hundred to three thousand theaters simultaneously, for maximum saturation), more than ever it behooves us to understand precisely how contemporary genre cinema shapes and mirrors our collective dreams and desires. What transformations of the basic cinematographic apparatus the coming century will bring we cannot accurately foretell, but one thing is certain: genre cinema will continue to be the dominant force in American cinema, if only because it is a tried and tested commodity that can reliably be called upon to entertain and satisfy an audience.

But there is much more going on than simply audience satiation, and it is this series of subtextual and metatextual concerns that occupies the essayists collected here. The American genre cinema will always be with us; but what genre films will we see in the coming century? Will the films of the 1990s give us some sense of what is to come, or will the concerns of the new century bring us a new set of generic requirements? Will digital imaging replace almost entirely the signification of the real, offering us wholly synthetic characters, locations, and voices that once again are called into play to satisfy our need for narratives that are both easy to follow, and yet unexpectedly complex? Will the cinematograph itself cease to exist in the coming century, to be replaced by something altogether beyond our collective experience? These are some of the questions we attempt to examine in this volume, and we hope that our meditations on genre are both useful and enlightening for the reader.

WORKS CITED AND CONSULTED

Altman, Rick. *The American Film Musical.* Bloomington: Indiana University Press, 1987.

Armstrong, Richard B., and Mary Willems Armstrong. *The Movie List Book: A Reference Guide to Film Themes, Settings, and Series.* Jefferson, N.C.: McFarland & Co., 1990.

Browne, Nick, ed. *Refiguring American Film Genres : History and Theory.* Berkeley : University of California Press, 1998.

Cameron, Ian Alexander. *Adventure and the Cinema.* London: Studio Vista, 1973.

Coates, Paul. *Film at the Intersection of High and Mass Culture.* New York: Cambridge University Press, 1994.

Dixon, Wheeler Winston. *The Films of Jean-Luc Godard.* Albany: State University of New York Press, 1997.

Fischer, Lucy. *Cinematernity : Film, Motherhood, Genre.* Princeton, N.J.: Princeton University Press, 1996.

Gehring, Wes D., ed. *Handbook of American Film Genres.* New York: Greenwood Press, 1988.

Grant, Barry Keith, ed. *Film Genre Reader.* 1st ed. Austin: University of Texas Press, 1986.

Grodal, Torben Kragh. *Moving Pictures : A New Theory of Film Genres, Feelings, and Cognition.* New York: Oxford University Press, 1997.

Lewis, Jon. *The Road to Romance & Ruin: Teen Films and Youth Culture.* New York: Routledge, 1992.

Lopez, Daniel. *Films by Genre : 775 Categories, Styles, Trends and Movements Defined, with a Filmography for Each.* Jefferson, N.C.: McFarland & Co., 1993.

Reed, Joseph W. *American Scenarios: The Uses of Film Genre.* Middletown, Conn.: Wesleyan University Press, 1989.

Silver, Alain, and Elizabeth Ward, eds. *Film Noir : An Encyclopedic Reference to the American Style.* Woodstock, N.Y.: Overlook Press, 1988.

Thomas, Tony. *The Films of the Forties.* Secaucus, N.J.: Citadel Press, 1975.

CHAPTER TWO

◫

New Wave Black Cinema in the 1990s

MARK A. REID

This chapter examines a representative group of black-oriented 1990s fiction films that are distributed by major film companies. I refer to these films and the community of black directors and writers as well as the black and nonblack technicians who produce these films as "Black Hollywood." The essay does not cover all Black Hollywood films made during this period. It does however focus on a selective group of films that are directed, written, or produced by African Americans who wear several different professional hats. They are not merely directors but are equally talented in other areas within the American film industry. In commenting on 1990s Black Hollywood, after almost a century of African American filmmaking, this essay addresses how particular films share or deviate from the themes, film styles, and iconography of previous African American directed, written, and produced black genre films.

Black-directed action films depicting urban life in Los Angeles, New York, Chicago, and elsewhere have been made since before the end of World War I. The purpose of this chapter, however, is very modest and in no way will it include a thorough analysis of the differences between 1990s African American Film and those films that predate this period. Still, it is important to note that before and immediately after World War I, black filmmakers, such as Noble Johnson and Oscar Micheaux, produced black action and family films that dramatize racial lynching, interracial intimacy, racial passing, black soldiering, urban poverty, and criminality. There are similar themes and social issues that black films of the 1960s through the 1990s dramatize. Admittedly, the early filmmakers had a cinematic style that was limited by the available technology and contemporary tastes of their respective period. In this sense, the films of the post–World War I era and of the 1960s–1970s are very different. But the themes, issues, and purposes of the films of these two periods are not that different. In total, the filmmakers wanted their films to attract, entertain, and educate their mostly black audiences.

A second wave of historically and thematically important black-directed documentaries and fiction films appears in the late sixties and early seventies. These black fiction films, as opposed to the documentaries, are made by college-trained independent filmmakers such as Charles Burnett, Julie Dash, Haile Gerima, Warrington Hudlin, and Alile Sharon Larkin and their non-film-school-trained contemporaries in Black Hollywood. These filmmakers use social realist and experimental film styles to explore urban poverty, police brutality, and, as in Dash's and Larkin's case, the life experiences of black women.

Another group of filmmakers of this second wave includes such Black Hollywood filmmakers as Gordon Parks (*The Learning Tree*, Warner Brothers, 1969 and *Shaft*, MGM, 1971), Melvin Van Peebles (*Watermelon Man*, Columbia, 1970), Gordon Parks Jr. (*Superfly*, Warner Brothers, 1972), Ossie Davis (*Black Girl*, Cinerama, 1972), and others. Though there exist a few exceptions, most of the Black Hollywood filmmakers of this period did not attend university film schools. Their films feature African American actors, employ popular black music forms, and, with the exception of Melvin Van Peebles's independently produced and mainstream-porno-distributed *Sweet Sweetback's Baadasssss Song* (Cinemation, 1971), borrow heavily from American film genres. Black Hollywood films, especially the African American action-film genre, exploit the more exotic elements that make up black inner-city life.

During the 1990s, blacks have directed many films but many of them began their careers as actors, writers, editors, cinematographers, assistant directors or film producers. For instance, Vondie Curtis-Hall, Bill Duke, Spike Lee, Kasi Lemmons, Mario Van Peebles, and Forest Whitaker are well-known directors who have important acting careers. Moreover, the actor-directors Curtis-Hall, Lee, Lemmons, and Van Peebles wrote the scripts for their respective films *Gridlock'd* (Polygram, 1997), *He Got Game* (Touchstone, 1998), *Eve's Bayou* (Trimark, 1997), and *Posse* (Polygram, 1993). Another significant number of African American directors started as cinematographers, producers or director-writers for black-directed films. Ernest Dickerson, the director-writer of *Juice* (Paramount, 1992), was Lee's preferred cinematographer during the 1980s. Douglas McHenry produced such black action films as *New Jack City* (Warner, 1991) and *The Walking Dead* (Savoy, 1995). McHenry also codirected *House Party II* (New Line, 1991) and directed *Jason's Lyric* (Polygram, 1994). Darnell Martin, one of the few black women directors in Hollywood, was second assistant camera on Lee's *Do the Right Thing* (Universal, 1989). She then went on to direct and write *I Like It Like That* (Columbia, 1994).

The African American's widening opportunities and interchangeable roles as director-writer, director-producer, or cinematographer of major American films indicate that Hollywood has certainly become an important outlet for a significant group of black film artists and technicians. Consequently, Hollywood's liberal capitalistic openness to employ talented blacks might also have its drawbacks. For instance, would-be black independent filmmakers, writers, and technicians are siphoned off by Hollywood's openness, all of which has an effect on the continued development of black independent film. One need only recall the effect that Hollywood had on black and interracial companies when major studios began producing black-cast films that were, from 1929 to 1961, exclusively directed and written by whites.

The lure of Hollywood took Spike Lee from his independent film beginnings but has done little to damage Lee's artistry. In fact, Lee has probably benefited from his more than a decade of filmmaking within Hollywood. However, major studio affiliation did little for the successful distribution and exhibition of Charles Burnett's *To Sleep With Anger* (Columbia, 1990). While the film industry has certainly acknowledged the existence of an African American film market, it has cautiously selected the films and filmmakers that receive financial backing and international distribution. Columbia's minuscule distribution of Burnett's *To Sleep* is but one example of how a studio can stifle its films. Yet indeed there are 1990s black-directed and written Hollywood films that present similar sociocultural themes and use innovative visual styles as the 1970s black independent films by Charles Burnett, Larry Clark, Julie Dash, Haile Gerima, and Alile Sharon Larkin.

Political concerns, black urban music, and visual styles simmer in the 1990s Black Hollywood films directed and written by such artists as

Bill Duke, Spike Lee, Kasi Lemmons, Darnell Martin, John Singleton, and George Tillman Jr. These filmmakers illustrate that resourceful and committed filmmakers can find honest work in an industry that produces for an international market. Their 1990s films are of critical importance to the growth of Black Hollywood and the American film industry. This should not be taken as an endorsement for audiences to applaud every black-directed and written film. One must distinguish which films are well made and why. Filmmaking requires several different talented individuals—director, writer, editor, cinematographer, producer, and others. One should not confuse or overestimate the decision-making power any member of the film crew may have over the final film product. One must always study several different sources. Still, studied criticism cannot escape the fact that it is far from being an objective act. Film criticism employs subjective criteria that particular groups of critics are in agreement with while other film critics may be in total disagreement. The African American audience's critical reception of *The Color Purple*—both Alice Walker's 1982 novel and Steven Spielberg's 1985 film—illustrates how diverse this reception can be within any community that is defined by singular-identity politics. (Important issues concerning feminist and black womanist film reception have been discussed in M. Watkins; Carson, Dittmar, and Welsch; and Bobo. In Harris, there is an equally important discussion of how African American audiences constitute many types of receptions.)

Yet and still, many 1990s Black Hollywood films create molotov cocktails containing black populist politics, rap music, and innovative camera techniques. After their visual and auditory explosions, filmgoers are left with images of mob rule and the results of black-on-black butchery. This abuse of opportunity by certain black filmmakers furnishes them with a fast buck and premature jouissance, just like in their films. The black-directed and written films that celebrate nihilism and senseless killing are far different from Black Hollywood films made by Lee, Lemons, Singleton, and black independent filmmakers who work with less financial support and fewer distribution outlets.

Many 1990s Black Hollywood films do not reflect the sociopolitical concerns found in the 1970s black independent films by Charles Burnett, Larry Clark, Haile Gerima, and Alile Sharon Larkin, Melvin Van Peebles, and others. Nevertheless, 1990s films focus on urban lower-class life and use social-realist camera styles like the earlier films. The 1990s films use similar black lower-class Los Angeles settings, long takes, and choppy editing styles. These elements are also present in such 1970s black independent films as Burnett's *Killer of Sheep* (1977), Clark's *Passing Through* (1977), Gerima's *Bush Mama* (1975), Alile Sharon Larkin's *A Different Image* (1981) and Melvin Van Peebles's *Sweet Sweetback's Baadasssss Song* (Cinemation, 1971). (For an in-depth discussion of these particular films see Burnett, Lott, Reid [*Redefining, Black Gangster*], Guerrero, Diawara, Kellner, and Chan.) The negotiation of these elements occurs especially in John Singleton's *Boyz 'n the Hood* (Columbia, 1991), Allen and Albert Hughes's *Menace II Society* (New Line, 1993), and F. Gary Gray's *Set It Off* (New Line, 1996). It also appears in 1990s Black Hollywood films with New York settings.

For example, Matty Rich's *Straight Out of Brooklyn* (Goldwyn, 1991) uses black-and-white cinematography, hand-held camera, claustrophobic interiors, and distraught black parents in very much the same manner as Burnett's *Killer of Sheep* (1977). *Straight Out* presents a sentry of tall public housing complexes that tower over their black inhabitants. Sounds are not of silence but of police sirens mixed with gunfire that echo off the housing development's cold hardened cement walls. The exterior daylight scenes infer the degree to which lower-class urban blacks have been contained in prisonlike architecture that police inspect as blacks receive and deliver indiscriminate violence. Rich's interior scenes are claustrophobic even though the rooms are scantily decorated. The sound of a loud drunken man abusing his wife replaces the police sirens and anonymous gunfire that awaits anyone attempting to escape this interior for the *Mean Streets*. Burnett's *Killer* invokes a similar picture of the souring of black families who suffer from unemployment and underemployment.

Burnett uses scenes of sheep at slaughter and empty exterior spaces that exist uncomfortably between dilapidated single-family housing. Burnett's interior scenes reveal the inner lives of the souls of blackfolk that he films. Theirs are the emptied private moments in which the black couple has nothing to say to each other. A single tear wells up in the eye of the mother, the father is speechless and full of hurt, their young preadolescent daughter witnesses not spousal abuse but something that is just as worse. The couple's long silence is as heartbreaking as Rich's scene of the loud fight between the couple in *Straight Out*. Are these two filmmakers predicting that the youths who witness their parents will soon become them? The two filmmakers stress how certain black families are destroyed by economic conditions. They avoid showy spectacles that celebrate images of imprudent young blacks who turn to crime to seek wealth, fast cars, and fine clothes.

Using the gritty color cinematography found in Van Peebles and in Gerima and Clark's 1970s works, Ernest Dickerson's *Juice* (Paramount, 1992) presents exterior scenes where concrete and brick buildings stand in close proximity to asphalt streets. Police are not immediately present in this film as they are in most scenes in *Sweetback*. Unlike the 1970s independent features, protagonists are usually African American male adolescents who are shown in fistfights and knife play. In hindsight, the violence dramatized in *Juice* is less spectacular than in such other adolescent male films as *Boyz 'n the Hood* and *Menace II Society*. In fact, the issue that generates most of the film narrative is an adolescent's need to own a gun to establish his bad-boy reputation. Guns are not freely distributed nor are they respected by most of the characters in this film. However, a gun will lead to the death of at least two black males. Recently, there have been several theoretical readings of the politics and aesthetics of the visual construction of urban black male figures (Herman Gray and S. Craig Watkins, in particular, offer innovative discussions on the ways in which the construction of black masculinity is treated by critics of film and popular culture).

In addition to family films such as *Straight Out of Brooklyn* and the gun-slinging adolescent male-centered films such as *Juice*, *Boyz*, and *Menace*, there were a few Black Hollywood films that feature young adult heroines. Black independent filmmakers have always made films that include black female heroines. Negotiation occurs between several types of visual and auditory elements in the early-1970s male- and female-centered independent works by Julie Dash, Alile Sharon Larkin and Haile Gerima, which also appears in Leslie Harris's *Just Another Girl on the IRT* (Miramax, 1992). Harris's film reflects 1990s popular music and clothing styles. She saturates *Just Another Girl* with hip-hop music and the loose-fitting clothing that is identified with this fashion. The central issue that generates this film is whether a pregnant teenager should undergo an abortion. She offers many reasons why she should. The most tangible reasons include her age and her plans to enter college next year. The film concludes with the girl accepting her child without relinquishing her plans to attend college at a later date. Certainly, the music and stylish dress are meant to attract a certain type of film audience. Additionally, the film dramatizes important contemporary social problems—teenage pregnancy and unwed teenage mothers. Black leaders have often criticized the presence of violence and sexual activity in black films. They might also criticize this particular film for its hip-hop style, the protagonist's devil-may-care attitude, and the fact that she represents all lower-class black teenage girls who become unwed mothers. However, if the viewer looks beyond the stylish décor of hip-hop music, dress, language, and attitude that colors most hip-hop films, s/he should see that this film particularly asks its teenage female spectators to avoid unwanted pregnancies by demanding that their male lovers use condoms.

Just Another Girl echoes the call for condom use that is also articulated in *House Party* (1990), another hip-hop black teen film. In broadening the issues covered in this subgenre, *Just Another Girl* presents a female-centered narrative in which sexual activity and childbirth are solely determined by a teenage black woman and not by her male lover or the State. The film empowers its lower-class teenage unwed mother who, in American news broadcasts and in the politics of both centrist Clinton Democrats and Reagan-Bush Republicans, has been demonized and held responsible for the deteriorization of the inner city and the black family.

On the other hand, when community leaders and critics ask Black Hollywood filmmakers to limit their films to middle-class upbeat images or progressive sociopolitical concerns, they are inadvertently asking these same filmmakers to ignore and leave undeveloped the *Just Another Girl* type of heroine. Ironically, this heroine shares similar womanist elements, admittedly in different forms, as the female protagonists in such black independent films as Alile Sharon Larkin's *A Different Image* (1981), Tracy Moffatt's *Nice Coloured Girls* (1987), and Julie Dash's *Daughters of the Dust* (Kino, 1991).

More to the point, if black filmmakers limit their work to art films, major studios would not finance and distribute their works, or would they? A too-easy response to this question would be no. But there are a few exceptions to this rule of thumb, which require comment. Indeed, there are instances when studios financed and distributed black-directed and written art films whose narratives address controversial issues in a somewhat avant-garde manner. However, this occurs to filmmakers who have acquired the Hollywood marketability of a Spike Lee, John Singleton, and Euzhan Palcy. Here, "Hollywood marketability" refers to and results from working within a major film organization,although, merely directing and writing a major studio-produced film does not guarantee any filmmaker this distinction. The film must attract a sizable box office that equals thrice or more the production and marketing costs of the film.

A case in point is Forest Whitaker's screen adaptation of Terry McMillan's 1992 bestselling novel *Waiting to Exhale*. Whitaker's 20th Century Fox-produced and distributed 1995 film adaptation of this best-seller grossed over $66 million in domestic rentals (the box-office receipts). The film's production and marketing costs amounted to about $15 million. The box-office success of *Waiting to Exhale* provides Whitaker and McMillan with Hollywood marketability. Consequently, Whitaker should acquire more options for his next project, its production budget, and his salary. Normally, he should also receive better choices over the talent and crew for his next project. This explains why Forest Whitaker might find better opportunities to direct; however, it does not explain why Spike Lee, after many box-office failures, retains a discernible amount of professional prestige in Hollywood. Lee has consistently made moderately important sociopolitical films for over a decade and has done this within Hollywood. His most flawed films still attract varying opin-ions on their critical merit. And Lee's critical and box-office successes— *She's Gotta Have It* (Island Pictures, 1986), *Do the Right Thing* (Universal, 1989) and *He Got Game* (Touchstone, 1998)—keep him afloat after his numerous Titanics have sunk. Finally, Lee's victorious struggles to direct, produce, and obtain distribution for *Malcolm X* (Warner, 1992) and *Get On the Bus* (Columbia, 1996) are unequaled among those of his Holly-wood contemporaries.

The iconography of many Black Hollywood films of the 1970s through the 1990s follows the traditions of various action-film genres. Thus, Gordon Parks Jr.'s *Superfly* (Warner Brothers, 1972) and Mario Van Peebles's *New Jack City* (Warner Brothers, 1991), two films dealing with black drug dealers and cops, include scenes of criminality, abundant sex-uality, and black-on-black violence. *New Jack City*, however, includes an African American, Asian American, and Anglo-American detective team who goes after a very dark-complexioned drug dealer. It is the light-com-plexioned detective who beats the dark-skinned dealer senseless. Yes, the story line provides reasons for this particular intraracial vengeance. Still, the light-complexioned black detective's violence is just another form of police brutality. In *Boyz 'n the Hood*, the self-hating black policeman is shown for what he is—a killer cop—and this particular film does not attempt to disguise this hateful violence by the demonization of black drug dealers and gang members.

Milton Friedman writes: "In 1970, 200,000 people were in prison. Today, 1.6 million people are. . . . The attempt to prohibit drugs is by far the major source of the horrendous growth in the prison population." Further in the article Friedman quotes Sher Hosonka, a former director of Connecticut's addiction services, who stated in 1995 that "Today, in this country, we incarcerate 3,109 black men for every 100,000 of them in the population." Sher compares the incarceration of black men in the United States to the lower figures, 729 black men for every 100,000, in pre-Mandela South Africa. And then he adds: "most customers do not live in the inner cities, most sellers do" (Friedman 19).

Audiences who frequent the black action "drug" films have yet to see a dramatization of this reality because the genre supports exotic images of the black inner cities. Black folks on coke are interesting if you view them at a nice suburban distance. Dirty cops, drug cartels, and the effects of incarcerating an excessive amount of young black men are rarely dramatized. These facts are mentioned only in passing. Images of white folk entering black communities in search of drugs are an unwanted fact and, consequently, films and articles like Friedman's are absent in these black action films, which are more truly whiteploitation films than blaxploitation. These visual taboos resemble a type of Hays Code against interracial drug intimacy.

Here, however, there are film-genre codes to adhere to that require no interracial intimacy between small-time black drug dealers and their white suburban clientele. What is definitely in this mix is a line of popular film forms, a few lines of exotic black inner-city content, and many lines of financing and distribution from an international cartel of entertainment companies (Columbia = Sony, Warner Brothers = Time-Warner and Polygram). Since the eighties, multinational companies that have transnational lines of interests in music, television, and other areas of the entertainment industry have increasingly consumed American film companies.

During the 1990s, African American men and their white male counterparts directed and wrote several black action films. In the 1970s such action films as Gordon Parks's *Shaft*, Gordon Parks Jr.'s *Superfly*, and Jack Hill's two Pam Grier vehicles *Coffy* (American International, 1973) and *Foxy Brown* (American International, 1974) were widely referred to as blaxploitation films. It is interesting to note that Quentin Tarantino's use of Pam Grier in *Jackie Brown* (1997) pays homage to Grier, her films *Coffy* and *Foxy Brown*, and their white director-writer Jack Hill. Both Hill and, more than twenty years later, Tarantino, write black action-film scripts that feature Grier as an intelligent and sexy black heroine. (For an interesting French critic's analysis of black action film and Quentin Tarantino's confessed love of 1970s black film culture see Samuel Blumenfeld ["Blaxploitation," "J'etais"]).

After more than twenty years' hindsight, these types of action films still incorporate interestingly varied plots and use different film styles. The breadth of black action films made in the independent and Hollywood film sectors indicates the continued popularity of this genre. Indeed, the genre has outgrown the term "blaxploitation" since it does not merely exploit blacks and never has. Black action films now include inner-city youth films, gangster films, heist films, and a group of films whose plots and iconography borrow heavily from film genres that were popular during the fifties and sixties. This last group of black films includes Mario Van Peebles's black western *Posse* (Polygram, 1993), which continues an earlier tradition of black westerns. For instance, Sidney Poitier's black western *Buck and the Preacher* (Columbia, 1972), and Gordon Parks Jr.'s *Thomasine and Bushrod* (Columbia, 1974) present blacks in a western setting. Even in the 1930s there existed black westerns such as the white-directed/black-scripted *Bronze Buckaroo* (Hollywood Productions, 1938), *Harlem on the Prairie* (Associated Pictures, 1939), and *Harlem Rides the Range* (Hollywood Productions, 1939). All three of these 1930s black-oriented independent films feature the black cowboy-singer Herb Jeffries. The black western might appear to be an anomaly to many viewers, but these westerns are most often based on African American experiences as cowboys, buffalo soldiers, and blacks—men and women—who migrated to the West before, during, and after the Civil War. (For more insight into this neglected history of African American life in the West see the following works: Durham and Jones; Porter; Tolson; Lapp; Dickson; and Grinde and Taylor.)

African American genre films of the 1990s blend themes and styles from black Hollywood and Black independent films. The inner-city youth film subgenre exemplifies this mixing of what was originally viewed as two distinctly separate paths within African American filmmaking—Hollywood or Independent. Matty Rich's *Straight Out of Brooklyn* (Samuel Goldwyn, 1991), John Singleton's *Boyz 'n the Hood* (Columbia, 1991), Ernest Dickerson's *Juice* (Paramount, 1992), Allen and Albert Hughes's *Menace II Society* (New Line, 1993), and Doug McHenry's *Jason's Lyric* (Polygram, 1994) are interesting in their style of dress, choice of language ,and documentary style. However, the narratives of these films offer little change from the nihilism of such black action films of the seventies as Larry Cohen's white-directed *Black Caesar* (American International, 1973), *Superfly*, and to a lesser extent, Wendell Franklin's *The Bus is Coming* (K-Calb, 1971) and Joe Manduke's white-directed *Cornbread, Earl and Me* (American International, 1975). Now, the black male protagonists are all of high-school age and many of them, according to these films, have fewer options than did their counterparts in the 1970s and 1980s black teen films. Most, if not all these youth films, portray physical aggression and gunfights between black male teenagers from the inner city. Still, there were other rap and hip-hop energized films that used comedy and black middle-class pursuit to portray black adolescent angst.

Possession of a large powerful low-riding car, and high-caliber, rapid-fire guns are the fetishes that conjure up an exotic black masculinity that emasculates through objectification. The black one's symbolic penis or in the case of women their clitoris length, strength as psychologically calibrated in the low-riding, rapid fire, black (wo)man machine. In these black male-directed, and many times written, films, the young black (wo)man's lack of the fetishistic signs—cars, guns, gold, clothes—indicates "the symbolic (b)lack of." Here I am especially thinking of Queen Latifah's role in F. Gary Gray's *Set It Off* (New Line, 1996) which offers a female slant to the typical black macho gangster hero. Latifah plays a macho (read stereotyped dyke) gangster in love with a sexy nubile black woman. This "(b)lack of" reminds filmgoers of the loss of selfhood that occurs in Ousmane Sembene's *La Noire de* (Senegal, 1966), also known as *Black Girl.* The black heroine remains anonymous but somehow knowable through her horrid urban experience. Unlike Sembene's depiction of the black heroine, this subgenre foregrounds the black subject's inhumanity and, even more to the point, nihilistic "by any means necessary" death wish. These fictional youths have lost their faith in the black community's and the capitalist system's ability to provide opportunities for their upward socioeconomic mobility. Admittedly, this loss of faith in America is also present in many of the independent and Hollywood films

There are three major elements that construct this type of antihero(ine) in most 1990s black action films. First, the protagonists express an unlimited appetite for objects that express their inner worth. These fetishes, according to their reasoning, provide them with sociopolitical importance within the local black community that is presently under their immediate control. Second, black nihilistic protagonists disdain any of their subjects who refuse a life of crime. They also fear local blacks who

FIGURE 2.1. (From left to right) Jada Pinkett, Kimberly Elise, Queen Latifah, and Vivica Fox celebrate the aftermath of a successful robbery in F. Gary Gray's *Set It Off.* Courtesy: Jerry Ohlinger Archive.

perform criminal activity without seeking their approval. Third, these protagonists consequently hate the very community leaders and the overall black underworld that were respected in most 1970s films. For instance, *Shaft* and *Superfly* presented elderly women and men who were free from harm, and black criminals were mostly shown fighting white policemen and Italian American Mafiosi. It was interethnic rivalry similar to *West Side Story* and not intraracial violence.

These newer films, for the most part, express the belief that young black adults have lost faith in their community's ability to assist them to better their lives. These films are racial lynchings of the mind. Their presentations of surreal images of black organized criminals replace the very real organizations of brutal policemen, overcrowded correctional institutions, and racist white thugs. These films tend to exaggerate black-on-black violence to hide the racist institutions and their practices that nurture the self-hatred of black-on-black crimes in this New Jack World Order.

There is certainly a more hopeful side to 1990s black film culture. There still exist middle-class black adolescent films that instruct. This group includes John Singleton's black adolescence-in-angst films *Poetic Justice* (Columbia, 1993) and *Higher Learning* (Columbia, 1994); each film features a Rapper, Tupac Shakur and Ice Cube, respectively. These films and others call to mind the 1950s films featuring James Dean and Marlon Brando. As black teen films, they more closely resemble Michael Schultz's black teen picture *Cooley High* (American International, 1975) since it focuses on black urban as opposed to white suburban student life.

Another subgroup is rap films of a particularly innocuous variety. This group of films includes *House Party* (Columbia, 1990), *House Party II* (New Line, 1991), *Just Another Girl On the IRT.* (Miramax, 1992), *CB4* (Universal, 1993), and *House Party III* (New Line, 1994). More than any other group of black 1990s films, this particular group enjoyed worldwide box-office success. The black urban clothing styles and the rap and hip-hop music scores popularized the dress and music of this new generation of Blues People of the Nineties. The international sales of rap and hip-hop music, dress styles, and films are strong in urban centers in Europe, Africa, and Asia. For instance, Mathieu Kassovitz's much heralded French film *La Haine* (Lazennec, 1995) borrows heavily in theme, dress, and music from such black action youth films as Lee's *Do the Right Thing* (1989) and Singleton's *Boyz 'n the Hood* (1991). It did not require much reflection for American and French critics to acknowledge this cross-cultural transnational borrowing.

The clothing styles in these action films include the rough urban dress, gold-plated chains, and ear, nose, and finger rings of urban street toughs, a type of spectacle of black urban in-your-face toughness. The oversized clothes resemble the zoot suits of the past and remind us how radical fashions can safely be normalized within the production-distribution-exhibition processes for consumption by an international middle class—the public of the multinational entertainment industry.

Similar to the popularization of dressing styles that such seventies action films as *Shaft* and *Superfly* spurred, 1990s black action films produce a similar crossover response among African American youths, white teenagers, and even among non-American teenagers. Each film's music score exploits popular black urban-music forms, such as rap and hip-hop, and the clothing that is identified with this music. Many of the actors featured in the films are notable for their previous work in black situation comedies or appearance in music videos featuring their music. Will Smith and Queen Latifah are two examples of this entertainment-marketing phenomenon.

The last group of films deals with the family and its struggles to survive the growing divisions in the black community between those who have succeeded and their brothers and sisters who have not yet received their piece of the African American middle-class dream. Of this type of narrative the films *Crooklyn* (Universal, 1994), *Soul Food* (20th Century Fox, 1997) and *He Got Game* (Touchstone, 1998) dramatize class divisions within black families and the community. Another group of black family films is more magical and not so easily placed into the traditional categories. Films such as Charles Burnett's *To Sleep With Anger* (Columbia, 1990), Kasi Lemmons's *Eve's Bayou* (Trimark, 1997), and, to a lesser extent, John Singleton's *Rosewood* (Warner, 1997) use African American mythology and magical imagery. Behind their mystical style they dramatize how black middle-class educated families in Los Angeles, New Orleans, and Rosewood, Florida, still encounter threats to their well being. Darnell Martin's *I Like It Like That* (Columbia, 1994) deals with the Afro-Hispanic family, an item that has yet not been clearly defined by critics who resort to traditional racial divides to describe what is a black film and what is not. This perhaps is the best conclusion to Black Hollywood films in the nineties. Many of them have been influenced by independent styles pioneered by both black and white filmmakers during the sixties and seventies.

WORKS CITED

Blumenfeld, Samuel. "Blaxploitation, le cinema du ghetto." *Le Monde* (March 31, 1998). 28, cols. 4–5.

———. "J'etais fier de posseder une culture noire." Interview withQuentin Tarantino. *Le Monde* (April 2, 1998). 31, cols. 1–4.

Bobo, Jacqueline. *Black Women as Cultural Readers*. New York: Columbia University Press, 1995.

Burnett, Charles. "Inner City Blues." *Questions of Third Cinema*. Ed. Jim Pines and Paul Willemen. London: British Film Institute, 1989. 223–26.

Carson, Diane, Linda Dittmar, and Janice Welsch, eds. *Multiple Voices in Feminist Film Criticism*. Minneapolis: University of Minnesota Press, 1994. 1–4.

Chan, Kenneth. "The Construction of Black Male Identity in Black Action Films of the Nineties." *Cinema Journal* 37.2 (1998): 35–48.

Diawara, Manthia. "Noir by Noirs: Toward a New Realism in Black Cinema." *African American Review* 27.4 (1993): 525–38.

Dickson, Lynda Fae. "The Early Club Movement among Black Women in Denver, 1890–1925." Diss. University of Colorado, 1982.

Durham, Philip, and Everett L. Jones. *The Negro Cowboys*. New York: Dodd, Mead, and Co., 1965.

Friedman, Milton. "There's No Justice in the War on Drugs." *New York Times* January 11, 1998: 19.

Gray, Herman. "Black Masculinity and Visual Culture." *Black Male: Representations of Masculinity in Contemporary American Art*. Ed. Thelma Golden. New York: Whitney Museum of Art, 1994. 175–80.

Grinde, Donald A., Jr., and Quintard Taylor. "Red v. Black: Conflict and Accommodation in the Post Civil War Indian Territory, 1865–1907." *American Indian Quarterly* 8 (1984): 211–25.

Guerrero, Ed. *Framing Blackness: The African American Image in Film*. Philadelphia: Temple University Press, 1993. 159–208.

Harris Trudier. "On *The Color Purple*, Stereotypes, and Silence." *Black American Literature Forum* 18 (1984): 155–61.

Kellner, Douglas. *Media Culture: Cultural Studies, Identity and Politics between the Modern and Postmodern*. London and New York: Routledge, 1995. 157–97.

Lapp, Rudolph. *Blacks in the Gold Rush*. New Haven: Yale University Press, 1977.

Lott, Tommy L. "A No-Theory Theory of Contemporary Black Cinema." *Black American Literature Forum* 25.2 (1991): 221–36.

Nichols, Peter M. "Climbing Toward the Domain of the Independent-Movie Elite." *New York Times* January 4, 1998, sec. 2: 26.

Porter, Kenneth W. "Negro Labor in the Western Cattle Industry, 1866–1900." *Labor History* 10 (1969): 346–64, 366–68, 370–74.

Reid, Mark A. *Redefining Black Film*. Berkeley: University of California Press, 1993. 109–36.

———. "The Black Gangster Film." *Film Genre Reader II*. Ed. Barry Keith Grant. Austin: University of Texas Press, 1995. 456–73.

———. *PostNegritude Visual and Literary Culture*. Albany: State University of New York Press, 1997.

Tolson, Arthur L. *The Black Oklahomans: A History, 1541–1972*. New Orleans: Edwards Print Co., 1972.

Watkins, S. Craig. *Representing: Hip Hop Culture and the Production of Black Cinema*. Chicago: University of Chicago Press, 1998.

Watkins, Mel. "Sexism, Racism and Black Women Writers." *The New York Times Book Review* (June 12, 1986): 1, 35–37.

CHAPTER THREE

◼

So Much is Lost in Translation: Literary Adaptations in the 1990s

JOHN C. TIBBETTS

D'Artagnan was the biological father of King Louis XIV.

This amazing revelation, coming at the end of Randall Wallace's screen adaptation of Alexandre Dumas's *The Man in the Iron Mask* (1998) constitutes, no doubt, one of the most startling screen moments of the 1990s. Who would have suspected it? Certainly not d'Artagnan's Musketeer comrades. Certainly not Louis's presumed father, King Louis XIII. Certainly not the historians. And certainly not novelist Dumas.

While viewers blissfully ignorant of the Dumas original might revel in such soap-operatic fabrications, the more informed purists surely cry foul! They charge that too many filmmakers perform such acts of sabotage on their beloved classics with impunity. They groan when Steven Spielberg's *Hook* (1991) forces Peter Pan to grow up; they weep when Alfonso Cuaron relocates Charles Dickens's *Great Expectations* (1997) to the sunny Florida Gulf; and they cringe when Disney turns *The Hunchback of Notre Dame* (1996) into a musical cartoon with cute gargoyle characters named "Victor" and "Hugo." A lame justification for these alterations comes from the narrator of *Great Expectations*: "This isn't the way things happened, it's the way I *remember* them happening." Director/writer Terry Gilliam expressed it more pointedly, regarding his screen adaptation of Hunter Thompson's *Fear and Loathing in Las Vegas* (1998): "My attitude was, 'I hate [Thompson], I hate the bastard, [I] don't want him near this thing, I'm going to fuck up his book if he comes near this thing.' And that was my approach" (Smith 78). Small wonder that some writers, like Nick Nolte in Keith Gordon's adaptation of Kurt Vonnegut's *Mother Night* (1996), might be tempted to hang themselves—with a noose fashioned from a typewriter ribbon.

By contrast, however, it should be remembered that more literary adaptations than ever before have displayed a faithfulness bordering on obsession—the conventional morality that regards anything less as "a kind of vulgar cannibalization, an abuse of the high art of fiction" (Admussen 58). Michael Winterbottom's *Jude* (1996), Bille August's *Les Miserables* (1998), Claude Berri's *Germinal* (1994), and Claude Chabrol's *Madame Bovary* (1991)—to cite just a few—have displayed such respect for the texts of Thomas Hardy, Victor Hugo, Émile Zola, and Gustave Flaubert, respectively, that the results fairly choked on their own literary bile.

Less easily categorized are those postmodernist confabulations that indulge in both extremes, simultaneously. Baz Luhrmann's *William Shakespeare's Romeo + Juliet* (1996), Richard Loncraine's *Richard III* (1995), Al Pacino's *Looking for Richard* (1996), and Peter Greenaway's *Prospero's Books* (1990) lock text and screenplay in a symbiotic embrace. Word and image coexist in a perpetually shifting, weirdly multisensory, multimedia equilibrium. Neither book nor movie, as a result, is the primary, or definitive text. Both proclaim themselves as independent alternatives. We have come to a fork in the road. And, as Yogi Berra once observed, we must take it.

No decade in the history of the motion picture, save perhaps the decade before World War I, has produced more literary and theatrical adaptations than the 1990s. Early in the decade, commentator Pat Dowell foresaw the boom. "Hollywood still loves a presold property," he wrote, "[and now] maybe even loves it more" (Dowell 29). Fees paid to authors by filmmakers and publishers have been steadily rising. Even though options, rather than an outright buy of a literary property, have comprised the vast majority of deals (ranging from an average of $25,000 to $50,000), increasingly six-figure deals are becoming commonplace. Agencies such as Creative Management, Creative Artists Agency, and William Morris are giving first-buy priorities to their filmmaker clients.

Spearheading what is becoming, in some quarters at least, nothing less than a literary takeover of movies, are writers like Tom Clancy,

Stephen King, Michael Crichton, and John Grisham. They all, at one time or another, have assumed control over scripts and directors; in some cases, they are serving as executive producers of these adaptations. Tom Clancy's CIA operative Jack Ryan has been portrayed by Alec Baldwin in John McTiernan's *The Hunt for Red October* (1991), and by Harrison Ford in two films by Philip Noyce, *Patriot Games* (1992) and *Clear and Present Danger* (1994). Ryan was predictably stalwart, a bulwark against slippery politics and murky ideologies. "It's a gray world," complains one of his associates in *Clear and Present Danger.* "No," retorts Ryan, "it's a matter of right and wrong."

In addition to many Stephen King adaptations for television miniseries (*The Tommyknockers, It, The Langolliers, The Shining*), there have been numerous theatrical films, including Mary Lambert's *Pet Sematary* (1992), which proposed that you have to die *twice* to be really dead; Frank Darabont's *The Shawshank Redemption* (1994), about Andy Dufresne (Tim Robbins), a messiah dispensing grace and hope to Maine's Shawshank Prison; Taylor Hackford's exemplary *Dolores Claiborne* (1995), which starred Kathy Bates in the eponymous role of a vengeful, abused wife ("Sometimes being a bitch is all a woman can hold on to"); George Romero's *The Dark Half,* in which writer Thad Beaumont (Tim Hutton) slays his wicked literary creation-come-to-life, "George Stark," with a leaded pencil.

Michael Crichton's books have been represented in Philip Kaufman's *Rising Sun* (1993), which sounded a warning note against the potential Japanese corporate takeover of America ("The Japanese are not our saviors, they are our competitors; we should not forget it"); two films by Barry Levinson—*Disclosure* (1994), a corporate takeover story disguised as a tract on sexual harassment, and *Sphere* (1998), an undersea science-fiction encounter with aliens, after which the three human survivors join hands and agree to forget all about it (!); and two blockbusters by Steven Spielberg, *Jurassic Park* (1993) and *The Lost World* (1997), both advertisements for a theme park at Universal City.

John Grisham's lawyer novels, meanwhile, are, in the opinion of commentator Mark Olsen, quickly becoming the most successful literary franchise in history: "Just like a new location for a fast-food chain, a Hollywood studio can purchase the rights to one of Grisham's stories and have a pretty solid idea of what they're going to get." (Olsen 76). No matter that their depictions of the letter of the law and the practices of judicial procedure usually stray far from home—these stories are no different from biographies and history films in that they conform their subjects to the formulas of popular entertainment. They are the stepchild of the conspiracy thrillers of the seventies, and, at the same time, like seismic readings, they reflect the changing face of the legal system and our growing concern, even distrust and confusion, about the efficacy of legal procedures in the nineties. Thus, in Sydney Pollack's *The Firm* (1993), Tom Cruise portrays brash young Mitch McDeere in a "Faust goes into a law firm" allegory. In Alan J. Pakula's *The Pelican Brief* (1993) newspaperman Gray Grantham (Denzel Washington) and law student Darby Shaw (Julia Roberts) uncover the conspiracy behind the assassination of two Supreme Court judges. Joel Schumacher's *The Client* (1994) and *A Time to Kill* (1996) throw maverick attorneys Reggie Love (Susan Sarandon) and Jake Brigance (Mathew McConaughey), into the clutches of mobsters and the Ku Klux Klan, respectively. James Foley's *The Chamber* (1996) pits fresh-faced Adam Hall (Chris O'Donnell) against a justice system determined to execute his convicted grandfather (Gene Hackman). Francis Ford Coppola broke a long dry spell with his hugely successful *The Rainmaker* (1997), which casts Matt Damon as a neophyte, shiny-faced idealist battling the wiles of a slick, big-city lawyer, Leo Drummond (Jon Voight) in a medical insurance case.

Certainly one of the major events of the nineties has been the continuing series of adaptations of novels by Jane Austen and Henry James. By the late 1990s, five Austen adaptations were playing in American theaters and on television. Their reception thus far has been profitable and has spread beyond the "art house" crowd. Ang Lee's *Sense and Sensibility* (1995) cost only $15.5 million to make and during its initial release grossed $42 million. *Persuasion* (1995), targeted as an art-house film, pulled in a respectable $5.3 million. Amy Heckerling's *Clueless* (1995) established Alicia Silverstone as a star and spun off an ABC television sitcom and a line of Mattel Toy Company dolls. The six-hour BBC/Arts and Entertainment *Pride and Prejudice* became A&E cable channel's fastest-selling video title. And Douglas McGrath's *Emma* (1996) prompted *People* magazine to proclaim Austen one of the "25 Most Intriguing People of 1995."

Austen's appeal resides in her finely honed dialogue and satiric thrusts at the follies of class, gender, and manners. Three of the Austen adaptations have been respectful, sumptuously mounted, impeccably-cast productions. Ang Lee's *Sense and Sensibility* benefited from crisp compositions, a sensitive response to the rural locations, and first-time screenwriter Emma Thompson's canny script. Lee was the perfect choice to helm the project. Like Austen, as Donald Lyons notes, Lee is "an artist of family and society, of the unending tension between ceremony and self" (Lyons 41). The misadventures of the two disinherited Dashwood sisters (Emma Thompson as the terminally demure Elinor and Kate Winslet as the dangerously headstrong Marianne) were retained as the central focus. Arrayed opposite them were Austen's admittedly shallow male characters (here transformed into more suitable foils), Hugh Grant as the retiring Edward Ferrars, Greg Wise as the dashing John Willoughby, and Alan Rickman as kindly Colonel Brandon. Retained is the satiric irony that was Austen's forte, that is, the sisters' delayed awareness of the dangerous extremes to which their respective temperaments are leading them.

An entirely different atmosphere pervades *Persuasion*, where sailors and the sea (the rainswept seawalls of Lyme Regis) play a significant role in the adventures of the Elliott family. Desperate to connect with the "proper" social set, Sir Walter (Corin Redgrave) subjects his daughters to the deceits and hypocrisies of society—all but Anne Elliott (Amanda Root), that is, whose intelligence and sardonic detachment from such frivolities is both her strength and her weakness. She's a Regency Cinderella who foolishly rejected her Prince Charming (Ciaran Hinds as Captain Frederick Wentworth) years before. Now, she presumes herself too plain to regain his attentions. There's a wonderful moment when the disconsolate Anne reflects on the inconstancy of the male gender: "All that privilege I claim for my own sex," she muses. "We love longest, when existence or when hope is gone."

It is *Emma*, written in 1816, the year before Austen's death, that has best borne out the timelessness of her work. Like the three novels that preceded it, it is preoccupied with the plight of young women desperate to be appropriately married. Spinsterhood and bad connections—such as marrying beneath one's station—are to be avoided at all costs. After a series of disastrous attempts to pair off her friends with men, Emma confronts a dilemma of her own: She falls in love with the noble Mr. Knightley, but hardly knows how to recognize, much less deal with her emotions. Two film versions, released in the same year, could not be more radically different. McGrath's film most closely preserves the story's period setting, story trajectory, and satiric sparkle. Perhaps its finest moment comes during the opening credits: An image of what appears to be a planet spinning in the star-spangled heavens turns out to be merely a small bauble dangling from Emma's delicate fingers. The tiny ornament is decorated with

34

FIGURE 3.1. Gwyneth Paltrow and Jeremy Northham take the floor at a fancy dress ball in Douglas McGrath's *Emma*. Courtesy: Jerry Ohlinger Archive.

Emma's miniature painted images of the people and places in her narrowly circumscribed world. It is a brilliant visual pun: What had at first appeared to be the cosmos is in reality a microcosm. It reminds us that Austen regarded her work as infinitely small in scale and dramatic compass (if not in pretension), declaring it to be "the little bit (two inches wide) of ivory on which I work with so fine a brush as produces little effect after much labor." However brittle and small Austen's images may be, they suggest truths of a universal proportion and scale.

The second film version, directed by Amy Heckerling, sets the sixteen-year old Emma (renamed "Cher" and portrayed by the unflappably ditzy and relentlessly sweet Alicia Silverstone) adrift in a modern milieu of Valley Girls and teen-speak. The title, *Clueless,* refers to her inability to deal with her own infatuation with her father's handsome law clerk, Josh (Paul Rudd). The use of language—always an important element in Austen's art—is the most interesting aspect of the film. If Austen uses language as a signifier of rank and social position, the teen vernacular of *Clueless* likewise functions as a codification of who is either "in" or "out" in Cher's insular circle. Far less mordant than Heckerling's other teen comedy, *Fast Times at Ridgemont High* (1982), *Clueless* suggests that the cynical "X-generation" has a sweet underbelly, after all.

Adapting Henry James to the screen has been the constant hope— and the inevitable bane—of many filmmakers over the last half century. "What to do with James," wails critic Daphne Merkin, "who, by his own admission, had trouble with what he called the 'solidity of specification,' and whose unique skill was his self-professed 'appeal to incalculability'— for intimating, in other words, that which is psychologically most oblique?" (Merkin 121) However, as commentator Laura Miller points out, James's relentless pursuit of the shadowy territories of human experience—"the imagined, the feared, the hoped for, the ignored, the undone"—is precisely the perverse challenge that filmmakers haven't been able to resist. (Miller 31) Moreover, it was James who understood the tensions between a European Old World, where class and money preordained the paths of individuals' lives, and the emerging New World whose new social liberties presented individuals with many competing and contradictory options.

Four Jamesian adaptations have appeared, and more are on the way. Jane Campion's *Portrait of a Lady* (1996) is an erotically idiosyncratic, feminist reconfiguration of the troubled relationship between "New World" Isabel Archer (Nicole Kidman) and "Old World" Gilbert Osmond (John

Malkovich). Agnieszka Holland's *Washington Square* (1997) examines the sexual politics underlying the relationship between wealthy heiress Catherine Sloper (Jennifer Jason-Leigh) and handsome idler Morris Townsend (Ben Chaplin).

The two screen versions of James's *Wings of the Dove* by Iain Softley (1997) and Meg Richman (1998) are especially interesting in that, like the two aforementioned versions of Austen's *Emma*, one is a faithful transcription, the other a free-form update. Iain Softley's *Wings of the Dove*, despite shifting the time period slightly forward to 1910, retains the settings of London and Venice, the core cast of characters, and the general plot outline. That shift forward in time, by the way, while attacked by many critics of the film, seems appropriate in the light of the fact that this is the most frankly erotic of James's novels, the one most conducive to the context of a world poised on the rim of modernism—when sexual mores and fashions are changing, the London Underground is running, and electricity is transforming urban life. Meanwhile, screenwriter Hossein Amini (*Jude*) ably sorts out the convolutions of the plot into a relatively straightforward story line; and director Softley rejects the sort of camera trickery, *outré* dream sequences, and other stylistic clutter that marred Campion's *Portrait of a Lady* (1996). The cast is exceptionally fine. As the target of the scheming Kate Croy (Helena Bonham-Carter) and the seemingly diffident Merton (Linus Roache), the wealthy but doomed American heiress, Milly (Alison Elliott), is a Pre-Raphaelite vision come to life. But as her affair with Merton develops, the very air grows darker and the rains fall harder, choking the brittle surfaces of Venice in the constricting coils of the unholy intrigue. Finally, it is Merton who is caught in the noose, as it were, and is left able only to love the dead Milly. He is obsessed with a passion more exquisite—and more hopeless—than anything he can feel toward the living Kate. This is reinforced by the penultimate scene, when Merton and Kate make love in his dingy apartment. Nowhere else in James is there a love scene like this, and the film perfectly captures his gruesome counterpointing of the blaze of sexual passion with the coldness of emotional paralysis. The figures grapple in the bed, in the shadows, but their faces remain turned away from each other. It is a moment that stands out in the catalog of Jamesian films. Surely, it haunts the viewer, rather like the memory of Milly that will haunt Kate and Merton forever after.

Meg Richman's *Under Heaven* isn't so much a story for the ages as a story for the "New Age." She has shorn James's book of its period trappings and thematic complexities. Updated to a modern Seattle setting, Kate and Merton are now Cynthia and Buck (Molly Parker and Aden Young), two slackers whose relationship meanders along in a haze of booze, drugs, and squalid poverty. The target of their intrigue, Milly, is now Eleanor (Joely Richardson), who lives alone in a mansion above Puget Sound. After the intrigue is discovered, no one seems to mind much. The threesome continue to live on harmoniously enough. Eleanor looks moodily on while Buck and Cynthia disport themselves in her bedroom. Finally, Eleanor has the grace and discretion to expire prettily in the garden. While the sex scenes—including a startling moment when Eleanor reveals her double mastectomy to Buck—are franker than anything in James, the rest of the movie has reduced the book's nastier implications into a kind of sentimental pabulum. No one, including the screenwriter/director, seems to have the slightest idea of what these characters are really about. Never mind the tangle of intrigue and deceptions, these folks are all a pretty sweet bunch after all. Like some episode of television's *Friends*, or *Melrose Place*, Cynthia and Buck love, conspire against their best friend, then drift apart again. Well, *whatever*. . . . Never mind, just think warm thoughts.

Shakespeare was undeniably one of the favorites of nineties filmmakers and viewers. The recent boom, according to Anthony Lane, is but the latest move on the part of filmmakers "not merely to bring him to the attention of the masses but to convince the masses that he is ready for immediate consumption" (Lane 65). Accordingly, several directors in the Nineties have flagrantly stamped Shakespeare's plays with a postmodernist sensibility. Only Trevor Nunn's *Twelfth Night* (1996), Oliver Parker's *Othello* (1995), and Kenneth Branagh's *Much Ado about Nothing* (1992) have kept the Bard within reach of traditional text and performance. Otherwise, Branagh's *Hamlet* (1996) and *A Midwinter's Tale* (1995), Al Pacino's *Looking for Richard* (1996), Richard Loncraine's *Richard III*, Gus Van Sant's *My Own Private Idaho* (1990), Baz Luhrmann's *William Shakespeare's Romeo + Juliet* (1996), and Peter Greenaway's *Prospero's Books* (1990), have wrought imaginative "takes" on their respective adaptations.

Pride of place necessarily goes to Branagh's four-hour *Hamlet* (1996), a reconstruction of the full text of the first folio plus portions of the second quarto. Despite this textual fidelity, never were Hamlet's lines upon hearing of the appearance of his father's ghost—"It bodes for a strange eruption of our status"—more appropriate. Branagh's adaptation looks and acts like no other Hamlet in screen history. Contrasted with Olivier's 1948 version, a spare, stark black-and-white chamber drama, and the 1991 Zeffirelli version, a Pre-Raphaelite conception with a drastically reduced text, this film is a big, bright, ornament throwing off a thousand glints of light. Most of the action takes place in blazingly lit castle interiors (a triumph of incandescent engineering!) teeming with courtiers and soldiers wearing a motley of Edwardian, mid-Victorian, and Ruritanian garb. And popping up everywhere are such modern appliances and props as photographs, newspapers, a steam engine, and a strait jacket for the mad Ophelia! Meanwhile, the indecision of Hamlet (Branagh), the machinations of usurpers King Claudius (Derek Jacobi) and Queen Gertrude (Julie Christie), and the connivings of Polonious (Richard Briers) transpire in huge ballrooms, where the mise-en-scène scatters the players about like chess pieces on a parquet checkerboard. Appropriately enough, in this weird Wonderland, the players strut and pose before galleries of mirrors, addressing their reflected selves as they declaim their famous soliloquies (including Ophelia's mad scene and the "To be or not to be" speech). In its unabashed theatricalism, in its sheer exhilaration of *performance*, it is metatheater on film, an event that enjoys its own mirror image as much as it solicits our applause.

But Branagh is not done with *Hamlet*. A necessary companion to his four-hour epic is *A Midwinter's Tale* (1995), a "backstage" version of *Hamlet* that Branagh released the year before. The glitches, twitches, and occasional glories behind a theatrical troupe's desperate preparations for a Christmas Eve performance of the play in an English country church constitute a rowdy commentary on the play in general (and in particular, the Branagh *Hamlet* to come). Meanwhile, when the actual play is enacted late in the film, it hurtles along in breathless leaps, rather like one of those Tom Stoppard breakneck versions of the Bard. (Branagh even gets in a private joke of his own, when the troupe's director reassures his players— many of whom appear in the aforementioned *Hamlet*—that they'll be allowed to perform the play *with cuts*.)

Many literary adaptations have introduced American audiences to the works of a group of relatively unknown international writers, old and new. Among the less touted screen "finds" of the decade is that self-proclaimed "galley slave to pen and ink," Honoré de Balzac. Although he produced more than one hundred major works before his death in 1851, he has been relatively ignored by filmmakers (only a *Masterpiece Theater* production of *Cousin Bette* comes to mind). Perhaps this has been due to a mistaken notion that the interrelationships among the characters of his *La Comédie humaine* series would present problems for audiences unfamiliar with him. Yet, Yves Angelo's *Colonel Chabert* (1995), Des McAnuff's *Cousin Bette* (1998), and Lavinia Currier's *Passion in the Desert* (1998) may bode well to make Balzac the *auteur du jour* for the future. *Colonel Chabert* was an absorbing character study of a man (Gerard Depardieu) claiming to be a long-lost (presumably dead) hero in Napoleon's campaign against Russia. By the story's end, he has lost everything except the integrity of his name. Cousin Bette was a high-toned soap opera, a dark fairy tale that cast Jessica Lange as a pale, tight-lipped, stiff figure of vengeance—a carnivorous bloom sheathed in black—against her boorish, selfish family. *Passion in the Desert* was the most interesting of the three; indeed, one of the most unusual literary adaptations of the nineties. Virtually a wordless meditation on the folly of art, society, war, and other human predilections, it confronted actor Ben Daniels with the most dangerous challenge faced by any actor of the decade—portraying a Napoleonic cavalryman who, after losing his way in the Egyptian desert, engages in a most peculiar relationship with a savage leopard.

Authors more contemporary to our time include several Chinese writers from the so-called New Realist period of the late 1980s. Zhang Yimou in his "breakthrough" films *Judou* (1990) and *Raise the Red Lantern* (1991) adapted, respectively, *Fuxi Fuxi*, by Liu Heng (the pen name of Liu Guanjun) and *Da hong denglong gaogao gua*, by Su Tong. Initially banned in China by the China Film Bureau, they are particularly distinguished by their sensitive portrayals of the repressed status of women in the patriarchal contexts of Chinese culture.

Jane Campion brought to the screen the three-volume autobiography of Janet Frame, New Zealand's foremost writer, under the title, *An Angel at My Table* (1990). Steven Spielberg and Steve Zaillian brought Australian writer Thomas Keneally's *Schindler's List* to the screen in 1993. Mexican author Laura Esquivel adapted the "magic realism" of her own *Como agua para chocolate* for her husband, Alfonso Arau, in *Like Water for Chocolate* (1993). From Australia came Gillian Armstrong's adaptation of Peter Carey's bizarre love story of two gambling addicts, *Oscar and Lucinda* (1997). From Scotland came Danny Boyle's adaptation of Irvine Welsh's ferociously trenchant portrait of drug trafficking in Edinburgh, *Trainspotting* (1996). And from Ireland several Irish writers have been represented—Maeve Binchy in Pat O'Connor's nostalgically bittersweet *Circle of Friends* (1995); Patrick McCabe in Neil Jordan's darkly surreal *The*

Butcher Boy (1998)—one of the most disturbing portraits of psychotic paranoia and mental integration in movie history; and Roddy Doyle's "Barrytown trilogy" in films by Alan Parker (*The Commitments*, 1994), and Stephen Frears (*The Snapper*, 1995, and *The Van*, 1996).

Some of the nineties' most controversial topics arose in literary adaptations. Mike Figgis's *Leaving Las Vegas* (1995), based on John O'Brien's 1991 autobiographical novel, portrayed the last days of a suicidal alcoholic. Neil Jordan's *Interview with the Vampire* (1994), drawn from Anne Rice's book, flirted with homosexuality and AIDS. Sex in general, both licit and illicit, graphic and suggested, was, as always, a recurring preoccupation in many other adaptations. Roland Joffe's *The Scarlet Letter* (1995) revisited Nathaniel Hawthorne's classic account of sex and adultery in Old Salem. Mike Nichols's *Primary Colors* (1998) adapted "Anonymous"'s political exposé about sex and adultery in the White House. And Adrian Lyne's *Lolita* (1997) took on Vladimir Nabokov's book about pedophilia and sexual obsession in the American Heartland. Significantly, all of them go soft, as it were, and shrug off their commitments.

Leaving Las Vegas opens promisingly enough: Fired from his job as a Hollywood screenwriter, and determined to drink himself to death, Ben Sanderson (Nicolas Cage) checks into a Las Vegas motel. Above the doorway is a sign that reads: "The Whole Year Inn." But the bleary-eyed Ben distorts the message into "The Hole You're Inn." Fair enough. Whereas the standard Hollywood formula had heretofore held out the promise of hope for a drunkard's redemption—or at least dramatically exploited his attempts to swear off the booze—this movie accepts alcoholism as a fatal fact in his life. Yet, in contradistinction to the book, the film softens the impact by enveloping the action in a romantic bloom of smeary, soft-focus images, time-lapse sequences, and gently skewed camera angles. Moreover, a bluesy soundtrack, consisting of Sting's rendering of all those Frank Sinatra-style, three-o'clock-in-the-morning laments (Figgis is himself a musician and fills in as keyboard man on the soundtrack), gently massages and comforts our distressed brow. After a lot of this, one gets the impression that Figgis is exploiting the story for the sake of yet another torch song from the midnight jukebox. So, "set 'em up Joe. . . ."

Interview with the Vampire was supposed to be about the seduction of a character named Louis by the Parisian vampire, Lestat. Their subsequent homosexual union, and a number of other liaisons, especially Louis's infatuation with Armand, the leader of a coven of vampires in the Theatre du Vampires, would seem to speak eloquently to a decade fraught with anxieties not only about homosexuality but about blood-related contagions, especially AIDS. Jordan's screen version with Tom Cruise, Brad Pitt, and Antonio Banderas (as Lestat, Louis, and Armand, respectively), however, mutes, if not entirely eliminates the homosexual overtones of their liaisons. Only in the scenes with the little girl, Claudia (Kirsten Dunst) whom Lestat and Louis "adopt"—in appearance a child but in practice a mature, ravenous, blood-drinking fiend—and in scenes with the darkly ferocious Antonio Banderas does the film transcend the trappings of yet another vampire movie and approach the perversities of the novel.

Surely no other literary adaptation of the nineties perpetrated a more bizarre, unintentionally comic spin on a literary classic than did Roland Joffe's version of Hawthorne's *The Scarlet Letter*. Demi Moore is Hester Prynne, and she swims in the nude, makes love in a grain bin, stands up for women's rights, and fights Indians. Gary Oldman is her lover, the Reverend Dimmesdale, and he also swims in the buff and makes love in a grain bin (when he's not fighting Indians). And Robert Duvall is the wicked Chillingworth (here named Dr. Roger Prynne), a guy who chops his hair into a Travis Bickle Mohawk and goes bare-bodied berserk at the full moon. Whereas Hawthorne chose to begin the story after Hester Prynne's adultery and concentrate upon the subsequent debilitating guilts suffered by both lovers (always a favorite theme of the author's), the movie chose to focus instead on the details of the erotic trysts (remember that business in the grain bin) and then prove the affair to have been a cleansing experience after all. The tougher issues, like the responsibilities Hawthorne insisted they must bear for their actions, are completely omitted. The happy pair escape at the end, of course, and ride off in a carriage toward the sunset, leaving in their wake savage Indians and vicious Puritans.

Primary Colors airs out the dirty political laundry and tarnished idealism that has attended American presidential politics over the past decade. Candidate Stanton (John Travolta) is portrayed not only as an opportunist who has indulged in shady campaign practices and the seduction of a young black girl, but as an idealist who believes that the end justifies the means. As a result, the film doesn't commit to a central viewpoint, or attitude toward its character. It's *shifty*, like Stanton himself. Still, it's great fun to watch Travolta as the big galoot who's running as hard for the presidency as he is from his own flawed character. In short, not only can he talk out of both sides of his mouth, but he can run in opposite directions, too.

Lolita was a film that promised to break out of the strait jacket of censorship that had plagued the Stanley Kubrick version of 1962. The subject of pedophilia has always been problemmatic, to say the least. In the "Crimes and Criminal Procedures" section of the United States Code, it is construed as a form of pornography. But although director Lyne and screenwriter Stephen Schiff did not have to knuckle down under the Production Code (which had been replaced by the Ratings Code of 1968), they had to face the reality of the Child Pornography Prevention Act that had just been passed in 1996. On a lawyer's advice, Lyne cut out most of Lolita's nude scenes, disallowed physical contact between actors Jeremy Irons and Dominque Swains (a pad or board discreetly separated them), and occasionally used a nineteen-year-old body double for Swains. Moreover, Humbert does not come across as a pedophile at all. Clearly, he is attracted only to Lolita (she reminds him of a little girl he had worshiped when he was a child but who had died tragically young); and at no time does he pay the slightest attention to the many other little girls who scamper about the edges of the story. It is the malevolent Clare Quilty (Frank Langella) who, by contrast, is the genuine pedophile. Lyne insures our antipathy to him by veiling him in infernal smoke and accompanying his scenes with the strains of Mussourgsky's *Night on Bald Mountain*. Thus, Humbert's slaying of Quilty at the end is seen to be more the action of an avenging angel than a deranged maniac. This is at variance with Nabokov's original conception, which neither justified Humbert nor attempted to diminished his wickedness. If anything, Humbert emerges here a victim of his own obsession and the target of Lolita's sexual aggressiveness and precocity. Director Lyne himself was quoted as protesting that his film took the moral high ground: "No one comes well out of it. They all *die* for chrissake" (qtd in Wood 9). Even the mainstream *Entertainment Weekly* carped at the result, calling the film a watered-down "Lolita," a "Lolita Lite": "It cowers before the morally self-righteous, sexually-spooked America of the late 1990s" (Tucker 54).

In closing, it's worth mentioning that, inevitably, the lives of writers themselves become grist for filmmakers and suffer the "sea change" of adaptation. One image in Bernard Rose's *Anna Karenina* (1997), based on the Leo Tolstoy novel, sums up the situation: In the prologue, Tolstoy himself is fleeing from a pack of wolves. He throws himself into a vast pit and clutches at a tree root to arrest his fall. There he dangles, midway between the hungry wolves crouching above and an angry bear waiting below. At the top, we might infer, are the filmmakers waiting to adapt his *books*; at the bottom are the filmmakers waiting to dramatize his *life*. . . . Either way, he's in trouble.

Indeed, the parade of images is varied and, occasionally, bizarre. In Brian Gilbert's *Wilde* (1998) a resplendently attired Oscar Wilde (Stephen Fry) lectures on aesthetics to scruffy miners in Leadville, Colorado. A gloom-haunted Franz Kafka (Jeremy Irons) lives out events in his novels in the night streets of Prague in Steven Soderbergh's *Kafka* (1993). Tweedy C. S. Lewis (Anthony Hopkins) mourns the death of Joy Gresham (Debra Winger) in Richard Attenborough's *Shadowlands* (1993). Algonquin Round Table wit Dorothy Parker (Jennifer Jason-Leigh) mourns life in general—"things always turn out worse than you think"—in Alan Rudolph's *Mrs. Parker and the Vicious Circle* (1994). Tightly-wound poet T. S. Eliot (Willem Dafoe) consigns his wife, Viv Haigh-Wood (Miranda Richardson), to an asylum in Brian Gilbert's adaptation of Michael Hasting's play, *Tom and Viv* (1995). Another poet, Pablo Neruda (Philippe Noiret), plays Cupid for the love-lorn postman, Mario (Massimij Troissi) in Michael Radford's *Il Postino* (1994). A hothouse bloom like Lytton Strachey (Jonathan Pryce) inhabits a dour Edwardian Wonderland in Christopher Hampton's *Carrington* (1995). Surly Arthur Rimbaud (Leonardo DiCaprio) declares himself a one-man poetry revolution in Agnieszka Holland's *Total Eclipse* (1995). And another revolutionary, the eighteenth-century playwright/swordsman/philanderer Pierre Caron de Beaumarchais (Fabrice Luchini), smuggles armaments to the American cause in Eduoard Molinaro's adaptation of Sacha Guitry's play, *Beaumarchais, the Scoundrel* (1997).

At this writing the flow of literary adaptations taking us into the millennium shows no sign of slowing down. Books are continually in motion. (In Greenaway's *Prospero's Books* a book in Prospero's library is entitled, "Books in Motion"; indeed, like Birnam Wood, it moves.). However, when virtual reality systems and holographic projections supplant conventional movie theaters and television screens, a plethora of new considerations regarding the adaptation process must arise. And then, perhaps we'll find out who the *real* father of Louis XIV was.

WORKS CITED

Admussen, Richard L., Edward S. Gallagher, and Lubbe Levin. "Novels and Films: A Limited Inquiry." *Literature/Film Quarterly* 6.1 (Winter 1978): 57–72.

Dowell, Pat. "Shooting Words." *American Film* 16.7 (July 1991):26–30, 46.

Lane, Anthony. "Tights! Camera! Action!" *The New Yorker* (November 25,1996): 65–77.

Lyons, Donald. "Passionate Precision: *Sense and Sensibility*." *Film Comment* 32.1 (January–February 1996): 34–41.

Merkin, Daphne. "The Escape Artist." *The New Yorker* (November 10, 1997): 121–22

Miller, Laura. "Henry James: Losing It at the Movies." *The New York Times Book Review* (January 19, 1997): 31.

Olsen, Mark. "Grisham Movies." *Film Comment* 34.2 (March–April 1998): 76–80.

Smith, Giles. "War Games." *The New Yorker* (May 25, 1998): 74–79.

Tucker, Ken. "Little Girl Lust." *Entertainment Weekly* 443 (July 31, 1998): 53–54.

Wood, Michael. "Revisiting Lolita." *The New York Review of Books* (March 26, 1998): 9–13.

CHAPTER FOUR

◉

Of Tunes and Toons:
The Movie Musical in the 1990s

MARC MILLER

To understand the precarious state of the movie musical in 1998, one has to travel back to 1964–65. Back then, there came in quick succession three enormous musical successes, one original (Robert Stevenson's *Mary Poppins* [1964]) and two adapted from 1950s Broadway smashes (George Cukor's *My Fair Lady* [1964], Robert Wise's *The Sound of Music* [1964]). All three won Oscars, racked up multimillions, and convinced studio executives that the masses would turn out for anything that sang and danced, be it a filming of a fustian mid-century stage property (Joshua Logan's *Paint Your Wagon* [1969], Francis Ford Coppola's *Finian's Rainbow* [1968]) or a special effects-laden version of a beloved children's book, festooned with cheery songs (Richard Fleischer's *Doctor Dolittle* [1967], Ken Hughes's *Chitty Chitty Bang Bang* [1968]).

To put it mildly, these executives misread their public. Usually costing $10 million to $20 million apiece when the average movie went for $4 million or less, most musicals of the late 1960s and early 1970s recouped less than half their budgets. For one thing, most weren't very good: Try sitting today through Andrew L. Stone's *Song of Norway* (1970) or George Sidney's *Half a Sixpence* (1967). For another, the traditional values they trumpeted were viewed as irrelevant or ridiculous in the era of

Vietnam, race riots, women's lib, and the King and Kennedy assassinations. Meantime, inexpensive works aimed at a growing "youth market" made all the money: good examples are Arthur Penn's *Bonnie and Clyde* (1967), Mike Nichols's *The Graduate* (1967), and Dennis Hopper's *Easy Rider* (1969).

The genre remained non grata throughout the 1970s and 1980s, with a new generation of moviemakers reflecting the darker, more cynical values of contemporary America. While there were still successful musicals, usually Broadway adaptations—Norman Jewison's *Fiddler on the Roof* (1971), Bob Fosse's *Cabaret* (1972), Randal Kleiser's *Grease* (1978)—these were the exception rather than the rule. For every *Grease* there were films like Robert Greenwald's *Xanadu* (1980); for every *Cabaret*, a film like Nancy Walker's *Can't Stop the Music* (1980); for every *Fiddler*, a film like Arthur Hiller's *Man of La Mancha* (1972). The movie musical, then, entered the '90s as a relic of an America that looked hopelessly naive and deluded to baby boomers, "Gen Xers," and the MTV crowd.

And so it might have remained, were it not for a single movie studio. For years, the only Hollywood outfit that could be relied on to release a musical every year or two was Walt Disney Pictures. Of course, that musical was nearly always a cartoon, and more often than not a reissue. A film such as David Hand's Disney production of *Snow White and the Seven Dwarfs* (1937), or Clyde Geronimi and Wilfred Jackson's *Peter Pan* (1953), or Geronimi and Jackson's *Cinderella* (1950) could always pull in a few million in rerelease, though the returns diminished as Disney began issuing its treasures on videocassette. Its new animated musicals, however, were languishing. While such efforts as George Scribner's *Oliver and Company* (1988) turned a profit, critics found the animation uninspired, the musical scores insipid, the storytelling witless (Canby C8; Carroll 57; French 42; Maslin, "In Today's" 13). Further, such fare lacked crossover appeal: While an *Oliver and Company* could mollify the undiscriminating six-year-old, it bored parents silly.

It was wise of Walt Disney Chairman Michael D. Eisner, then, to demand better product—and hire the talent to deliver it. For its twentninth full-length animated feature, Ron Clements and John Musker's *The Little Mermaid* (1989), Disney began cobbling together a stable of musical-making artists something like the fabled Freed Unit at the old MGM. Producers such as John Musker and Don Hahn; directors such as Kirk Wise and Gary Trousdale; screenwriters such as Linda Woolverton and Carl Binder; and, most of all, the composer-lyricist team of Alan Menken and Howard Ashman—all brought to their jobs a fine sense for musical storytelling, as well as an instinct for material that could beguile kids, "Gen X," and even the old fogies who grew up with *Easy Rider* (1969) and *The Graduate* (1967). The result was a genuine renaissance in the movie musical—albeit one unable to cross over from cartoonland into live-action cinema.

Like most good musicals, the better Disney efforts of the '90s begin with strong stories, quirky and interesting characters, and songs that advance plot or delineate character. The protagonist is inevitably young and energetic, but somehow dissatisfied with life. Aided by a mentor, who is frequently endowed with magical powers, he/she ventures out into the world, discovers love (cue the Oscar-winning ballad), and is thwarted by a villain. With the help of mentor and anthropomorphic sidekicks, the hero/heroine survives a titanic struggle with the forces of evil. In triumph, he/she embodies timeless American values (regardless of the movie's setting or the protagonist's nationality), such as hard work, sacrifice, love of parents/home, or that Disney staple, belief in wishes (Cochran 64).

Such was the formula with which Disney entered the 1990s, thanks to *The Little Mermaid*'s overwhelming success. Though *Mermaid* originally had been planned as a nonmusical (pressbook 8), critics and audiences agreed that the Menken-Ashman score helped immeasurably—indeed, was the film's driving force. The team had had a long apprenticeship off-Broadway, culminating in the long-running *Little Shop of Horrors* (later a successful movie musical in 1986), and *Mermaid*'s score revealed that their lessons had been well learned. From expository opening number ("Daughters of Triton") to heroine Ariel's "I want" ballad ("Part of Your World") to Busby Berkeleyesque production number ("Under the Sea") to villainess Ursula's plot-forwarding tour de force ("Poor Unfortunate Souls") to comic divertissement ("Les Poissons") to choral love song ("Kiss the Girl"), it carefully hit all the marks of a classic Broadway score. Citing "Part of Your World"'s yearning melody and protofeminist lyrics, *The New York Times* observed that "any Broadway musical would be lucky to include a single number this good. *The Little Mermaid* has a half dozen of them" (Maslin "Andersen's" C17). Lest his heroine's political correctness spoil the fun, Ashman leavened his lyrics with a winking note of self-parody that recalled Lorenz Hart or E. Y. Harburg. *Mermaid*'s musical riches did not end with its songs: Menken punctuated the story with a forceful musical underscoring recalling Max Steiner or Erich Wolfgang Korngold.

The Little Mermaid won two Oscars, earned $84 million in its initial domestic theatrical release, and laid the foundation for a marketing franchise that turned Disney from a profitable but moldering old-guard corporation into an unstoppable entertainment phenomenon. Impressive as that $84 million was in 1989, it was chump change compared to the millions to be made from *The Little Mermaid*'s international rights, video sales and rentals, cable showings, fast-food tie-ins, and, especially, product licensing: *Little Mermaid* toys, clothes, watches, trinkets, books, even a Saturday morning TV series. Disney had stumbled on a gold mine, and it spent the rest of the decade extracting the riches.

With newfound confidence, newfangled computer animation, and a record-crashing $35 million budget, Disney put six hundred people to work on Gary Trousdale and Kirk Wise's *Beauty and the Beast* (1991) (*Beauty* pressbook 2). The first animated feature ever to be nominated for Best Picture, *Beast* had been on Disney's back burner for decades, and was green-lighted when the ever-inventive Ashman came up with a solution to what Disney executives saw as the principal problem: a too-gloomy, claustrophobic second act (*Beauty* pressbook 5–6). By assigning lifelike qualities to the inanimate objects of the beast's castle—Mrs. Potts the teapot, Cogsworth the clock, and so forth—Ashman brightened the story, gave more characters more to sing about, and, not incidentally, sired a myriad of marketing possibilities. Too, he and screenwriter Woolverton amplified the feminist subtext that had served *Mermaid* so well: Belle, a rather passive heroine in the original story, is transformed into a bookish, inquisitive miss who rejects her handsome, empty-headed suitor Gaston for the brutish Beast, a sensitive soul who needs but a little nurturing to be changed into a (rather too-pretty) prince. Cannily, Disney fashioned a two-track marketing campaign for *Beast*, stressing the romance for the adults and the fun for the kids. All generations were bowled over, and even Disney was a bit surprised to find it had a lucrative "date movie" on its hands. Gushed *Variety*: "They just don't write 'em like they used to? Oh, yes they do. They're just not writing 'em for Broadway" (Gerard 35).

Producer Kirk Wise gave most of the credit to Ashman. As he told *The New York Times*, "Howard felt very passionately that the American musical theatre was sort of the spiritual ancestor of the animated feature—and that the animated feature had become the last refuge of musical theatre. It's the only place where you can still get away with a character bursting into song. Howard helped us structure the story so that the songs support it and grow out of it, rather than feeling tacked on"

(Solomon 83). Wise was wiser than he knew, for as studios ventured into live-action "bursting into song," audiences balked. Also, as lesser talents than Ashman wrote movie musicals, scores became less organic to the storytelling.

While writing *Beauty and the Beast*, Ashman was harboring a horrible secret; he was dying of AIDS (making the lyrics of the title song, with their implicit promise of regeneration through love, all the more poignant). For Disney's next animated musical, Ron Clements and John Musker's *Aladdin* (1992), only three Ashman songs made final cut; the rest were done by Broadway-West End lyricist Tim Rice (whose best known shows are perhaps *Evita, Joseph and the Amazing Technicolor Dreamcoat*). "You'll know right away who wrote what," warned the *New York Post*. "The songs by Ashman are marked by his crafty wit and urbane grace, his uncanny unexpected puns and rhymes. The other songs are your basic boilerplate show tunes" (Bernard 23).

Aladdin was still an enormous success, spawning another Saturday morning TV show, an "Aladdin on Ice," and enough toys to fill FAO Schwarz. The movie took in over $200 million at the box office (IMDB), and counting everything, Disney accountants reckoned, it was responsible for a cool billion in revenues. But commercial success this time had little to do with adroit musical storytelling and everything to do with *Aladdin*'s glib pop satire. While most of the movie's voices were filled in by a decidedly B-team cast (headed by Scott Weinger as Aladdin and Linda Larkin as Jasmine), superstar Robin Williams took the role of the genie and made it forever his own. The studio turned on the tape recorder and let Williams run wild, improvising some twenty to thirty hours of comic riffs, and boiled it down to a pop gallery of some seventy celebrity impersonations, with Williams's genie morphing rapidly into Ed Sullivan, Harpo Marx, Jack Nicholson, Arsenio Hall, Dr. Ruth, and others. While audiences ate it up, it was clear that *Aladdin* was no heartwarming musical fairy tale but a calculated pop-culture artifact from a large corporate structure. Wrote David Denby in *New York Magazine*: "The movie is so filled with grinning references to television, movies, and old Disney films that it's practically a celebration of the magic-carpet ride of modern entertainment. . . . To make still better animated films, [Disney] would have to recapture something like innocence, and for this group of Hollywood artisans, innocence may no longer be possible" (Denby 110).

But movie executives read bottom lines before they read critics, and other studios viewed Disney's returns and divined the message: Animated musicals sell. Within a year after *Beauty and the Beast*, half a dozen non-Disney cartoon musicals were released: Bill Kroyer's *Ferngully: The Last Rainforest* (1992), Phil Nibbelink and Simon Wells's *An American Tail: Fievel Goes West* (1991), Ralph Bakshi's *Cool World* (1992), Don Bluth's *Rock-a-Doodle* (1991), Bruce W. Smith's *Bebe's Kids* (1992), and Masanori Hata and Misami Hata's *Little Nemo: Adventures in Slumberland* (1992) (Corliss 75). Lacking the budgets, merchandising savvy, and storytelling acumen of Disney's best, most flopped. Nor were their scores as distinguished as the Ashman-Menken movies, settling for a few wannabe pop ballads and derivative production numbers.

As *Aladdin* outgrossed even *Beauty and the Beast*, Disney's entertainment machine was happily puffing and roaring. Roger Allers and Rob Minkoff's *The Lion King* (1994) was in production (under the working title *King of the Jungle*), Mike Gabriel and Eric Goldberg's *Pocahontas* (1995) was on the drawing board, and lucrative direct-to-video sequels to *Beauty and the Beast* and *Aladdin* were hastily concocted. The studio was also preparing something far more ambitious: the first live-action, big-budget, all-out movie musical in years.

This was Kenny Ortega's *Newsies* (1992), a daring attempt to musicalize the story of a New York newsboys' strike of 1899. With a pleasant score by Menken and Jack Feldman, the two-hour, eight-song extravaganza had all the ingredients of an old-fashioned hit along the lines of Sir Carol Reed's film of the musical *Oliver!* (1968): traditional, Rodgers and Hammerstein-styled musical storytelling; a sweet young-love story; loads of dancing boys tearing through high-energy production numbers; a starry supporting cast (Bill Pullman, Robert Duvall, and Ann-Margret); an extraordinary old-New York set; and trendy touches designed to mask the undeniably recherché air. These included peppering the score with a rock beat, enlivening the dances with MTV cutting and *Footloose* (1984, dir. Herbert Ross) / Flashdance (1983, dir. Adrian Lyne) leaps and jabs, and presenting an ethnically diverse newsboys' dancing chorus—unthinkable in 1899. Its underdog-fighting-the-system theme was a perceived crowd-pleaser, and its first-time director, Kenny Ortega, had recently choreographed a successful semi-musical, Emile Ardolino's *Dirty Dancing* (1987). All the planets, then, seemed in alignment for *Newsies*.

What happened, instead, was disaster. While critics praised *Newsies* for its energy and good intentions, they found it antiquated and bland. *The Christian Science Monitor* summed it up: "Going to see *Newsies* is like running into a dinosaur in your local park. It's a healthy, friendly, good-looking dinosaur. But it's a dinosaur nevertheless, and its future is definitely not bright" (Sterritt 12). U.S. audiences were downright hostile, plunking down less than $3 million in theaters (IMDB), and other studios thought twice before proceeding with their own live-action musicals.

And there were a surprising number in the pipeline. Disney was planning a sequel to *Mary Poppins* and a musical adaptation of *The Little Princess*. Castle Rock was prepping *Singing Out Loud*, with a remarkable pedigree: Stephen Sondheim (music and lyrics), William Goldman (screenplay), and Rob Reiner (direction). Barry Levinson was preparing *Toys* as a big-budget musical (it was released as a nonmusical in 1992, starring Robin Williams, and in any event suffered a box-office fate even worse than *Newsies*). Broadway adaptations in various states of preproduction included *Evita*, *Cats*, *The Phantom of the Opera*, *Les Miserables*, *Sweeney Todd*, *Into the Woods*, and *Miss Saigon* (Haithman 82). Most of these projects died aborning, the victims of studio nervousness, which could be backed up all too well with recitations of the fate of *Newsies*.

Yet the live-action musical was not entirely dead—it was just being watered down and labeled something else. Several big-budget titles of the early and mid-1990s were packed with songs or dances, and some did quite well. Eschewing the character-bursting-into-song formula, their musical moments were strictly presentational: Hi, we're doing a number. And for some reason, audiences found this easier to swallow. Bette Midler's war-with-songs epic *For the Boys* (1991, Dir. Mark Rydell) didn't set box offices on fire, but Whoopi Goldberg's singing-nun comedy *Sister Act* (1992, Dir. Emile Ardolino) was a smash, and Disney's *What's Love Got To Do With It* (1993, Dir. Brian Gibson) profitably revived a genre that had laid mostly dormant since the 1950s, the suffering-songbird biopic (in this case, Tina Turner).

All the same, live musicals were in sad shape. Exhibits A and B: James L. Brooks's *I'll Do Anything* (1994) and Michael Ritchie's *The Fantasticks* (1995, unreleased). The former was a pet project of writer/director Brooks (*Terms of Endearment* [1983], *Broadcast News* [1987]), a would-be hybrid of Hollywood satire, story-songs (by Carole King and others), and comedy. Preview audiences howled at the singing (Ebert); whether this was due to the old-fashioned story-musical concept or the singing voices of the leads (Nick Nolte, Joely Richardson, Albert Brooks, Julie Kavner) is open to speculation. In all events, Columbia lost its nerve and released *I'll Do Anything* with only one musical number. What remained was a plodding romantic comedy laced with songless song cues.

The Fantasticks' fate was even sadder. The delicate off-Broadway smash by Tom Jones and Harvey Schmidt, running since 1960, had seen several false starts as a movie over the years. With its mixture of fantasy, pantomime, fourth-wall elimination, and theatrical styles running from Kabuki to Shakespeare, it seemed virtually impossible to adapt to the screen. But veteran movie director Michael Ritchie (*Downhill Racer* [1969], *The Candidate* [1972], *Smile* [1975]), a *Fantasticks* fanatic, delivered the authors a concept that made sense to them: begin the story in a realistic setting, in a small Midwestern town in the 1920s, bring in a traveling carnival, and gradually introduce elements of fantasy. That way, he felt, audiences wouldn't be too jarred by the rampant stylization. Ritchie envisioned something both grand (Panavision, Technicolor, Dolby) and intimate (small, unstarry cast, $10 million budget), and Jones and Schmidt penned a screenplay that found room for virtually all their classic stage songs. Filming in Arizona went smoothly and came in under budget; everyone involved was satisfied with the result; and MGM/UA initiated previews (Miller 5). But disaster struck again. Audiences loathed the mixture of reality and fantasy, laughed in the wrong places, and found the piece's Kennedy-era innocence far too disingenuous for the hard-edged '90s. A wounded UA kept pushing back the release date and eventually scrapped *The Fantasticks* altogether.

Which makes the last MGM musical to date, by default, Paul Verhoeven's *Showgirls* (1995). "Musical" may seem a misnomer, but it was conceived and marketed as such, with MGM promising "a soundtrack by Dave Stewart that will include original songs by David Bowie, Thrill Kill Cult, and the artist formerly known as Prince," not to mention "three lavish production numbers, one of them an S&M fantasy, all of them featuring wall-to-wall nudity" (Grimes 20). This heady brew was the joint inspiration of screenwriter Joe Eszterhas and director Paul Verhoeven, both coming to the project with a parade of lurid, similarly titled movie hits between them: *Fatal Attraction* (1987), *Total Recall* (1990), *Basic Instinct* (1992). They envisioned not a character-bursting-into-song format but a straightforward melodrama of Las Vegas' porn demimonde, punctuated by the promised naked dancing girls.

It was certainly a try at something different, and for a brief moment MGM's publicity machine puttered joyously with prerelease anticipation. The official *Showgirls* Web site received a then-record 1 million hits. Bus stations were plastered with the movie poster, a nude woman peeking artfully from behind a show curtain. Free eight-minute trailers were dispensed at video stores ("Showgirls" 5). Then, on September 22, 1995, the hype was drowned out by derisive laughter. Critics ripped apart the acting, direction, writing, musical sequences, and, above all, the Esterhazs-Verhoeven dirty-old-men notions of eroticism (Mathews, "Tasteless" B3). Audience curiosity helped *Showgirls* to a strong opening weekend, but the box-office falloff was so precipitous that the movie never made back its $35 million cost (IMDB).

Disney's animated musicals, meanwhile, were doing splendidly. *King of the Jungle*, retitled *The Lion King* (1994) when the studio realized that lions don't actually live in the jungle (Posner 82), had been in the works since 1991, an unusually serious, *Hamlet*-like tale of a lion cub avenging his father's death while romancing his lioness childhood sweetheart. Disney hired Tim Rice to pen the lyrics, Elton John to write the melodies, and Hans Zimmer to give the light-rock score an authentic African sound. And to inject more comedy, screenwriters Irene Mecchi, Jonathan Roberts, and Linda Woolverton beefed up the supporting roles of Timon the meerkat and Pumbaa the warthog. Aided by the crack timing of Nathan Lane and Ernie Sabella, and entrusted with the hit tune "Hakuna Matata," the burlesque-influenced duo became audience darlings (O'Mahony 31).

Musically, however, critics mourned Ashman's passing and Menken's absence. The songs were fewer than *Mermaid* and *Beast* had boasted and, many felt, inferior. *The New York Times* deemed them "nondescript" and added, "the fact that *The Lion King* has become the Disney studio's biggest hit, despite its mediocre songs, is not a happy sign for the artistic future of the animated musical" (Holden 22). But the strong story and breathtaking animation carried the day, and *The Lion King* breezed on to total revenues approaching $1 billion (Hofmeister D1). In 1997, imaginatively rethought by Julie Taymor for the Broadway stage, it became an even bigger hit than Disney's previous movie-to-stage transcription, *Beauty and the Beast.*

The Lion King's runaway success helped Disney forget *Newsies* and plow with renewed vigor into musical production. Besides the cartoons *Pocahontas* (1995), Gary Trousdale and Kirk Wise's *The Hunchback of Notre Dame* (1996), and Ron Clements and John Musker's *Hercules* (1997), the studio helped midwife the long-delayed screen version of Alan Parker's *Evita* (1996). But, profitable as all these projects proved, none was as successful or as praised as *The Lion King*. Beginning with *Pocahontas* and continuing through *Hercules*, most critics felt, the Disney formula was going slightly sour.

The descent was gentle and subtle. *Pocahontas* was a shrewd blending of fact and fiction—and Disney's sometimes incompatible impulses toward art and commerce. In telling the story of Captain John Smith's exploration of Virginia and the squaw who guided him, Disney hired new screenwriters and a new lyricist to work with Menken: Stephen Schwartz, of *Pippin* and *Godspell*. On the one hand, the writers were politically correct to a fault, bluntly depicting the Virginia Company's ruthless pursuit of gold and willingness to ravage the land they had plundered. With Russell Means, who had led the seventy-one-day resistance at Wounded Knee in 1974, on hand as technical advisor and voice of Pocahontas' father, it scrupulously avoided Hollywood noble-savage clichés. The heroine's mentor this time was no jolly crustacean or maternal teapot, but Grandmother Willow, a wise rather than wisecracking old tree, with Linda Hunt's voice. The movie even went in for a bittersweet ending, a first-ever for a Disney cartoon, with the romantic leads parted forever.

On the other hand, the love story was a total fabrication to begin with: The real Pocahontas was about eleven when she met Smith, and certainly not the curvaceous maiden dreamed up by Disney. Further, kids were put off by the history lessons and lack of snappy supporting characters, and adults resented "the heavy-handed sermonettes contained in [the songs]" (Mathews, "Disney" B3). Even with the usual barrage of publicity and merchandising, *Pocahontas* crept to a $140 million gross domestically—no disgrace, but a letdown after *The Lion King*'s $313 million. But if *Pocahontas* lurched backward at the box office, it was a return to form musically, with Menken's colorful underscoring and Schwartz's thoughtful lyrics miles ahead of *The Lion King*'s pop twitterings.

The same team brought the same integrity to *The Hunchback of Notre Dame* (1996), penning a Broadway-style collection of comic numbers, character songs, and ballads. This time, too, there was an unusually somber tone to the score, with song titles such as "God Help the Outcasts" and "Hellfire." In the latter, the villainous Frollo sings frankly of his lust for the gypsy girl Esmeralda and fondles her scarf, while her sensuous image taunts him in the fire of the hearth. This was too much for many adults, including *The Los Angeles Times*' Mark Silver, who called *Hunchback* "a beautiful, powerful film that I would not recommend for children under eight or nine years old" (Silver 25).

All the same, the film was hardly unadulterated Victor Hugo; as in *Pocahontas*, Disney tried to steer both the high and low roads, and wobbled. The darkness of the story was not slighted, with both the plight of the gypsies and the unbearable ostracism of Quasimodo given full weight. But, perhaps with an eye to *Pocahontas*' declining box-office receipts, Disney hedged its bets with broad comedy. In what *Magill's Cinema Annual* called "the adapters' most contrived touch" (Hopp 265), the screenwriters invented three talking gargoyles, Victor, Hugo, and Laverne. To many, this conceit hit the wrong note: "appallingly flippant," *Newsday* called the trio (Anderson B3). As with *Pocahontas*, Disney catered to several audiences, but without the fluid grace it had shown in *Beast* or *Mermaid*. And as with *Pocahontas*, it paid for it at the box office: a worldwide take of $318 million, less than half of *The Lion King's* (IMDB).

Sensing that it was overburdening its animated musicals with purpose, Disney next sought actively to lighten up. *Hercules* had a zippy Menken score with sassy David Zippel lyrics, a Supremes-style Greek chorus in a series of music-video-influenced production numbers, a devil-and-his-pretty-disciple motif borrowed from George Abbott and Stanley Donen's *Damn Yankees* (1958). It also had a hip, self-mocking tone that disarmed many critics. They chuckled at the "Air Herc" athletic-shoe billboards, action-figure and theme-park references, and '90s catchphrases dotting the ancient-Greek landscape. But the relentless jokiness didn't fare any better with audiences than did the portentousness of *Hunchback* or *Pocahontas*; *Hercules* was the weakest box-office performer in the bunch (IMDB).

Along with its cartoon spectaculars, Disney dabbled in other forms of computer animation over the decade. Henry Selick's *The Nightmare Before Christmas* (1994) and John Lasseter's *Toy Story* (1995) were not exactly cartoons and not exactly musicals, just cyber-animated comedies with a few incidental songs. In the meantime, though, the studio was getting ready to release another expensive live-action musical. *Evita* (1996) had attracted Hollywood's interest virtually from its opening on Broadway in 1979. Among the tantalizing possibilities announced over the years: Franco Zeffirelli directing Diane Keaton; Ken Russell directing Liza Minnelli; Michael Cimino directing Meryl Streep; Barbra Streisand as Evita and Elliott Gould as Juan Peron; Pia Zadora, Bette Midler, Olivia Newton-John, Michelle Pfeiffer, or West End original Elaine Page as Evita (Greenberg 22).

Eventually, director Alan Parker, backed by producer Robert Stigwood and Cinergi Pictures Entertainment, assembled a $60 million package anchored by what seems, in retrospect, the inevitable Evita: Madonna. The press had a field day pointing out the obvious parallels between

Peron and Ciccone: fashion plates with a gift for self-invention, publicity hounds with erotic public personas. To the delight of Disney subsidiary Hollywood Pictures, which released the movie, miles of column inches were generated before and during filming. Most of it centered not on the differences between the real and reel Evita, or even the stage and screen Evita, but on those two world-shattering issues, Madonna's pregnancy and Madonna's acting ability.

Clearly, Parker was thinking big. Filming mostly in Budapest—a better stand-in for old Buenos Aires than the new Buenos Aires was—he employed as many as four thousand extras, shot for eighty-two days (Dwyer 29), made a song-and-dance man of Antonio Banderas, persuaded Argentine President Carlos Saul Menem of Argentina to grant permission to use the real Casa Rosada for the "Don't Cry for Me, Argentina" sequence, and never met an interviewer he didn't like. This was, he assured the press, an *Evita* reinvented for film, with a Parker-Oliver Stone screenplay that represented "a new film genre—not opera, not an old MGM musical with people speaking, then bursting into song" (Gritten C17). Exactly what he had in mind was first unveiled at Cannes in May, 1996, when a ten-minute preview, according to several press reports, was greeted rapturously. Disney announced a Christmas Day opening, the hype crescendoed, and the world held its breath: *Evita*, it seemed, would either be the greatest smash in movie history or a laughingstock.

Surprisingly, it emerged as neither. Reviews were all over the map, with the highbrow critics generally slamming Parker for watering down history and misusing Madonna, or using her in the first place (Krauze 34). As for the "new film genre," it turned out to be a completely sung musical, careening schizophrenically between realism and artifice, shot with rapid MTV-style cuts. While this did remove those "character-bursting-into-song" moments that make audiences so uneasy these days, for many it placed the action at an emotional distance. Describing the movie as "the biggest, loudest, most expensive music video ever made," *The New Yorker* complained, "the real world has been deposed and exiled from this picture" (Lane 75). Nevertheless, there were also some fine reviews, and *Evita's* $8.6 million weekend opening at only seven hundred theaters made it look at first like a runaway hit (Weinraub, "Don't Cry" C15). But once the furor died down and the curiosity seekers had been satisfied, the box office fell off—a pattern repeated around the world as Evita went into international release. It stalled out at about $135 million worldwide

(IMDB), leaving questions about the movie musical's future viability frustratingly unanswered.

Middling boxoffice was also the fate of that Christmas' other big movie musical release, Woody Allen's *Everyone Says I Love You* (1996). This, too, attracted herds of reporters, for its all-star cast (Julia Roberts, Drew Barrymore, Alan Alda, Goldie Hawn, Edward Norton,and others), and even more for its writer-director, Woody Allen, making his first musical. "I'd always wanted to do some musical things," he told *The Los Angeles Times*. "I wanted to do a musical where it was like my parents at their anniversary, where they just dance and your heart goes out to them, but they can't dance. . . . People do sing privately. It's an expression of emotion, and I wanted the actor or actress to act the scene and then, when it came to a certain point, sing the thing rather than just go on with the dialogue" (Clark 3).

For this quaint approach, Allen concocted a lighthearted, thin story, depicting multiple love affairs among New York's privileged classes, with Paris and Venice sequences folded in. Behind the camera if not in front, he hired top musical talent: Broadway's Graciela Daniele to choreograph, jazz great Dick Hyman for the musical arrangements. The songs were mostly from the pens of B-list writers of the '20s and '30s. (There were so many that Allen's first cut ran three hours and twenty minutes, leaving such actors as Liv Tyler and Tracey Ullman on the cutting-room floor [Clark 92].) All the actors except Barrymore did their own singing, including Allen, whose toneless rendition of "I'm Through With Love" prompted giggles in many audiences.

At $20 million—cheap for a movie musical, expensive for a Woody Allen movie—*Everyone Says I Love You* opened to mostly positive reviews, with critics charmed by its sing-your-heart-out conceit and even the game performances of its vocally challenged cast (Kauffman, Sarris). Inarguably, it's a traditional movie musical, from its opening shot of Edward Norton warbling "Just You, Just Me" (badly) to Drew Barrymore, in front of the Metropolitan Museum of Art. The artifice begins immediately, and swiftly escalates, as Yves St. Laurent mannequins in a window come to life, passersby sing random lines of the song, and production numbers build in such unlikely venues as Harry Winston, the Frank E. Campbell Funeral Home, and a hospital wing. For a pas de deux between Alda and Hawn along the Seine, Allen deliberately evokes Vincente Minnelli's *An American in Paris* (1951)—then undercuts the already fragile reality of the moment by having Hawn suddenly fly.

FIGURE 4.1. Drew Barrymore and Edward Norton in Woody Allen's *Everyone Says I Love You.* Courtesy: Jerry Ohlinger Archive.

For those willing to buy into its fairy-tale aura and limited lung power, *Everyone Says I Love You* offered many incidental delights. Hawn and Alda aside, however, it denied its audiences one of the chief pleasures of musicals: watching talented singers and dancers strut their stuff. As with many Allen pictures, some were put off by its narrow wealthy-white-urban milieu; and the arbitrariness of musical placement, with songs occurring randomly rather than at emotional peaks, reveal it to be no well-thought-out musical narrative, but merely a casual homage to the tightly constructed musicals of the past.

To date, *Everyone Says I Love You* is the last major, nonanimated movie musical. Cartoons, on the other hand, are alive and kicking. Disney's production of *Mulan* (1998), directed by Tony Bancroft and Barry Cook, has already topped both *Hunchback* and *Hercules* in domestic returns, its feisty heroine and wiseacre dragon (with Eddie Murphy's voice) audience favorites. As a musical, however, it's skimpy goods: four songs, no hits. Meanwhile, more studios are braving the animated arena. Twentieth Century Fox's *Anastasia* (1997), directed by Don Bluth and Gary Goldman, had a big Broadway score by Stephen Flaherty and Lynn Ahrens (*Ragtime*), along with a bizarre take on Russian history: The Romanovs, it seems, were basically a nice nuclear family, and the Revolution was fueled by an evil curse leveled by Rasputin. Assembled at an expensive new Fox facility for animation in the Southwest, *Anastasia* cost an alarming $53 million and performed indifferently at the box office (IMDB). Warner Brothers' *Quest for Camelot* (1998), directed by Frederik Du Chau, was a financial and artistic disaster; and recently we have seen Richard Rich's animated remake of *The King and I* (1999), and Dreamworks' ambitious Moses toon-epic, *Prince of Egypt* (1999), directed by Brenda Chapman and Steve Hickner.

At this point, animated musicals continue to look like the better bet, financially, for studios. But however disappointing a decade it has been for live-action musicals, the genre never quite dies. Currently, the press is buzzing with rumors that Antonio Banderas, having acquitted himself so well in *Evita*, will film *The Phantom of the Opera* (first filmed in 1925 as a silent). A twentieth-anniversary rerelease of *Grease* pulled in over $28 million on a minimal investment. Warners and David Geffen are preparing the stage hit *Dreamgirls* for a 1999 filming, and speculation about casting for Miramax's proposed movie of *Chicago* has generated nearly as much newsprint as the *Evita* saga (Weinraub, "New Life" C14). Of course, *Chicago* is tricky material, and how its theatrical devices (vaudeville-style musical numbers, Brechtian commentary, in-your-face choreography) can be translated to film is anybody's guess. Will it be the genre-reviving blockbuster *Evita* wanted to be, or the *Newsies* of 2002? The amount of ink already spilled on the project proves that the movie musical, no matter how seemingly moribund, always has an encore left in it.

WORKS CITED

Aladdin. Pressbook. Los Angeles: Walt Disney Productions, 1992.

Anderson, John. "A Cute Hunchback." *New York Newsday* (June 21, 1996): B2, B3, B9.

Beauty and the Beast. Pressbook. Los Angeles: Walt Disney Productions, 1991.

Bernard, Jami. "That Old Disney Magic." *The New York Post* (November 11, 1992): 23.

Canby, Vincent. "*Oliver*, with Twists, from Disney." *The New York Times* (November 18, 1988): C8.

Carroll, Kathleen. "*Oliver* is a Grim Disney Tale." *New York Daily News* (November 18, 1988): 57.

Clark, John. "Citizen Woody." *The Los Angeles Times* (December 1, 1996): Calendar, 3, 92.

Cochran, Jason. "Sum of Their Parts?" *Entertainment Weekly* (February 6, 1998): 64–65.

Corliss, Richard. "Aladdin's Magic." *Time* (November 9, 1992): 74–76.

Denby, David. "Boy Wonders." *New York Magazine* (November 30, 1992): 110.

Dwyer, Michael. "Don't Cry for the New Eva, Either." *The New York Times* (May 5, 1996), sec. 2: 19, 29.

Ebert, Roger. "I'll Do Anything." *Chicago Sun-Times* (February 4, 1994): www.suntimes.com/ebert/ebert_reviews/1994/02/902949.html.

French, Philip. "Oliver and Company." *London Observer* (December 17, 1988): 42.

Gerard, Jeremy. "*Beauty, Nick and Nora*: Tuneful Tale of Two Cities." Variety (November 18, 1991): 35, 37.

Greenberg, James. "Is It Time Now to Cry for *Evita?*" *The New York Times* (November 19, 1989), sec. 2: 1, 22.

Grimes, William. "In the Wings: A Movie with Few Clothes and No Regrets." *The New York Times* (February 12, 1995), sec. 2: 1, 20, 21.

Gritten, David. "Madonna Stars in *Evita.* Eva Peron Herself Would Have Loved the Commotion." *New York Newsday* (May 12, 1996): C13, 17.

Hackett, Larry. "Granting Disney's Wish." *New York Daily News* (November 22, 1992): City Lights, 3.

Haithman, Diane. "With a Song in Its Heart." *The Los Angeles Times* (April 26, 1992): Calendar, 5, 82, 89.

Hofmeister, Sallie. "In the Realm of Marketing, *The Lion King* Rules." *The New York Times* (July 12, 1994): D1, 17.

Holden, Stephen. "Why Two Soundtracks Are Music to Boomers' Ears." *The New York Times* (September 4, 1994), sec. 2: 22.

Hopp, Glenn. *The Hunchback of Notre Dame* entry. *Magill's Cinema Annual 1997* (Beth A. Fhaner, ed.), New York: Gale, 1997, 264–67.

IMDB. Internet Movie Data Base Search Engine, at <http://us.imdb.com/search>.

Kauffman, Stanley. "The Food of Love." *The New Republic* (November 11, 1996): 40–41.

Krauze, Enrique. "The Blonde Leading the Blind." *The New Republic* (February 10, 1997): 31–37.

Lane, Anthony. "Immaterial Girls." *The New Yorker* (January 6, 1997): 74–75.

Maslin, Janet. "Andersen's Mermaid, by Way of Disney." *The New York Times* (November 15, 1989): C17.

———. "In Today's Animation, It's Dog Eat Doggie." *The New York Times* (November 27, 1988), sec. 2: 13.

———. "Target: Boomers and Their Babies." *The New York Times* (November 24, 1991), sec. 2: 1, 16.

Mathews, Jack. "Disney Has a Go at History." *New York Newsday* (June 23, 1995): B2–3.

———. "Tasteless Tribute to Skin Game." *New York Newsday* (September 22, 1995): B3.

Miller, Marc. "I Can See It: The Fantasticks on Film." *Stages* (Fall 1995): 4–5.

O'Mahony, John. "They're the Talk of the Jungle." *The New York Post* (June 15, 1994): 31.

Pocahontas. Pressbook. Los Angeles: Walt Disney Productions, 1995.

Posner, Ari. "The Mane Event." *Premiere* (June 1994): 80–84, 86.

Sarris, Andrew. "Woody Sings, Julia Doesn't . . . A Casual, Endearing Musical." *The New York Observer* (December 2, 1996): 37.

"Showgirls Site Sets Web on Fire." *Variety* (September 18, 1995): 5, 6.

Silver, Mark. "*Hunchback*: Sex, Lies—and Videotapes, Too." *The Los Angeles Times* (June 23, 1996): Calendar, 25–27.

Solomon, Charles. "Building a Magical *Beast*." *The Los Angeles Times* (November 10, 1991): Calendar, 3, 83, 84, 90.

Sterritt, David. "*Newsies*." *Christian Science Monitor* (April 17, 1992): 12.

Weinraub, Bernard. "Don't Cry for the Musical: *Evita* Has a Big Weekend." *The New York Times* (January 13, 1997): C15.

———. "New Life for Musicals." *The New York Times* (July 24, 1998): C14.

CHAPTER FIVE

◼

Political Film in the Nineties

STEPHEN PRINCE

American cinema has long possessed a vibrant and energetic tradition of political and social filmmaking (Combs; Crowdus; Davies and Neve; Neve; Polan; Prince), and the cinema of the nineties was no exception. While it has become somewhat fashionable to bemoan the hegemony of blockbuster filmmaking in contemporary cinema, this alleged hegemony is less total than is commonly realized. While blockbusters tend to dominate media coverage and yearly grosses, the industry's productions remain diverse. This diversity contains much politically pointed and socially critical filmmaking. In this regard, the films of the nineties have maintained the tradition of topicality and salience that picture making in previous decades has established. To appreciate this tradition, it will be helpful to note some of the socially conscious filmmaking of prior decades. This filmmaking has established a national, critical cinematic context in which the works of the nineties belong.

The muckraking tradition of socially conscious filmmaking has roots in the silent period (e.g., Griffith's riffs in *Intolerance* [1916] against self-appointed guardians of public morality), but it saw an efflorescence in the thirties. The gangster films of the 1930s showed a society of unequal opportunity and an economic system that rewarded the violent and ruthless behavior of Caesar Enrico Bandello (*Little Caesar* [1931]), Tony Camonte (*Scarface* [1932]), and Tom Powers (*The Public Enemy* [1931]).

63

In these films about the building of criminal empires, the gangster became a Horatio Alger hero enacting a twisted American dream. These gangsters met violent ends, allowing Production Code morality to claim that the pictures showed that crime doesn't pay. But everyone knew otherwise. They showed all too well that crime can pay and that the American dream of wealth and abundance had its dark and sordid components.

In the 1940s, Hollywood mobilized around the war effort and its pictures explicated the need for a united front against a common enemy. Much of this period's production is a masterpiece of agenda-setting filmmaking. However, the collective imagery in these films of a united America was offset in the postwar years by film noir, which suggested a fractured, anxious, and fearful culture. In the 1950s, Robert Aldrich linked noir with Cold War anxieties about the bomb in the penultimate film noir *Kiss Me Deadly* (1955), which suggested that noir had one of its roots in Cold War culture.

The repressive conformity of fifties culture, splendidly evoked in *The Man in the Gray Flannel Suit* (1956), led to its dialectical opposite in the sixties. And American film participated in the sixties currents of protest and rebellion. *The Graduate* (1967), *Bonnie and Clyde* (1967) and *Easy Rider* (1969) were pitched to a young, antiestablishment audience impatient with conventional society and its films. These late-sixties pictures were hip, stylistically audacious, and they celebrated nonconformity. They also had a strong sense of the limits of rebellion. Their narratives often concluded with the death or diminishment of the rebel hero.

The paranoia thrillers of the seventies (*The Parallax View* [1974], *Capricorn One* [1978], *All the President's Men* [1976]) signaled a shift away from the celebration of outlaw heroes in late-sixties cinema. More despairing about the prospects for democratic society, these were films in the shadow of Watergate. They showed governmental corruption and conspiracy, and their narratives were parables of defeated heroes in which shadowy cartels and power brokers maintained pervasive social control. The paranoia thrillers were common throughout early and mid-seventies production, and collectively they portrayed an America dominated by a power elite composed of state and corporate interests.

The Spielberg-Lucas feel-good science fiction and fantasy blockbusters helped remove some of the bitterness and cynicism from popular film in its late-sixties and seventies incarnations. (*Jaws* [1975], however, shows its mid-seventies paranoia thriller lineage in its subplot about the efforts by Amity officials to conceal the shark's presence and deny its threat, lest the tourist business be threatened.) Fantasy villains—a giant shark, Darth Vader, Nazis searching for the Ark of the Covenant—substituted for the more politicized visions of American society in previous decades of film.

But mindless as the new pop blockbusters were, they did not curtail the sociopolitical impulses of American filmmaking. Just as the industry was turning to the fantasy blockbusters, Martin Scorsese made *Taxi Driver* (1976), an exceptionally powerful portrait of psychological and social alienation. Moreover, the eighties featured an abundance of political filmmaking. The 1980s saw large cycles of films devoted to the era's front-burner social issues (Prince; Ryan and Kellner). These included the Vietnam War, the first time Hollywood had examined this event in a sustained and ambitious manner (*Apocalypse Now* [1979], *Coming Home* [1978], *Rambo: First Blood Part II* [1985], *Platoon* [1986], *Hamburger Hill* [1987], *Born on the Fourth of July* [1989]). Eighties topical filmmaking also included cycles of production manifesting Reagan-era Cold War politics (*Red Dawn* [1984], *Invasion USA* [1985], *Top Gun* [1986], *Iron Eagle* [1986]), as well as productions from a liberal perspective that sympathetically portrayed the revolutionary movements in Latin America (*Salvador* [1986], *Under Fire* [1983]). Dystopic science fiction (*Blade Runner* [1982], *Escape from New York* [1981], *Robocop* [1987]) pictured a quasi-fascistic America, with a crumbling infrastructure and authoritarian political control.

As this brief summary shows, the social and political impulses of American filmmaking have been very strong throughout decades of production. The reasons for this are very basic. While Hollywood has traditionally defined its product as entertainment and has pooh-poohed "message" filmmaking, in practice the industry has consistently relied on topicality as a crucial ingredient of box-office success. While moviegoers want entertainment, the public has also demonstrated that it will respond to timely and topical filmmaking, provided these attributes are embedded in a compelling story populated by interesting characters. Thus, for the industry topically oriented filmmaking has an inherent marketing hook, provided the subjects in question have genuine salience for the public and can be given successful narrative form. The best examples of American topical filmmaking succeed as narrative films *and* as portraits of the nation and society.

With this in mind, one should expect that nineties filmmaking would carry on the topical impulses of the American film tradition. And, indeed, political filmmaking is very much alive in nineties cinema. Oliver Stone has continued to occupy his solitary position as the only major filmmaker who is a consistent and vocal critic of the nation's domestic and foreign policy. Stone's achievement in this regard is apparent in that he is out there, by himself, making large-budgeted studio pictures that arouse political controversy.

Stone has been the most visible and consistently political of contemporary American directors. *Salvador*, his first mature feature, was a searing exposé of the U.S. role in propping up a brutal regime in El Salvador during the eighties. Stone quickly followed this feature with *Platoon* and *Wall Street* [1987], both impassioned treatments, respectively, of the Vietnam War and capitalist rapacity. He intended *Platoon* as a rebuttal to *Rambo: First Blood Part II*, which he called "a fascist comic book" (Breskin 141). Stone returned to the war for a third Vietnam film, *Heaven and Earth* [1993], but his major political works of the nineties focused on the institutions of American power as revealed in the workings of the Kennedy and Nixon presidencies.

JFK (1991) caused a furor over its treatment of the Jim Garrison (Kevin Costner) investigation of Kennedy's assassination. Garrison, a New Orleans District Attorney, concluded that Kennedy had been killed as part of a conspiracy and that the Warren Commission's single-bullet theory was hopelessly flawed. Stone's film reopened this issue for Americans and stimulated extensive media debates about the case and the Warren Commission's findings. These debates and controversies extended to Stone's film itself and particularly to the ethical issues raised by his filmmaking techniques. Throughout the film, Stone blended real historical footage with "fake" footage that he had filmed so it would look as if it were part of the archival record. Within the film's complex montage design, viewers could hardly tell the difference between the real and the faked footage. Furthermore, Stone included some clearly fictionalized characters in the story and offered a speculative thesis about what caused Kennedy's killing, namely, that he was planning to withdraw U.S. forces from Vietnam, angering the hawks who wished to pursue the war.

While *JFK* had an extraordinary public impact and helped lead to an official reexamination of the Warren Report, Stone's treatment of history struck many as being overly cavalier. His use of bogus footage, fictional characters, and a fanciful hypothesis about Kennedy's plans for Vietnam seemed at odds with the film's exhaustive marshaling of the documentary and historical evidence connected to the assassination. Was the film real or fictional, and how did its maker view the patchwork of history and rumor that he had assembled?

Stone was singularly unhelpful, saying that he had intended to create a "counter myth" to the reigning myth of a single bullet and a lone assassin. While the film's fluid blend of fiction and fact makes it a postmodern work, many viewers were not ready to discard these distinctions because they cared about the truth claims of images and the veridical status of the events they purported to document. *JFK* is a landmark film of the nineties, demonstrating how powerful cinema can be in its topical function. But it also showed that viewers valued the distinctions between historical fact and mythic invention and that they expected filmmakers to respect these differences.

Stone continued his examination of the presidency and the inner workings of American power in *Nixon* (1995). Stone surprised everyone by offering not a strident denunciation but a compassionate portrait of this politician who trampled on the Constitution and who vigorously pressed the Vietnam War while proclaiming his intent to end it. Stone's direction of Anthony Hopkins's masterful performance evokes Nixon's anguish and his tortured psychology in a manner that is disturbing and humanizing. Stone's Nixon emerges as both monster and victim, a haunted and driven man who tragically realizes that he does not control the power of the war machine but that it uses and controls him. In its Watergate sequences, as Nixon under siege withdraws into the shadows of the White House, the film expands on the ornate conspiratorial vision of *JFK*. The ultimate players in this political drama remain cloaked in secrecy, and the chain of decision making aims for "plausible deniability." Most sinister of all are a group of ultra-right-wing Texas businessmen (the leader of which is played with palpable menace by Larry Hagman) who have ties to the Kennedy killing and who try to intimidate Nixon into taking a hard line on communism and the nation's internal security. In its acute paranoia, Stone's political vision in *JFK* and *Nixon* vividly points toward the antidemocratic impulses within American political culture and its institutions. Kennedy and Nixon become, in these films, victim and exemplar of this dark current.

Stone's other major political work of the decade was a grim and nasty satire of mass-media influence, the cult of celebrity, and the rampant violence of contemporary popular culture. *Natural Born Killers* (1994) followed the exploits of two multiple murderers, Mickey (Woody Harrelson) and Mallory (Juliet Lewis), as their killing spree lands them on the covers of national news magazines and gains them a legion of fans attracted by their celebrity. Unfortunately the film's satire and its moral tone and point of view are insufficiently controlled. As a result, the picture and the filmmakers become too fixated on these sociopaths and the audience too closely identifies with them. To work properly, irony is a distancing mode and requires distance of the reader or viewer, but Stone's filmmaking technique here is immersive, plunging the viewer into the maelstrom of violence the film unleashes and offering Mickey and Mallory as the most engaging characters in a gallery of otherwise repugnant and smarmy personalities. As cinematographer John Bailey has observed, the film "places you inside the violence, makes you a part of it. Its point of view is that of the killers, not because of a clear critical or moral perspective but because that's where the action is. The defining aesthetic is MTV" (Bailey 28). As a consequence, the film becomes what it aims to critique, yet another ugly manifestation of the pop cultural obsession with violence.

Stone is clearly the major political filmmaker at work in the industry today, and his films can be studied as part of an evolving career. But, as noted, he is the only industry figure whose work is consistently and explicitly political. Our survey of political film in the nineties, therefore, now takes us away from directors and toward individual pictures situated by topic rather than by filmmaker. These are films, for the most part, by directors who are much less ideologically inclined than is Stone and whose work is less tied to an abiding personal political vision but who have nevertheless helmed one or more pictures that are pointed in their social address.

A spate of urban dramas etched complex portraits of the interlocking nature of city life and of urban blight and decay. In *City Hall* (1996), Al Pacino is John Pappas, a flamboyant and compassionate mayor who believes in the potential of his city. Aided by his idealistic deputy mayor, Kevin Calhoun (John Cusack), Pappas has run the city in an efficient and humane way, and he now angles for national political office. But things come apart when a gun battle between an off-duty cop and a gangster kills an innocent child. Pappas responds to the tragedy in a compassionate manner and makes an impassioned speech at the boy's funeral against urban crime. But in the aftermath of the killing, the otherwise devoted Kevin Calhoun learns that Pappas has cut deals with the Mob, and that one of these deals has inadvertently produced the tragedy.

Director Harold Becker and his screenwriters construct a fine, multilayered narrative that shows the everyday moral compromises that the exercise of political power entails. Even though Calhoun manages to preserve his idealism by film's end, Becker and company have shown the ways in which the political art of compromise degrades the quality and erodes the character and caliber of urban life.

Becker's film is not well known, but its view of the inevitable compromise of one's integrity and one's ideals in a political career links it with two fine political films released at the end of the decade. In *Bulworth* (1998), director Warren Beatty stars as a politician who has a psychological breakdown, the ironic result of which is his decision to speak the truth, as he sees it, irrespective of his audience or the cost to his career. He quickly insults all of his major ethnic, racial, and demographic constituencies and thereby discovers how incendiary politics can be when its rhetoric is stripped of the pabulum and obfuscation that normally cloak it. At the end, Bulworth (Beatty) is killed by an assassin and becomes thereby a kind of martyr to an alternative vision of social life. In *Primary Colors* (1998), John Travolta plays a Bill Clinton-esque presidential candidate whose voracious appetites for life, sex, and power are fed by his political aspirations. Director Mike Nichols shows with genial and wicked wit the gulf between a candidate's public political persona and his daily actions, a division that the Monica Lewinsky sex scandal has reinforced in real life. *City Hall, Bulworth,* and *Primary Colors* point toward a widespread public sense that the institutions of the polity no longer serve the people, for reasons that range from bureaucratic ineptitude to moral evasion and criminal duplicity.

The American city is an even darker place in Sidney Lumet's *Night Falls on Manhattan* (1997), Costa-Gavras's *Mad City* (1998), John Sayles's *City of Hope* (1991), and Kevin Reynolds's *187* (1997). Lumet is an established master of complex urban dramas (*Dog Day Afternoon* [1975], *Serpico* [1973], *Prince of the City* [1981]), and he again depicts the tangled web of corruption that these contemporary dramas find so inevitable at the heart of urban life and public institutions. A young district attorney (Andy Garcia) is appointed to prosecute a small-time drug dealer and cop killer. The D.A., however, discovers that the dead cop was on the take and that the trail of payoffs leads to his own father, an otherwise respectable and distinguished policeman. The D.A. learns the lesson that these films have been collectively elaborating, that few are clean in today's urban metropolis.

Mad City, directed by Costa-Gavras, elaborates this collective tale of social breakdown by indicting sensation-mongering news media for corrupting the quality of American life. Museum guard Sam Bailey (John Travolta) takes hostages to protest the museum's decision to fire him. Because his hostages are children, the news media swarm on the story, and Sam's fate is determined by a well-meaning reporter (Dustin Hoffman) and a slimy national news anchor (Alan Alda). When the media coverage turns public opinion against him, Sam commits suicide, prompting the reporter (Hoffman) to utter the film's last line—"We killed him"—as an indictment of broadcast journalism.

Sayles's *City of Hope* employs a daring narrative gambit. It is not structured, like a conventional movie narrative, in a linear fashion and with a central protagonist. Instead, the story is episodic and features an ensemble of characters, including cops, City Hall politicians, a building contractor and his disaffected son, an idealistic but ambitious black city councilman, his constituents, a thug and arsonist who operates an auto garage, and a white college professor falsely accused by two black youths of sexual assault. Sayles's film moves fluidly among these characters and their subplots, intercutting the separate narrative lines to create a montage of urban disaffection. A central plot event involves the mayor's plan to demolish a block of low-income apartments to make room for an office complex. Reluctantly, the contractor hires the arsonist to torch the buildings, and two people die in the fire. Although Sayles shows the rapprochement of the professor and one of his accusers, this modest affirmation cannot outweigh the economic and political rapacity he has shown among the city's officials. He ends the film on a bleak note. The contractor finds his son gut-shot in an empty office building. Unable to reach a phone and unwilling to leave his son, the contractor screams into the night, "We need help," over and over again. His cry is unanswered, and it becomes the filmmaker's lament and warning regarding the precarious fortunes of America's cities in the early years of Reaganomics.

The film *187* is the bleakest of these city films, showing the degradation and destruction of an idealistic high school teacher. Trevor Garfield (Samuel L. Jackson) is a Brooklyn science teacher who assigns a failing grade to a troublesome student. Anticipating trouble after learning that the student is a gang member, Garfield tries to enlist support and protection from the school administration but is rebuffed. As Garfield walks the crowded school halls between classes, the student attacks and repeatedly stabs him. Garfield nearly dies. When he recovers, he transfers to a Los Angeles high school where he confronts the same bleak conditions: burned-out teachers, sullen and homicidal students, an impoverished school system, and the impossibility of teaching or learning in such an environment. As Garfield says, it is a world where chaos rules, not order, and where righteousness is not rewarded. The film offers no solutions, only the dark portrait of social breakdown and personal destruction among the economically disenfranchised.

In *City of Hope,* in the subplots dealing with the black city councilman and his constituents, Sayles shows the black-white racial tensions that are entwined with economic disenfranchisement. The film *187* depicts the hostilities of Hispanic and black youth leading ghettoized lives. Race in America remained a major social issue during the nineties, as the Rodney King incident, the Los Angeles riots, and the O. J. Simpson trial demonstrated. Several striking films addressed contemporary racial relations, and many of these were tied to the emergence, for the first time in American cinema, of black filmmakers with major studio distribution. The most visible of these, of course, was Spike Lee who worked prolifically during the nineties and whose films consistently brokered the race question, often to the discomfort of Middle America. Lee felt that the topical focus of his films made them fundamentally different from the works of such movie-obsessed directors as Steven Spielberg and Martin Scorsese.

> See, I wasn't really raised on movies. I went to see them, but I wasn't like Spielberg and the rest of these guys. They wanted to be filmmakers when they were still in Pampers. That wasn't my case. And in a lot of ways this might be an advantage, because for a lot of these guys, their films are about films they've seen. Their films are *about* films. (Breskin 179)

A director as prolific and impassioned as Lee has occasional misfires. *Jungle Fever* (1991) was a reactionary warning that all sorts of bad things happen when lovers cross the color line. A black architect (Denzel Washington) has an affair with a white Italian woman and realizes, after much tribulation, that likes should stay with likes. One of Lee's lesser efforts, the film winds up being a racist picture about racism.

Lee fared better with *Malcolm X* (1992), an epic and surprisingly conventional biopic about the fiery black leader. Lee had campaigned vigorously in the industry to ensure that this picture would be made by a black director, and when he got the assignment, he fashioned a heartfelt picture that charted the events of Malcolm's life and offered black audiences a hero of their own at the center of an epic Hollywood picture.

Crooklyn (1994) showed black family life in 1970s Brooklyn, while *Get on the Bus* (1996) was an original, low budget allegory about black manhood told through a gallery of characters enroute via bus to the Million Man March in Washington, D.C. Lee switched effortlessly to documentary for the affecting *Three Little Girls* (1997), a moving examination of three black children who lost their lives in a church bombing.

Lee kept difficult racial issues on the nation's movie screens, but he was assisted by other black filmmakers who, like Lee, brought vital new perspectives to American cinema. John Singleton's *Boyz 'n the Hood* (1991) was a vivid portrait of dead-end lives and the random violence in South Central Los Angeles that was wiping out a generation of youth. Allen and Albert Hughes chronicled gang violence and urban crime in *Menace II Society* (1993) and *Dead Presidents* (1995), the latter an epic portrait of a young man's bleak life in the Bronx from the 1960s through the Vietnam years and after. Violence in the Hughes brothers' pictures is disturbingly graphic but it is presented in a moral context and with a moral point of view that is quite rare in contemporary film.

In *Straight Out of Brooklyn* (1991) Matty Rich, a teenaged director making his first feature, crafted a powerful portrait of the ruin of a black working-class family whose son is unable to escape the drug culture of the streets. These pictures by Rich, Singleton, and the Hughes brothers strikingly demonstrate the results of the new voices at work in American cinema. Before the nineties generation of black filmmakers, American pictures had ignored the milieu of south-central Los Angeles and other black inner-city communities, and the new black directors now claimed these for themselves.

But they also refused to be confined there. In *Rosewood* (1997), John Singleton brought to vivid life a little known but horrific incident, the torching by white racists of a prosperous black Florida town in the early 1920s. Singleton cast a black actor (Ving Rhames) as the strong silent cowboy hero so often played by whites in Hollywood melodramas. While this character does introduce Hollywood formulas into the narrative, Singleton's portrait of black heroism is nevertheless stirring, as Rhames does battle with the town's attackers and helps lead a small band of survivors to safety. Stepping outside the urban milieu that the new black filmmakers often depicted, Singleton proved to be very adept at evoking this time period and its rural setting.

Ghosts of Mississippi (1996), another Hollywood depiction of past racial incidents, dramatizes the effort of the widow (Whoopi Goldberg) of slain civil rights leader Medgar Evers to bring his killer (James Woods) to justice. Woods turns in a stunning performance as Byron De La Beckwith, a satanic racist consumed by his hatred for blacks. But while the films of Spike Lee and the other new black directors take chances in their approach to race and grapple with difficult issues, *Ghosts of Mississippi*, as directed by Rob Reiner, remains a well-intentioned, comfortingly liberal film about a well-meaning white man (District Attorney Bobby DeLaughter, played by Alec Baldwin) attempting to help black folk. As such, DeLaughter, rather than Myrlie Evers, becomes the protagonist. *Ghosts* is earnest, but it plays the issues safely and builds its black story around a white protagonist.

Racial rage from a white perspective was powerfully portrayed in *Falling Down* (1993). Michael Douglas plays a recently fired aerospace worker whose world crumbles with the loss of his job. Alienated by his perception that nonwhites and immigrants have stolen opportunities from deserving Middle Americans, he embarks on a violent odyssey across Los Angeles, venting his anger on blacks, Hispanics, and Asian Americans. Directed by Joel Schumacher, the film is exceptionally strong at depicting Douglas's rage, but it treats the character with some ambiguity, as if undecided whether Douglas is victim, villain, or frustrated hero. Moreover, it invites the viewer to scapegoat the minorities who are the targets of Douglas's attacks and to applaud Douglas's rage. At the same time, the movie shows that Douglas's character intends to murder his family once he reaches home. His delusions have become homicidal and suicidal. This unresolved presentation of the character makes for an ambivalent film and an ambiguous point of view. But herein lies the film's power. It is often the messy films, those not fully in control of their own contradictions, that achieve a visceral poetry. This *Falling Down* does, and it remains an essential nineties touchstone about the personal alienation and social confusion in segments of white America.

One of the sharpest political films of the late nineties focused, like *Falling Down*, on the alienation of white executives. Writer-director Neil Labute's *In the Company of Men* (1997) is an audacious and acidic portrait of sexual cruelty that links the callous behavior of its characters to the predatory ethic of corporate capitalism. Frustrated by job insecurity and rampantly misogynist, two junior business executives, Chad (Aaron Eckhart) and Howard (Matt Malloy) plot to pick a woman at random, get her to fall in love with them and then dump her. Their intent is to deliberately hurt her. Chad tells Howard that this would give them a comforting memory that would be a buffer against future experiences of being passed over for promotion or left by a wife or girlfriend. Chad points out that they'd always be able to say no one got us like we got her.

They pick Christine, a deaf secretary in their firm. Both men woo her, and she falls in love with Chad, who then reveals the game and confesses that he has no feelings for her whatsoever. As they planned, Christine is badly hurt by the betrayal. What gives this extraordinary film its sting is the outrageously sadistic nature of Chad and Howard's game and the way in which the game is contexualized in terms of a capitalist ethic. As Chad says, in terms that could also apply to the emotional scam he runs with Howard, "That's what business is all about: who's sporting the nastiest sack of venom and who is willing to use it." Chad clearly has the biggest sack of poison, as it transpires that, simultaneous with the game on Christine, he is betraying Howard to the company bosses. With his machinations, Chad surreptitiously makes Howard look like a fool and ruins his career in the firm. Sexual politics and economic politics become as one in an ugly portrait of the manner in which personal pathology, sanctioned by and in a social system, can rise to sublime heights of expression. Few contemporary American films have given us so ruthless a picture of the connections between personal and economic predation.

As these films depicting Washington politics, race relations, and social and economic opportunity demonstrate, socially conscious filmmaking was thrived in the nineties. Thus, this decade joins those others in American film history in which the cinema has been both mirror and commentary on the state of the nation. Despite the box-office dominance of fantasy blockbusters, American film maintained a socially engaged stance, and filmmakers continued to look about at the nation's streets and communities, finding there abundant material to nurture a socially conscious cinema. This inflection redeems and distinguishes American film. Without a topically engaged outlook in the film industry, without a commitment by filmmakers and distributors to pictures that seek to depict and transform social problems, the industry is strictly a money-making enterprise.

WORKS CITED

Bailey, John. "Bang Bang Bang Bang, Ad Nauseum." *American Cinematographer* 15.12 (December 1994): 26–29.

Breskin, David. *Inner Views: Filmmakers in Conversation* Boston: Faber & Faber, 1992.

Combs, James. *American Political Movies* New York: Garland, 1990.

Crowdus, Gary, ed. *A Political Companion to American Film* Lakeview Press, 1994.

Davies, Philip, and Brian Neve, eds. *Cinema, Politics and Society in America* New York: St. Martin's Press, 1981.

Neve, Brian. *Film and Politics in America: A Social Tradition* New York: Routledge, 1992.

Polan, Dana. *Power and Paranoia* New York: Columbia University Press, 1986.

Prince, Stephen. *Visions of Empire: Political Imagery in Contemporary American Film* New York: Praeger, 1992.

Ryan, Michael, and Douglas Kellner. *Camera Politica* Bloomington: Indiana University Press, 1988.

CHAPTER SIX

◼

The Martial Arts Film in the 1990s

DAVID DESSER

The martial-arts film, as a distinct American film genre, can be clearly dated as beginning in 1979, though it has antecedents in the immediate preceding years. It is an offshoot, a borrowing, and an outright co-optation of the Hong Kong martial-arts film popularized in the United States in 1973 with the release of a large handful of dubbed imports, including and especially *Five Fingers of Death* and Bruce Lee's *Fists of Fury* (a.k.a. *The Big Boss*) and *The Chinese Connection* (a.k.a. *Fist of Fury*). As the section on the genre's history will reveal, Hollywood immediately jumped on the martial-arts bandwagon, but Bruce Lee's untimely death before the release of what would be his blockbuster, mainstream hit, *Enter the Dragon*, put the genre on hiatus in Hollywood until Chuck Norris established it as a legitimate, American genre with *Good Guys Wear Black* in 1979. It is a genre that remains virtually unexplored, indeed undefined, by academic criticism. But as a genre with mainstream, cult, and exploitation appeal it has much to offer as cultural mirror and cultural critique, if less often as artistic or aesthetic currency.

By martial-arts film, we mean specifically films that feature Asian martial arts that, though broad and varied, represent fighting styles quite distinct from Western martial arts such as boxing or fencing. Variously known as kung fu or karate, the martial arts more broadly contain both unarmed and weapons styles, sometimes in combinations that were traditionally nowhere found in Asia, but that in a cinematic and cultural melange may be reasonably called "martial arts." While it is possible to see the martial-arts film as an offshoot of the broader, action/adventure film, in fact, an examination of the large corpus of films that feature martial arts reveals that there are both commonalities across this corpus of films that define it as a unique genre, while at the same time, it is something of a megagenre itself, with variations enough to justify categorization by subgenre. Similarly, the martial-arts film has influenced the broader category of the action film, making hard and fast categorization of any individual film a difficult, but also probably pointless task.

The martial-arts film may be said to be one in which the protagonist or protagonists are skilled in Asian martial arts and put such skill to use in the resolution of the plot. There are five major variations of the martial-arts film, which I shall call (1) the "arena" subgenre; (2) the "law-enforcement" subgenre; (3) the "juvenile adventure fantasy"; (4) the "video/cartoon fantasy"; and (5) the sci-fi subgenre. The arena subgenre concerns protagonists who fight within diegetic arenas in organized (legal, quasi-legal, or illegal) competitions; the law-enforcement subgenre concerns protagonists who are members of police, armed services, or other such agencies, or are vigilantes working where such agencies are corrupt or unable to intervene; the juvenile adventure fantasy concerns children or young teens who are budding or accomplished martial artists; the video/cartoon fantasy consists of films that are derived from video games or animated television series (or, sometimes, both); the SF martial-arts film is rather self-explanatory: an SF setting, usually a post-apocalyptic future. Of course there are some overlaps, such as the arena film or law-enforcement plot set within a fantasy or science-fiction setting. Or there are variations of any individual subgenre, a law-enforcement film with an arena component, or a popular variation on the law-enforcement subgenre that consists of a reluctant hero or wandering chivalric do-gooder who, while not connected with any official law-enforcement agency, serves on the side of the right, the weak, the oppressed. The largest number of martial-arts films may be comfortably placed within these subgenres, with the arena and law-enforcement subgenres dominating in numbers, while the juvenile adventure and video/cartoon fantasy variation have proven to be among the most commercially profitable of the films.

Like many "exploitation" genres, the martial-arts film, while it has many high visibility stars and individually successful films, derives its bread and butter from B features, essentially low budget, formulaic films that are usually released in regional playdates or, more often, direct-to-video and pay-TV. Like other exploitation genres, too, it is given over not simply to highly formulaic repetitions, but to sequels (a general feature of the action film, too, such as the *Die Hard* or *Lethal Weapon* series, and, of course, of the horror film, for example, the many sequels to *Halloween, A Nightmare on Elm Street,* and *Friday the 13th*). Most of the films, especially those intended for immediate pay-TV and direct-to-video playoff tend to be rated R by the MPAA, for violent content. Unlike other pay-TV and direct-to-video exploitation forms, the martial-arts film does not particularly rely on sex and nudity for its R rating and audience appeal (even those films that feature some nudity and sexual situations rely far more on violence, precisely on the martial, as opposed to, shall we say, the marital, arts).

The major martial-arts films within the broad subgenre of the arena version include most of the early films of Jean-Claude Van Damme, of which *Bloodsport* (1987) and *Kickboxer* (1989) may be taken as paradigmatic; *Hard Target* (1993, directed by Hong Kong's master of violence, John Woo) is an interesting variation on the arena subgenre. So, too, *Sudden Death* (1995), which takes place in a hockey arena, is a variation on the arena setting. Low-budget knockoffs of *Bloodsport* include the *Bloodfist* series (eight films between 1989 and 1996, all starring Don "The Dragon" Wilson), while *Kickboxer* has given rise to three sequels itself (none featuring Jean-Claude Van Damme). Other significant films within the arena variation include the first two films of the *Best of the Best* series (1989, 1993).

The law-enforcement subgenre has been the particular province of Steven Seagal, who has ranged across a wide variety of law-enforcement agencies, including the CIA, the Chicago PD, the DEA, the LAPD, the NYPD, the U.S. Navy, and even the EPA in such films as *Above the Law* (1988), *Marked for Death* (1990), *Hard to Kill* (1990), *Out for Justice* (1991), *Under Siege* (1992), *The Glimmer Man* (1996), and *Fire Down Below* (1997). Second-line stars, such as Cynthia Rothrock (the only woman to emerge as a genuine star in American martial-arts films, in contradistinction to the Hong Kong industry where female martial artists have been prominent since the 1960s) often utilize this subgenre such as in the two *China O'Brien* films (1990, 1991), the two *Lady Dragon* films (1992, 1993), *Tiger Claws* (1992), and *Guardian Angel* (1994). Similarly, Jeff Speakman has found this variation to his liking in *Street Knight* (1993) among other films.

There is, to a certain extent, a fine line between the juvenile adventure fantasy and the video/cartoon fantasy. Films such as *The Karate Kid* series (1984, 1986,1989), the *3 Ninjas* series (1992, 1994, 1995) and *Sidekicks* (1992) would perhaps most properly fit into the former category, while *Teenage Mutant Ninja Turtles* (1990—from cult comic book, to mainstream animated series, to hit movie), *Double Dragon* (1993), *Street Fighter* (1994), *Mortal Kombat* (1995), and *Mortal Kombat II: Annihilation* (1997) are all overtly derived from cartoons and video games and thus define the latter subgenre.

The element of fantasy within the martial arts, which has made it so popular and profitable within the realm of video games, has also impacted the martial-arts film in terms of science-fiction settings. Cyborgs and multiple variations on that theme, have proven particularly popular within the martial arts, the in- or extrahuman dimension of cyborgs helping to account for the spectacular martial skills often displayed by the protagonists within these films. Olivier Gruner (the low-budget Jean-Claude Van Damme), for instance, got his break in *Nemesis* (1993), a tale of cyborgs and terminators in a post-apocalyptic universe; even Van Damme himself made use of this genre. Though he is not a cyborg in *Cyborg* (1989), he is a cyborg in *Universal Soldier* (1992), with sometime martial-arts star Dolph Lundgren helping the mayhem along. Other cyborg-SF martial-arts films include *Knights* (1993) with the diminutive, kickboxing Kathy Long taking on a cyborg army with the help of pro-human cyborg Kris Kristofferson, and *Omega Doom* (1996), with Rutger Hauer starring in this *Yojimbo*-derived martial arts/Cyborg adventure. The plots are often law-enforcement or arena variations, while much of the imagery is derived from video games (and from video technology itself). A film like *The Crow* (1994) contains elements of the law-enforcement, juvenile fantasy, and SF/fantasy varieties and shows some of the problems and limitations of defining these subgenres too finely.

The line between the martial-arts film and the broader action film may sometimes be difficult to discern. Certainly Asian martial arts have had a tremendous impact on the action film. The *Lethal Weapon* series, for instance, promulgates Mel Gibson's Martin Riggs as a martial artist, and the first film in the series (1987) features a good deal of karate/kung fu action, including the climactic fight between Riggs and Gary Busey's Mr. Joshua. Similarly, the fourth entry in the series (1998) actually features Hong Kong martial-arts superstar Jet Li as a criminal skilled in the martial arts. Sylvester Stallone's John Rambo in the *First Blood* series

(1982, 1985, 1988) is also a skilled martial artist, in addition to his proficiency with modern weaponry and technology. If an important feature of the action film is the use of contemporary weaponry and a reliance on explosive effects, these elements are also familiar in many films that can be considered martial arts. In particular, the line between action and martial arts is fairly permeable within the law-enforcement subgenre. Similarly, the line between the martial-arts film and the science-fiction film can often be quite confusing as in the aforementioned "cyborg" or post-apocalyptic films. Thus we need one further provisional definition of the genre. One way of bringing a more definitive sense of categorization to this quandary is to recognize the importance of an acknowledged martial artist as the star of a martial-arts film. This becomes a factor not only for fans of the genre by which to judge the films, but also aids in defining the genre itself. As we will see below, the consequences of featuring an accomplished martial artist impacts the narratives, settings, and motifs of the films themselves.

The American martial-arts film owes its origins and the majority of its defining characteristics to Hong Kong martial-arts films. It is quite possibly the most derivative genre in Hollywood's history and amounts to nothing less than a virtual stealing, a cultural co-optation, of another country's popular cinematic culture. Of course, the Hong Kong martial-arts film did not arise in a cultural vacuum and it owes as many of its characteristics to outside cultural and cinematic influences as to the particularities of Chinese culture and cinema. The Hong Kong martial-arts film certainly derived features and resemblances from the Hollywood western, while in the 1960s it was hugely influenced by Japanese Samurai and gangster films (themselves influenced by American westerns and gangster films). Nevertheless, the Hong Kong martial-arts film exists as a definable genre with deep roots in Chinese tradition and strong lines throughout the history of Chinese and Hong Kong cinema. There was virtually nothing resembling an American martial-arts film until an influx of highly successful Hong Kong imports in the spring and summer of 1973 planted the seeds of a future American co-optation.

If by martial arts we mean specifically Asian martial arts, then the traces of a martial-arts film within the Hollywood cinema are easily noticeable for their rarity before 1973. A single sequence in Raoul Walsh's *White Heat* (1949); a sustained tenor of the martial arts in John Sturges's *Bad Day at Black Rock* (1955); Sam Fuller's exploration of Japanese karate and kendo in *The Crimson Kimono* (1959); the James Bond films of the

1960s and their many imitators; Tom Laughlin's biker-who-knows-karate thriller, *The Born Losers* (1967), and, perhaps most notably, TV's *The Green Hornet* in the 1966–67 season, mark the mere traces of the martial arts within Hollywood cinema. Those watchful for the martial arts would have seen its presence in films such as *The Mechanic* (1972) and *Superfly* (1972) where their appearance is minor, but noticeable. This minor presence of the martial arts would change dramatically, first, with the introduction of the television series *Kung Fu* in the fall of 1972 (first as a made-for-TV movie, then as a monthly program for its first season), second, with the tremendous success of Tom Laughlin's *Billy Jack* (which opened regionally in the South in 1972, but did not score big nationwide until 1973), and third and most importantly, the influx of Hong Kong imports in the spring of 1973.

Following the immediate and sensational box-office success of *Five Fingers of Death* (beginning in March) and Bruce Lee's *Fists of Fury* in May, Hollywood immediately jumped on the clear kung fu bandwagon and put *Enter the Dragon* into production. Before its release in August of '73, American screens were flooded with Hong Kong imports, hastily and inexpertly dubbed, but among the season's box-office champs. Bruce Lee's untimely death in July of that year put a damper on Hollywood's martial arts mania, for he was the only genuine superstar to emerge not only in the United States, but worldwide within the martial-arts film. But *Enter the Dragon* was a smash, while throughout the remainder of 1973, Hong Kong imports continued to pull in many U.S. dollars.

The success of *Billy Jack* (whose martial arts component is significant, but one is not sure if its success was dependent on that), of TV's *Kung Fu*, and of the dozens of Hong Kong imports, Bruce Lee's films in particular, set the stage for a martial-arts genre. Though *Enter the Dragon* established a recognizable pattern for future martial-arts films to follow— a combination of the arena and law-enforcement variations, the use of a multiracial cast (Asian, white, Black), exotic locale, and so forth—the genre would actually be somewhat delayed, most probably by Bruce Lee's death. The genre would take a number of detours before finding a solid basis on which to build.

The first detour of the martial arts genre-to-be was through the black action film (blaxploitation). If martial arts was a minor component in *Superfly*, it was the major raison d'être of *Black Belt Jones* (1974), produced and directed by the team who created *Enter the Dragon*, Fred Weintraub and Robert Clouse, and starring Jim Kelly, who made his film debut in *Enter the Dragon*. The martial-arts film found a welcome and solid response among black film-goers and, in some ways, replaced blaxploitation. By 1974, when *Black Belt Jones* was released, blaxploitation's days were numbered and so, therefore, were Jim Kelly's. *Three the Hard Way* (1974, directed by Gordon Parks Jr. who had helmed *Superfly*) and *Hot Potato* (1976) could not sustain blaxploitation nor Kelly's karate-film career. Neither could the introduction of karate wielding, statuesque Tamara Dobson in two *Cleopatra Jones* films (1973, 1975) sustain blaxploitation, with a feminine and feminist angle.

A second detour of the martial arts was through international coproductions with genre-bending peculiarities: kung fu/horror (*Legend of the Seven Golden Vampires*, 1974) or the kung fu western (*The Stranger and the Gunfighter*, 1976). These were little more than curiosities that led virtually nowhere. Similarly, the brilliant Sam Peckinpah combined martial arts with the action film in *The Killer Elite* (1975). Peckinpah demonstrated a familiarity with martial-arts choreography and some understanding of the spirit of the martial arts, but audiences, overall, ignored the film. Only Bruce Lee continued the box-office clout of the martial-arts genre in America, first with his last Hong Kong film, *Way of the Dragon* (a.k.a. *Return of the Dragon* [Meng long guo jiang], 1972, not released in the States until 1974), and then *Game of Death* (1978), completed and released some five years after his death. By the time Lee's friend Stirling Silliphant completed *Circle of Iron* (a.k.a. *The Silent Flute*, 1979), conceived by Lee and originally set for him to star in, the genre would find its true American hero, the star the genre apparently needed to set it on track, a particularly American track: Chuck Norris.

Chuck Norris would set the tenor for a number of the central components of the martial-arts film, not the least of which would be the presence of an acknowledged martial artist in the starring role. The success of his early films demonstrated the viability, if not of a martial-arts genre per se, at least of Chuck Norris's starring in martial-arts films. But when the inevitable low-budget rip-offs appeared to considerable success, the genre was established and so it remains.

Norris, appropriately enough, was introduced to American film-goers via Bruce Lee in *Way of the Dragon*, where he played the role of Colt—the western-genre derivation of his name was all too deliberate. This film, also a variation on the law-enforcement subgenre like *Enter the Dragon* (Lee is a martial artist who comes into a situation where actual law-enforcement agencies are powerless to stop the criminal gang), climaxes in one of the genre's most memorable arena sequences, in the Roman Colosseum. As in many Hong Kong films, part of the pleasure and significance of the film rests in the fact that the Chinese hero defeats a foreign villain (in this case a white American). Norris's martial-arts credentials were established by supporting discourses surrounding the film, when perhaps for the first time many Americans learned of the existence of karate championships of various sorts. The off-screen viability of the martial arts of both hero and villain would play into the pleasures of the on-screen fight sequences.

In 1977, Norris attempted a big-screen star-making role in *Breaker! Breaker!*, part of the short-lived cycle of Citizen's Band (CB) radio films, which included *Citizens Band* (a.k.a. *Handle with Care*, 1977), *Smokey and the Bandit* (1977), and Sam Peckinpah's *Convoy* (1978) among a few others. *Breaker! Breaker!* was a flop, but Norris's next effort would virtually inaugurate not only his solid and respectable film career, but the American martial-arts film.

Good Guys Wear Black (1979) was Norris's big break, an appropriate vehicle for his solid martial arts skills and his screen presence as a likable guy with something smoldering underneath (the persona of almost every male martial-arts star, a limited, but successful range of emotions and abilities). It also introduced a number of crucial elements to the genre, including the legacy of the Vietnam War, both as origin of the hero's special skills and as a paranoid backdrop of governmental cover-up and corruption. Hugely successful as a lower-budget film, it enabled Norris and studio American International Pictures to proceed with a number of films in its wake, including *A Force of One* (1979), a law-enforcement type, and *The Octagon* (1980), which brought the arena variation to the fore once again. Norris would mostly continue in the law-enforcement subgenre, with films like *An Eye for an Eye* (1981), *Silent Rage* (1982, which brings an element of horror into the genre), *Lone Wolf McQuade* (1983), and *Code of Silence* (1985). These films would culminate in the TV series *Walker, Texas Ranger*, which premiered in 1993 and continues to run both in syndication and in prime time, making it the first martial-arts prime-time television series since *Kung Fu*, and the longest running ever on network TV.

As Norris's career progressed and solidified, he would introduce an important variation on the martial-arts film, one that would have great impact on the action film in general and on America's cinematic coming to terms with the legacy of the Vietnam War. His *Missing in Action* (1984) was part of the mid-1980s cycle of Vietnam War films, especially those concerned with the MIA/POW issue. *Uncommon Valor* (1983) set the tone for these films, an essentially conservative tenor which accused the U.S. government of cowardice and betrayal in abandoning the alleged POWs still remaining in Vietnam. The best-known, most notorious of these films is, of course, *Rambo: First Blood II* (1985), but *Rambo* oddly owes much of its plot, iconography, and stereotypical characterizations to *Missing in Action*. This film, successful on its lower-budget terms, spawned two sequels (1985, 1988), and many imitators. In particular, the Vietnam setting, utilized as backdrop for the paranoid thriller that is *Good Guys Wear Black*, is more central to these films and would form the underpinning to literally dozens of cheaper, more exploitative genre entries. But along with the earlier law-enforcement films, Norris's Vietnam action thrillers solidified the martial-arts genre and paved the way for other important '80s martial-arts stars such as Sho Kosugi and Michael Dudikoff before the breakthrough success of Steven Seagal and Jean-Claude Van Damme.

As claimed above, the viability of a genre rests less with the bigger-budget or star vehicles than with routine, low-budget derivatives or second-line stars who emerge from these sorts of films. Thus the successful films of Sho Kosugi and Michael Dudikoff helped demonstrate that the martial-arts film was a viable, money-making structure, that is, a genre. Critically neglected and despised, the martial-arts film nevertheless was set on a consistent production path that continues unabated into the 1990s. Kosugi, a native Japanese actor with considerable martial arts skill, began his career playing the villain in *Enter the Ninja* (1981). Its title obviously recalled *Enter the Dragon*, but few could perhaps have imagined that a veritable "ninja" craze would follow, not only through two sequels to this film and three other "ninja"-titled films starring Kosugi, and through the "American Ninja" series (five films, three starring Michael Dudikoff), but through the megatext that became *The Teenage Mutant Ninja Turtles* (more of that soon). It was significant that Kosugi's film debut was as a villain and that a white, non-martial-artist actor (Franco Nero) was the film's star. This was part of a pattern already seen in Chuck Norris's films where Asian actors and martial artists were utilized mostly as villains. But in Kosugi's film, it was the martial art of ninjutsu that caused the greatest excitement from martial-arts fans and thus helped introduce a Japanese dimension to what was still being thought of as kung fu, a Chinese martial art. Ninjutsu relies not only on karate and jiujitsu, but also on a dazzling array of exotic weapons and skills. The samurai sword, throwing stars, throwing knives, staffs, and sticks were introduced into the arsenal of martial-arts films, becoming quite as popular as Bruce Lee's nunchuks ever were. Kosugi's films would thus increase the iconography of the genre and expand its geography away from China/Hong Kong.

The sequels to *Enter the Ninja* allowed Kosugi to be the hero. It was his martial-arts skills, after all, that made the original film so memorable. Thus Kosugi become the first Asian star in the American cinema since Bruce Lee. He would thus, also provide a model for other Asian and Asian American actors to attempt to achieve stardom in American cinema, some through martial-arts films and many in more mainstream efforts. It is notable that at this time (1980–81) Hollywood filmmakers attempted to make an American star out of Jackie (then Jacky) Chan, a major star of the Hong Kong cinema since 1978 (Chan resurrected the martial-arts film in Hong Kong much as Chuck Norris did in the United States). Chan's stardom would not take hold in the States, but Kosugi's would, at least for a decade, but only in low-budget genre efforts. In a more prestigious film, such as *Blind Fury* (1989), an Americanization of the Japanese blind swordsman "Zatoichi" series, Kosugi again plays the villain, this time to Rutger Hauer (whose own career never lived up to the expectations placed on him following *Blade Runner* [1982]). Similarly, in 1984, Kosugi was instrumental in the TV series *The Master*, focusing on a ninja master and his younger protégé. However, the master was played by Lee Van Cleef (who had starred in *The Stranger and the Gunfighter*), the protégé by Timothy Van Patten. While this brought ninjutsu to the home screen and thus to more mainstream audiences, Kosugi was again essentially the villain and the show itself lasted only one season. Still, Kosugi made a dozen films in the 1980s, setting the martial-arts film on a course that enabled it to showcase Japanese martial arts and a Japanese martial artist within the context of the Hollywood cinema.

The career of Michael Dudikoff revealed even more clearly how the martial-arts film would work to co-opt Asian film genres and Asian film stars, tying into timely American concerns sifted through the needs and practices of the low-budget exploitation genre. Sho Kosugi's films were made by the once tremendously successful production pair of Menachem Golan and Yoram Globus, whose Cannon Films was one of the real success stories of the 1980s. Their cheap and fast production methods enabled them to capitalize on every fad, real or imagined, missing as often as they hit. But if they hit with Sho Kosugi, they hit even bigger with Michael Dudikoff. A bit player in such films as *Making Love* (1982), *I Ought to Be in Pictures* (1982), *Uncommon Valor*, and *Bachelor Party* (1984), his starring role in *American Ninja* (1985) set him on a course of low-budget martial-arts stardom.

American Ninja was Cannon's derivation of its own ninja series with Sho Kosugi but with a strictly American star and inexpensive Philippine locations. The Asian locale brought along Asian villains once again; even Dudikoff's fellow ninjas are "American" (i.e., white) ninjas, thus helping to prepare for the future genre in which Caucasian stars would dominate. A sequel to *American Ninja* in 1987, also with Dudikoff, was no less successful, relying on by-now standard plot devices such as evil drug lords and marauding armies of evil martial artists. While Cannon produced *American Ninja 3* (1989) without Dudikoff, Dudikoff himself entered Chuck Norris's territory with *Platoon Leader* (1988), derived both from *Platoon* (1986) and from Norris's *Missing in Action* series (the third of which was released the same year as *Platoon Leader*). Aaron Norris, Chuck's brother, directed Dudikoff in this film, making the Norris connection both obvious and palpable. The *American Ninja* series would continue, both with Dudikoff (*American Ninja 4: The Annihilation* [1991]) and without him (*American Ninja 5* [1993]). But by the time of *Platoon Leader*, other more significant figures would enter the martial-arts canon.

The films of Chuck Norris, Sho Kosugi, and Michael Dudikoff demonstrate the viability of a martial-arts genre in the 1980s, but at a low-budget, mostly exploitation level. Norris would never have a genuine blockbuster hit, while Kosugi's and Dudikoff's careers were almost strictly video and pay-TV fodder. The same could not be said, however, of a mid-'80s film that attained genuine blockbuster status and inspired three sequels: *The Karate Kid* (1984). If the proximate model was *Rocky* (1976; John G. Avildsen helmed both the Stallone film and this one), *The Karate Kid* also added an important new wrinkle in the emerging American martial-arts genre: the wizened Asian martial-arts master and the white hero whom he trains.

Whatever martial-arts purists may have thought of *The Karate Kid* (neither Noriyuki "Pat" Morita nor Ralph Macchio possess any discernible martial-arts skill), mainstream American audiences ate it up, lending the genre the kind of commercial, if not critical, respectability that would inspire larger budgets and bigger stars to enter the fray. With a box-office gross of more than $90 million in the United States, *The Karate Kid* obviously offered up a palatable means of expressing martial artistry within a Hollywood context. Essentially a juvenile adventure fantasy with a fairly benign arena component, *The Karate Kid* allowed audiences to experience some of the training and the philosophy of the martial arts (important semantic features of the genre as we will see below) while delivering up a new kind of supporting character within the genre: the seemingly and deceptively harmless, wizened, crafty, benevolent, a little bit mysterious Asian man who is in reality a martial-arts master. This figure would become both a common component and a cliché of the genre, ranging from Joel Grey's "yellowface" portrayal of a Korean martial-arts master in *Remo Williams: The Adventure Begins. . . .* (1985) to the rat/ninja master, Splinter, in the *Teenage Mutant Ninja Turtles* series. (The paradigm for this relationship had been introduced in TV's *Kung Fu*, where Keye Luke's blind Master Po would refer to hero Kwai Chang Caine as "grasshopper"—the inevitable joke in every martial-arts spoof.) The significance of this figure will be discussed below, but the appearance of this figure is owed to *The Karate Kid*.

The *Karate Kid, Part II* (1986), though generally critically dismissed as a pointless sequel, actually outgrossed its predecessor, pulling in an astounding $115 million in domestic grosses (making it the second most successful martial-arts film in U.S. box-office history). Much more geared to the arena subgenre even than the first film, it not only added mainstream respectability to that particular variation, but added the "exotic locale" to the arena subgenre's discursive field. Set in Okinawa, *The Karate Kid II* certainly devotes much of its screen time to Orientalizing the Okinawan locations and characters (though Asian Americans play the leading roles, aside from Ralph Macchio's reprise of the title character). *The Karate Kid III* (1989) added little to the genre, but its respectable domestic box-office gross ($39 million) continued to demonstrate a certain mainstream appeal of the genre, and it did add a *soupcon* of martial-arts respectability with the addition of Thomas Ian Griffith to the cast. Griffith would go on to become one of many second-line stars of the martial-arts genre, which was poised for its breakthrough around the time of this third entry into the series. It is worth noting that the fourth and final sequel to *The Karate Kid, The Next Karate Kid* (1994), focused on a female fighting protagonist and grossed a pitiful figure of less than $9 million in the United States. Whether this is owed to the fact that the series was played out, that the protagonist was female, or whether by 1994 the heyday of real martial artists in martial-arts films was already triumphant is difficult to say.

By the middle of the 1980s, the martial-arts film had established a certain hybridity, testimony to the genre's solidity and its protean nature. We have already seen how the martial arts film intersected with the Vietnam War film; Chuck Norris attempted an Action-Adventure film with *Invasion USA* (1985) and an even more traditional genre entry with *Firewalker* (1986), a variation on the standard search-for-buried treasure film like *King Solomon's Mines* (which had most recently been filmed in 1985) or even the *Indiana Jones* trilogy, which started in 1981. Michael Dudikoff tried the same action-adventure variation with *River of Death* (1989). John Carpenter's *Big Trouble in Little China* (1986) acknowledged the American genre's roots in the Hong Kong cinema and betrayed something of a knowledge of where the genre had gone in Hong Kong. Perhaps one of the oddest of these hybrid films was *The Last Dragon* (1985, a.k.a. Berry Gordy's *The Last Dragon*), an attempted revival of blaxploitation, the musical (Gordy was founder and then-Chairman of the board of Motown Records), and the new martial arts fantasy. Then there was *Gymkata* (1985), a disastrous effort to make a star out of Olympic gymnast Kurt Thomas, attempting some sort of gymnastics-cum-martial-arts melange. Director Robert Clouse, who had done so well with Bruce Lee in *Enter the Dragon* and with Jim Kelly in *Black Belt Jones*, had far less luck with Thomas. Still, such a film is tribute to the existence of a genre that would soon hit even bigger.

The films of Chuck Norris, Sho Kosugi, Michael Dudikoff, *The Karate Kid* series, TV's *The Master*, and the sort of hybridity in films like *The Last Dragon* testify to a lively interest in martial-arts films. Similarly, the impact of martial arts on action films (*Rambo*, *Commando* [1985], *Lethal Weapon*, etc.) show the martial arts sifting throughout mainstream cinema. But mainstream cinema was not only the venue where Asian martial arts had an impact. Action-adventure comic books, especially those from the Marvel Comics group, had felt the impact of martial arts. The on-going popularity and legacy of Bruce Lee was the primary engine behind this continuing cult fandom. By the 1980s, kung fu, ninjutsu, bushido (Japanese martial arts and spirituality) had found their way into such cult comics as *Daredevil*, *Dr. Strange* and *The X-Men*, among others. American comic books and Asian martial arts would merge in 1984 to create *The Teenage Mutant Ninja Turtles*. A cult success right from the start, few could have imagined the astonishing popularity that the Turtles would attain. What Marsha Kinder calls a "supersystem" (122) of Turtle-mania emerged in the late '80s, culminating, for our purposes, in the 1990 feature film that became, and remains, the highest grossing martial-arts film in history, taking in over $135 million in the domestic U.S. box office. Even the much-inferior sequel (1991) grossed almost $80 million in the United States, making it the fifth-highest grossing martial-arts film of all time.

A full appreciation of Turtlemania requires a recognition not only of how martial arts had found its way into films, television, and comic books but of how, more generally, Asian popular culture profoundly impacted American culture. Perhaps the primary engine of this impact came not through any of these sources, but through the introduction of the Nin-tendo Entertainment System to the United States in 1985. Perhaps it is coincidental that this introduction coincides with the 1980s boom in martial-arts films—Chuck Norris, Sho Kosugi, *The Karate Kid*, and oth-ers—but the relationship between martial arts and home video would be one of a profound mutuality of influence and impact. Video games, in arcades and then in the home, had been a fact of life since the early 1970s, breaking through in 1979 with the introduction of hardware from the likes of Atari, Midway, and Mattel among others. (Kinder 88) But a video bust occurred in 1982, mostly due to a lack of software. Nintendo, a Japanese videogame maker, put the home video market back on track in 1985 and has kept it there ever since (joined by the likes of Sony and Sega more lately). Though the "Mario Brothers" games are among the most popular, martial arts, especially for older players, is one of the dominant genres. *Street Fighter* and *Mortal Kombat*, for instance, are ubiquitous both in arcades and in home systems. *The Teenage Mutant Ninja Turtles* spawned home video games, along with the television cartoon and live-action film series, the sort of megatext or supersystem that drives the entertainment and culture industries. This idea of a supersystem imported, adapted, and transformed for American uses reached its height in the *Power Rangers* phenomenon of the early '90s. Sci-fi fantasy, martial arts, and cheesy special effects never had it so good as on the Fox Televi-sion program derived from a popular Japanese children's series. Interest-ingly, the feature film was not simply a disappointment, but something of a flop. Whether this signaled the end of the craze or it came just as the craze was fizzling out cannot be known.

As *The Teenage Mutant Ninja Turtles* supersystem began to establish itself in the mid-'80s, the martial-arts genre in film found two stars who would bridge the gap between cult fandom and mainstream success: Steven Seagal and Jean-Claude Van Damme. Seagal made his film debut in *Above the Law* in 1988. It was a moderate commercial success with some critical respect given it as well. If it is reminiscent of Chuck Norris's *Code of Silence*, it is doubtless deliberate, both relying on director Andrew Davis and on Chicago locales and actors. Van Damme had appeared in bit parts in a handful of minor films previously, but his starring breakthrough came in 1987 with *Bloodsport*. Though he would take a supporting role (to Sho Kosugi) in *Black Eagle* the next year, in 1989 he achieved his solid stardom with *Kickboxer* and *Cyborg*.

Starting in 1990, both Van Damme and Seagal would appear in at least one film every year, with Seagal's films, in particular often attaining blockbuster status (*Under Siege, Under Siege 2* [1995], *Hard to Kill*, and *Marked for Death* especially). With the continued and ongoing success of Seagal and Van Damme, other stars would follow. Cynthia Rothrock, gainfully and successfully employed in Hong Kong since 1986, would achieve her American success with *China O'Brien* in 1990; Don "The Dragon" Wilson would make his starring debut with *Bloodfist* in 1989; *Bloodfist II* in 1990 would solidify his career. Phillip Rhee would try to become the first Asian martial artist to succeed since Sho Kosugi with *Best of the Best* in 1989; Jeff Speakman in *Perfect Weapon* (1991); Thomas Ian Griffith in *Excessive Force* (1992), and Jeff Wincott in *Martial Law* (1992) were only some of the many who tried their hands in cinematic martial-arts combat in the wake of Seagal's and Van Damme's success. Both the martial-arts film and the influence of martial arts on the big-budget action film were here to stay in the '90s.

By the middle of the '90s, the line between Hollywood and Hong Kong martial-arts films was becoming a bit blurred. Jean-Claude Van Damme worked with Hong Kong masters John Woo (as noted above), who also created such films as *Blackjack* (made-for-TV, 1995) and *Once a Thief* (1997); Ringo Lam (*Maximum Risk*, 1996), and Tsui Hark (*Double Team*, 1997, *Knock Off*, 1998). Ronnie (a.k.a. Ronny) Yu created a video/cartoon fantasy with *Warriors of Virtue* (1997). Jackie Chan's more recent Hong Kong films were increasingly being released to mainstream theaters with dubbed soundtracks. *Rumble in the Bronx* (1995) was a substantial hit; *Mr. Nice Guy* (1997), with an Australian setting, revealed something of the internationalization of the genre. A major Hollywood film, *Rush Hour*, appeared in the fall of 1998. Hong Kong star Chow Yun-fat starred opposite Mira Sorvino in *The Replacement Killers* (1998), a

FIGURE 6.1. Chow Yun Fat and Mira Sorvino in Antoine Fuqua's *The Replacement Killers*. Courtesy: Jerry Ohlinger Archive.

somewhat disappointing variation on the John Woo gangster film. Not everyone proved sanguine about Hollywood's importation of Hong Kong filmmakers and film stars: it certainly had deleterious effects on Hong Kong's indigenous industry and continues to reveal the manner in which Hollywood both borrowed and co-opted the Hong Kong genre.

No survey of the martial-arts film, however brief, would be complete without acknowledging the tragic career of Brandon Lee, Bruce Lee's equally ill-fated son. He made his film debut in Hong Kong with *Legacy of Rage* (Long zai jiang hu) in 1986, the same year he appeared in the made-for-TV *Kung Fu: The Movie*, which starred David Carradine, reprising his role as Kwai Chang Caine from the original television series of the '70s. He then appeared in the pilot for *Kung Fu: The Next Generation* (1987) playing the son of the grandson of Kwai Chang Caine (neither Brandon Lee nor star David Darlow would appear in the syndicated television series, which would again star David Carradine). The irony here, of course, is that the original *Kung Fu* was inspired by an idea of Bruce Lee's, who had hoped to star in the series, but was rejected by Warner Brothers who was unwilling to have an Asian star on a regular prime-time show. *Showdown in Little Tokyo* (1991) made Brandon a minor star in Hollywood and the modest success of *Rapid Fire* (1992) solidified that status. Brandon died accidentally on the set of *The Crow*, which, upon its release in 1994 became an immediate cult favorite. A competent martial artist (trained as a child by his father) and extremely handsome and personable, Brandon Lee might very well have become a star to rival Seagal or Van Damme. But we will never know.

The martial-arts film owes little, on the semantic level, to classical Hollywood genres—it has little in common with "fight-oriented" genres such as the boxing film or the swashbuckler, for instance. Though these films feature, respectively, hand-to-hand or weapons-oriented fights, the narrative drive of those genres work toward very different ends. The boxing film is almost always concerned with issues of the sport's corruption or the physical damage it may do to the fighter (or both), while the swashbuckler is essentially a romance (where the martial-arts film is virtually never concerned with the formation of the heterosexual couple). The genre with which the martial-arts film perhaps shares the most semantic features is the western. The western, as it has the world over, profoundly influenced the Hong Kong martial-arts film, which, in turn, gave direct rise to the Hollywood version. Thus there is a kind of circularity of influence at work here, and the martial-arts film in Hollywood could, and did, take over the action genre which the western had vacated by the middle 1970s. Motifs of wandering through dangerous landscapes, of civilization versus savagery, of chivalrous acts undertaken selflessly, of a vengeance-seeking loner, and a climactic showdown between hero and villain show the martial arts film's indebtedness to the western.

A more profound resemblance, if not influence, however, may be found on the syntactical level, where the martial-arts film has much in common with, of all things, the classic musical. Like the musical, it is primarily star-driven, with plots built around the particular musical/martial talents of the star. Each film must work in a specific number of fight sequences with feature the star's martial talents, leading to a final fight sequence, closer in spirit to the finale of the musical than the showdown of the western. As in the musical, the fight scenes are, literally, chore-ographed, and much of the pleasure within these texts relies on the star's bodily performance, his (or hers) "to-be-looked-at-ness" both within fight scenes and as physical specimens. Fred Astaire's soft-shoe or his duets with Ginger Rogers or Cyd Charisse, Gene Kelley's acrobatic or balletic feats, Eleanor Powell's or Ann Miller's eye-popping tappings, and so forth, find their homologies in the aikido of Steven Seagal, the kickboxing of Jean-Claude Van Damme and Don "The Dragon" Wilson, the Eagle Claw kung fu of Cynthia Rothrock or the kenpo of Jeff Speakman. This reliance on choreography and the specifics of the star's talents, reveals that, like the musical, the martial-arts film is a star-driven genre and that the films are primarily star vehicles. Thus, as in the musical, the plot of any individual film must literally make room for the star's talents, the dis-play of martial arts. To question this syntactical feature is to ignore the demands of genre.

Each of the subgenres within the martial-arts film may be defined not simply by the large plot motivations and character types that it fea-tures, and not simply by the presence of an acknowledged martial artist, but also by recurring patterns of setting and motif. The arena subgenre tends to set itself within an exotic or hidden locale, often Hong Kong, sometimes Thailand or the Philippines, sometimes a vaguely defined "Asia." Van Damme, as we have noted, tends to favor the arena subgenre. Thus we see *Bloodsport* and *Double Impact* set in Hong Kong, *Kickboxer* in Thailand; *Lionheart* utilizes illegal fighting arenas in New York and Los Angeles; *The Quest* is set in some mythical Asian never-never land. *Best of the Best* climaxes in an arena (a legal and legitimate one) in Korea; less legal and legitimate is the Philippino arena utilized in *Bloodfist*. Since the arena film specializes in scenes of man-to-man combat, isolated, overt arenas are best suited to allowing this sort of action to occur.

The law-enforcement subgenre tends to be set within urban environs, focusing on big-city police or other law-enforcement agencies. Seagal has favored Los Angeles for *Hard to Kill* and *The Glimmer Man*; Chicago for *Above the Law* and *Marked for Death*; New York for *Out for Justice*. He has also utilized exotic or hidden locales: a battleship for *Under Siege*; a moving train for *Under Siege 2*; the Kentucky coal mine country for *Fire Down Below*. Most other law-enforcement films rely almost exclusively on urban settings. Such settings are not only the home of large law-enforcement agencies, but allow for the sorts of car chases that also typify the genre, along with a handful of subsettings common to urban life and frequently utilized by the law-enforcement subgenre.

The juvenile adventure fantasy is almost always set within a recognizably contemporary middle-class environment. Familial relations—parent-child, sibling-sibling—school, friendships, status and image, and other typical juvenile concerns not only predominate the plots of these films, but impact the setting. Daniel's adjustment to his new life in southern California with his single mom provides the impetus for *The Karate Kid*; Barry's desire to fit it at school leads to the hijinks of *Sidekicks*. The *3 Ninjas* series focuses on three quite well-to-do brothers, their very wealth making them the targets of a kidnapping in the first entry. The middle or upper-class settings of these films provided both title and setting for a recent martial-arts spoof, *Beverly Hills Ninja* (1997), starring the late Chris Farley. That a spoof could be made in the first place demonstrates the generic familiarity of this subgenre. *Teenage Mutant Ninja Turtles* provides something of a transition, so to speak, between the juvenile adventure fantasy, with its setting in New York City and its plot of runaway or abandoned children, and the video/cartoon fantasy, the Turtles themselves and their rat-master providing the obvious cartoonlike iconography. *The Crow* would also fit into this subgenre with its setting in a dangerous (if highly stylized), recognizable contemporary urban dystopia, the iconography inspired by the comic book that gave rise to the film.

The video/cartoon fantasy attempts to narrativize what is essentially nothing more than the constant, nonstop combat of the videogames. Of course, the games themselves tend to provide something of a "backstory," some sense of narrative, certainly of quest, if only of a rudimentary sort (games have beginnings, goals, and ends). But the two-dimensional backdrops of the videogame needs something greater in the cinematic translation, yet it is precisely fans of the games whom the film versions hope to attract. To this end, they reproduce the fantastic/mythological settings of the games. Thus a mythical Shadaloo in *Street Fighter*, some other-worldly realm in *Mortal Kombat*, the sewers beneath the streets of Manhattan for the haunts of the Turtles; some vaguely futuristic Los Angeles for *Double Dragon*.

Finally, there are the overtly futuristic settings of the SF/martial-arts films. Such films rely almost exclusively on post-apocalyptic settings—burnt-out and ruined cities or vast stretches of desert wasteland. Since the budgets of these films tend to be low, such settings are obviously cheaper than the complex and detailed cityscape of, say, *Blade Runner*, or the high-tech future of the *Star Trek* films. Inexpensive computer-generated imagery and special effects help create the SF atmosphere, but the post-apocalyptic settings not only help bring about the overall tone of lawlessness and loss, but also help motivate the hand-to-hand combat or simple weaponry of the fight sequences.

In addition to similarities of settings among members of the various subgenres, we may point to recurring narrative patterns and plot devices. Thus in the arena subgenre there is a focus on the rigorous, demanding, sometimes exotic training the hero must undergo to prepare for his final showdown. These training sequences are mini-narratives within the film itself as the hero progresses in skill from failure, to moderate success, to success within the training regimen. This training regimen is (usually) administered by an aging Asian master, as in *The Karate Kid* films as noted above, and in many of Jean-Claude Van Damme's films: *Bloodsport* (where the training by the Asian master occurs in flashback), *Kickboxer*, and in the low-budget knockoff *Bloodfist*. Such training may involve unique apparatuses to develop the hero's skill or flexibility; many regimens often involve training the hero to fight blind (cf. *Star Wars*, for instance); sometimes these sequences are comic. Whatever the case, a rigorous training regimen, usually administered by an aging Asian master, is a virtual commonality in virtually every arena film.

Training sequences are far less frequent in the law-enforcement subgenre, but they do occur. Flashbacks reveal how Jeff Speakman's hero became a kenpo specialist in *Street Knight* (through training by an Asian master). Don "The Dragon" Wilson undergoes rigorous training at the hands of an Asian master in order to overcome a villain with seeming superpowers in *Red Sun Rising* (1993). Jalal Merhi learns the dreaded and deadly Tiger Claw style from a secretive, aging Asian master in *Tiger Claws*.

More particular to the law-enforcement subgenre as a recurring narrative moment is the barroom brawl. The urban settings of these films allow them to include the pool hall, the bar, the hangout for local toughs and thugs. Inevitably the hero enters such a domain and is attacked with fists, knives, cue sticks, beer bottles, and so forth, by appropriately large stunt men in carefully choreographed movements. Oftentimes, the cue sticks are used as staffs or, broken in half, as fighting sticks; even the billiard balls may get into the act. Much breaking of glass, stools, and bones proceeds. Seagal is particularly fond of such scenes and notable ones may be found in *Above the Law*, *Marked for Death*, *Out for Justice*, and *Fire Down Below*. *Street Knight* relies on one such scene as do many of the earlier films of Chuck Norris, among others. The barroom brawl is a clear derivation of the Hollywood western of course, and it found its way quite frequently into the Hong Kong martial-arts films that were Hollywood's most immediate models. Coming early in the films, such scenes serve to establish the hero's martial skills, functioning much the same way as training sequences or preliminary fights before the climax in the arena subgenre.

The juvenile adventure fantasy is much less violent than the law-enforcement films or the arena films. Of course, an arena component is common to many of these films (*The Karate Kid*, *Sidekicks*), but the preliminary and final confrontations are much less deadly. Most common to these films are moments in which the protagonist's newfound martial skills are put to use in saving a friend or a potential romantic interest. Following rigorous training (which may yet have a long way to go) the hero is confronted by local toughs or bullies, at the school yard, the beach, the playground, and the young protagonist defeats them, sometimes to his own amazement as well as his enemy's. Gradually, the stakes of these confrontations escalate, but never to the point that they do in the other subgenres and usually up to a point where a moral or ethical lesson can be imparted both to protagonist and audience.

The video/cartoon fantasy relies strongly on a series of escalating combats, where opponents appear ever stronger, ever more skilled and the hero or heroes must continually undergo training or self-determination in order to defeat the ever-greater threat. The more overtly SF films tend to follow the pattern of the law-enforcement subgenre, providing the hero with narrative moments where he must prove himself against less skilled, thuglike enemies in bombed-out bars and pool halls or their futuristic equivalents.

The most common plot devices in the arena subgenre are the pursuit of the championship, which involves a series of preliminary fights (and, as we have seen, often further training); the winning of the final competition in the arena; a physical injury or risk of death for the hero; and an element of revenge on the hero's part, often against the chief competitor. This chief competitor, whose preliminary bouts we also see, which establish his fighting credentials, is not only a clearly skilled antagonist, but is just as often an imposing physical specimen, perhaps best exemplified by "the Chinese Hercules," Bolo Yeung (who made his American film debut in *Enter the Dragon* as "Bolo" and changed his name thereafter to reflect that character; formerly he was Yang Sze). The hero seeks revenge against his chief opponent because, typically, the opponent has, in the past or during the present competition, injured or killed the hero's brother or friend (it's the friend in *Bloodsport*; the brother in *Bloodfist* and in *Best of the Best*, as examples). To make this final confrontation even more dramatic, the hero is often wounded (legitimately or through cheating) by his opponent, or the injury he has sustained earlier comes back to haunt him. Bloodied, almost broken and battered beyond belief, sometimes even blinded (hence the training regimen described above) he rallies himself to defeat his opponent. Jean-Claude Van Damme, in particular, climaxes his films with fight sequences in which his character is often bloodied and battered (a motif he borrows from Sylvester Stallone, who is perhaps overly fond of this often sado-masochistic focus on the maimed body of the hero). Notably, the hero does not kill his opponent, even if the opponent had maimed or killed his friend/brother or other ring opponents earlier. *The Karate Kid II* and *III* show this motif clearly, where even if the villain/opponent has been dastardly and cruel, the hero rises above his feelings of vengeance.

The law-enforcement subgenre also utilizes, as one might expect, a confrontation between hero and villain as its most common narrative thread. The film's events are set in motion precisely because the hero is a member of a law-enforcement agency whose job it is to fight crime and corruption. By the time the film's end rolls around, there is often an element of revenge on the hero's part for the killing or wounding of a partner most particularly; sometimes, though far less often, the killing of the hero's wife or family. (*Hard to Kill* relies on the death of the hero's wife, but that is more unusual; partners are the most commonly wounded or killed.) Revenge is only a small element here, however. The climax is the natural culmination of the hero's relentless pursuit of the villain for his wrongdoings. Since the chief villain is usually an older man, a powerful, entrenched member of the status quo or a seemingly untouchable crime boss, the final confrontation is not the film's most exciting climactic battle. This comes when the hero confronts the villain's chief henchman, like the hero, a martial artist of some considerable skill.

The most common narrative engine of the juvenile adventure fantasy is the hero's pursuit of his own growth and development. These films are mostly coming-of-age melodramas, with martial arts as the key component to maturity. In films that focus on younger children, like the *3 Ninjas* series, the plot revolves around the youth defeating members of the adult world, making buffoons out of the villain's henchmen, and foiling the plot of the wicked, if ultimately harmless, grownups. In films focusing more on adolescents, the adult world is seen as both menacing and supportive, but the hero's true test comes when he must face up to his peers. *Sidekicks* is the best example of this, where the hero's father is kind but ineffectual; Barry looks to Chuck Norris (literally—he plays himself) for inspiration, but Barry must defeat his peers. Norris defeats the evil grownup.

The most common narrative engine, indeed virtually the only narrative engine, of the video/cartoon fantasy appears to be the villain's attempt at universal control over the entire planet or at least the city where the action takes place. In *Mortal Kombat* and its sequel and in *Street Fighter*, world domination and enslavement is the order of the day on the part of the cartoonlike villains. The cartoonlike heroes, the familiar characters from the video games, band together to stop him. In *Double Dragon* and *Teenage Mutant Ninja Turtles* it is control over the city that occupies the villain. In these latter films, the heroes are closer in age and temperament to the protagonists of the juvenile adventure fantasy (teenagers, that is to say), while the villains are grownups. Of course, the villains in the video/cartoon fantasy are as much mythological creatures with near-super powers as they are human grownups, but such is in keeping with the image of adults held by the juvenile audience these films hope to attract.

The video/cartoon fantasy relies strongly on fantastic elements, including nonhuman creatures or extrahuman powers possessed by heroes and villains alike. This is the foundation, of course, of the *Teenage Mutant Ninja Turtles* themselves and their Master Splinter, the human-size rat. To combat the Turtles, their archenemy, Shredder, creates mutated animal/teenagers in the second film of the series, *The Secret of the Ooze*. In *Double Dragon*, the pursuit and attainment of a special talisman endows the wearer with magical and super powers. Most of the villains in *Mortal Kombat* are nonhuman creatures, many of them out of the Ray Harryhausen school of monsters (multiple arms, wings, etc.). These films inevitably climax in a final fight scene between villains and heroes with, of course, the inevitable triumph of the heroes, significantly without particular losses (not only to make room for a hoped-for sequel, but also in keeping with the different sensibilities of the younger audiences these films must attract).

The SF/martial-arts film tends to rely, as noted above, on post-apocalyptic settings; the hero tends to be engaged in the protection of the weak and innocent, in something of a variation on the law-enforcement subgenre. The villains and antagonists in these films are often nonhuman or extrahuman: Cyborgs, terminators, computer-enhanced soldiers, mutations, and the like. The SF setting allows something of the look of the video/cartoon fantasy and permits the introduction of these fantastical sorts of creations. Occasionally, even the hero is cyborg-like, such as in *Universal Soldier* or *Nemesis*. These films follow the same plot structure of the other genre films, with the hero demonstrating his martial capabilities and his heroic status along the way while pursuing the villain to the inevitable fight to the finish.

The law-enforcement subgenre brings with it more subtleties of theme than the other forms. For instance, endemic to the genre is the corruption of the law-enforcement agency for which the hero works. There is inevitably someone on the inside working for the villains, a crooked cop, for instance. Or the head of the governmental agency is, in fact, the villain. This is representative of the post-Vietnam, post-Watergate sensibilities of much Hollywood cinema. The political sensibilities of these films tend to be generally left-of-center (with the exception of the Chuck Norris films of the '80s and his television series). Thus, along with the corruption of the status quo, of the wealthy, comes an element of social class-consciousness. The hero not only sides with the little guy, as heroes are wont to do, but the little guy is usually expressly coded as working-class and the hero's roots are within this class. The films of Steven Seagal are exemplary here and he often brings an even more overtly leftist stance to his films in which other social issues are addressed, particularly environmentalism. The only thing comparable to this corruption of the status quo and the hero's working-class roots may be found in the arena subgenre, where the professional fighter is often exploited by the idle or cruelly rich. This element of social class is an important factor in the martial-arts film that is unique to the action genre as a whole, which tends to be much more conservative or middle-of-the-road.

Finally, a word should be said about the use of "fantasy" even within the martial-arts films that have a more realistic tone and tenor to them. Such a fantasy revolves around the seemingly impossible physical feats that the hero and villains seem routinely capable of performing. These feats have become routine in the Hong Kong martial-arts film, the films of King Hu (e.g., *Touch of Zen*, Xia Nu, 1969) and, following him, Tsui Hark (e.g., *Zu: Warriors of the Magic Mountain*, Shu Shan, 1980), in particular. People who can fly, are impervious to ordinary weapons, can jump from impossible heights, and so on, are routine in Hong Kong films and easily explainable in the video/cartoon and SF subgenres. Yet such feats often appear in the arena or law-enforcement subgenres. An example here would be *Red Sun Rising*, whose villain possesses a seemingly magical ability to kill his enemies with the mere touch of his fingertips. Such an image here is in keeping with the appearance of other so-called magical/mystical abilities and images in martial-arts films—special healing or debilitating herbs, ancient secrets and applications of acupuncture, and near-impossible powers known only to a few. In Hong Kong films this often functions as a kind of cultural marker of superiority, a compensation for the West's superior technology (viz., in Tsui Hark's multipart *Once Upon a Time in China*, Huang Fei-hong, 1991–96); in Hollywood films, it participates in the continued "Orientalizing" of Asian culture, a sense of its foreignness, its primitivism, but also its potential, secretive superiority.

Similarities of setting and motif help define a genre. But sometimes there are elements that are not quite reducible to diegetic concerns, not necessarily dependent on plot or character, which also help in defining a genre. One such element in the martial-arts film is a reliance on what might be called "beefcake": the display of the nude or seminude male body. If feminist film theory has claimed that a foundational element of the classical Hollywood cinema is a reliance on the specularization of the female form (not necessarily nude, but within the overall context of "pleasure in looking"), critics more lately have pointed to something similar occurring within other genres that rely on the physical pleasures of the male body. The musical, for instance, has been identified as one genre in which this occurs. Our comparison above between the martial-arts film and the musical can also be extended to this level, where the physical performance of the male star is part and parcel of the pleasure of the text. But the martial-arts film extends this pleasure in performance to a pleasure in looking, looking at the nude male body. This nude or seminude body has been variously called the "hard body" (by Susan Jeffords) or the "spectacular body" (by Yvonne Tasker). "Spectacular body" seems closer to the mark for its double entendre of the impressive musculature of the protagonist and of this musculature as spectacle.

If Jean-Claude Van Damme has been among the most insistent of martial arts stars in having his body beaten, battered, and bruised in the climactic fight scenes of his films, he has equally been the most insistent on showing off this body. His nickname, "the Muscles from Brussels," is both an accurate one and one he insists on demonstrating in film after film. Both through costuming that emphasizes his hips, buttocks, and genitals (tight jeans or leotards in particular, and the splits he manages to do at least once in each film which may be a demonstration of his flexibility, but force attention to the genital area), and through plot devices that enable him to remove his shirt or all of his clothes (the "butt shots" of his films have become notorious; see Clarke and Henson 140), Van Damme's body is always on display. This has variously been explained as an attempt to woo women audiences to his films (the standard audience demographic for martial-arts films is said to be males between fifteen and twenty-five—no different than the majority of films) or to attract or appeal to a gay male audience (Clark and Henson). Whatever the case, it is undeniable that male nudity is very much present within the genre. Don "The Dragon" Wilson, Jeff Speakman, Richard Norton (an Australian martial-arts star who has worked in both Hong Kong and Hollywood), and others can be counted on to display their torsos (if not more) in their films. Indeed, only Steven Seagal has shied away from this feature of the genre (he is the oldest of the martial-arts stars, aside from Chuck Norris, and, although big and athletic, is not heavily muscled).

What is most interesting about this male nudity, or beefcake, is that it does not find much equivalence in cheesecake, the use of female nudity. While her sexuality and physical attractiveness are certainly emphasized (especially via a propensity for low-cut blouses), Cynthia Rothrock has never appeared nude or topless in her films. Kathy Long has a brief nude/sex scene in *The Stranger* (1994), but none in *Knights*. Costuming emphasizes her sexuality to be sure, but nudity is extremely rare. Similarly, *Streets of Rage* (1994), a very low-budget exploitation effort written, produced, and starring Mimi Lesseos, offers up one brief (completely gratuitous) nude scene. The *Nemesis* films (1993–96) of female bodybuilder Sue Price toy with cheesecake and certainly put her hard body on display, though the nudity is rather coyly handled. Perhaps this propensity for male rather than female nudity, is seen best in the first *Lady Dragon* film (1992). Star Cynthia Rothrock has no nude scenes; costar (as the villain in this film) Richard Norton does. For a genre that allegedly appeals to adolescent boys and young men, this might seem a surprising twist.

Sex scenes featuring male stars are relatively rare in martial-arts films. That is to say, the beefcake is not usually associated with overtly sexual scenes. Jean-Claude Van Damme has utilized such scenes most frequently (*Double Impact, Maximum Risk*), but even those are rare, and seem more in keeping with the display of his own body and, also, to establish his heterosexuality given the allegedly gay or homoerotic appeal his films are said to have. The martial-arts film is very much a homosocial genre, like the action film in general. And, like the bodily displays of Arnold Schwarzenegger and Sylvester Stallone in their films, the genre emphasizes the male figure in ways classical Hollywood rarely, if ever, did.

Genres are said to be popular precisely because they answer, within structured fantasy, social, historical, psychological, or cultural issues within the culture that produces and consumes them. A genre may rise when societal issues coalesce around its particular patterns of setting, theme, and motif and fall when these issues seem no longer relevant. Of course, a genre's rise and fall is dependent on other issues, as well, such an industrial ones: the ability of an industry to produce similar films cheaply and quickly; the emergence of a space, a niche, in a marketplace, and so on. Thus it is unlikely that the Hong Kong martial-arts film could have found a home on American screens were it not for the fragmentation of the mainstream audience, the downturn of the Hollywood industry in the '60s, and the shortage of homemade product at the time—similarly, the emergence of smaller studios, such as American International Pictures, New World, Cannon, and others, whose lower budgets and specialized product could take advantage of niche or cult marketing. But the industrial factors that gave rise to the appearance of Hong Kong movies on American screens and of American martial-arts movies themselves must take a dim second place to the importance of historical and cultural factors giving rise to the genre.

The appearance of martial arts within the Hollywood cinema and the Hong Kong martial-arts film on American movie screens coincides with U.S. troop withdrawals from Vietnam in 1972–73. Unlike the case of World War II, Hollywood had done virtually nothing in support of the Vietnam War, unquestionably America's most unpopular overseas venture. Thus when Richard Nixon announced the gradual withdrawal of American troops beginning in 1972 (along with the virtual end of the military draft), followed by the removal of all troops and the closing down of the American embassy in Saigon in 1973, there was a sigh of relief on the home front. Yet the sense that the war had been lost (Nixon's advisors told him for his second term as president to declare victory and get out) was a bitter pill for many Americans to swallow. The legacy of Vietnam would not show up for some time in the Hollywood cinema of the '70s (not until 1976 or so). There might have been some irony, then, or it might have been all too appropriate, that for the first time in America's history mainstream theaters were flooded not simply with foreign films, but with Asian films.

One cry heard again and again in the discourse surrounding the Vietnam War was raised against the nature of the enemy: physically smaller, technologically inferior, how could such an army defeat the American military, the best-trained, best-equipped fighting force the world had ever seen? Was such a fighting force mirrored in Hong Kong martial-arts films where the lone (Asian) fighter, of not very imposing stature, can single-handedly take on groups of men, some much bigger, some well armed? Was the use of exotic or casual weaponry on the part of martial arts heroes not something of a corollary to the Vietcong and their primitive weaponry and booby traps? We might understand the attraction of the Hong Kong martial-arts film, then (along with the introduction of Japanese martial-arts films, especially the *Streetfighter* series, 1974–79, starring Shinichi [Sonny] Chiba), as a kind of coming to terms with a seemingly inferior enemy. Such an enemy might very well be understood to have possessed secret, ancient, mystical fighting techniques by way of explanation for the U.S. defeat. Co-opting those techniques, at least through the structured fantasy of genre over the course of the next decade, would help alleviate those cultural tensions.

Meanwhile, however, the immediate appeal of Hong Kong martial-arts films was not to mainstream audiences struggling with the legacy of the Vietnam War, but precisely to those subcultural, disillusioned, disaffected audiences who had opposed the war or who were, more radically and generally, alienated from much of mainstream culture. That is to say, the appeal of martial-arts movies was to inner-city and rural audiences, to African American, Latino, and Asian American youth nationwide, and to the younger remnants of the counterculture who had already evinced an interest in Asian culture (if not necessarily Asian popular culture, e.g.,

Zen Buddhism). This appeal to black audiences in particular led, unacknowledged of course, to the critical denigration of the genre. But for audiences of color, the sight of Asian men, and women, starring in action-packed movies filled with attractive and dynamic heroes and suave and sophisticated villains was a welcome relief from years of stereotypical characterizations and outright exploitation of their like. Similarly, the Hong Kong films with their plots of exploited workers and subaltern peoples resisting the forces of exploitation and colonialization doubtless struck an allegorical nerve. Indeed, Hong Kong martial arts movies virtually replaced the blaxploitation cycle and, as we have seen, attempts were made almost immediately to revive blaxploitation through the use of martial arts. It didn't take hold, and by 1976 both blaxploitation and the martial arts were gone, the latter only temporarily. It was precisely this subcultural appeal, along with marginal and fly-by-night companies that often released the films, that led to the rather sudden decline of Hong Kong imports.

The legacy of Vietnam, the cultural trauma, lay dormant in American cinema (save through allegories of the war, such as *M*A*S*H* [1970], or *Ulzana's Raid*, [1972]). The first appearance of what might be called the return of the repressed came through in a cycle of films focusing on returning Vietnam vets: *Taxi Driver* (1976), *Heroes* (1977), *Rolling Thunder* (1977), among others. It was during this period that the martial-arts film lay virtually dormant, as outlined above. But when it appeared in the form of Chuck Norris, it did so among a host of films that brought the Vietnam War back into America's consciousness, powerful retrospective examinations of the war focusing primarily on what had gone wrong: *The Boys in Company C* (1978), *The Deer Hunter* (1978), *Coming Home* (1978), *Apocalypse Now* (1979) most memorably. It is no accident that Norris's *Good Guys Wear Black* is very much a Vietnam-themed film, no accident that so many martial-arts films take Vietnam as their literal starting point.

Vietnam functions as a moment of origin for the martial-arts film much the way the Vietnam War functions within the diegesis of so many films as the origin of the hero's exposure to Asian culture, his training as a killer, his sense of betrayal by his country, and a certain legacy of rage. If the Vietnam War itself introduced the concept of the Army's Special Forces (better known as the Green Berets, and later offshoots in the other services such as the Navy SEALS) it provides a rationale within many martial-arts films for the hero's special skills. For Chuck Norris, Vietnam functioned as training ground in films like *Good Guys Wear Black* and *A Force of One*; later in the *Missing in Action* series, it functions much as it does in the *Rambo* films, as a site of incoherent rage and a sense of betrayal. The films thus represent deft attempts at mastery of the Vietnam trauma. In a sense, the hero becomes his enemy. Following this logic, his defeat in Vietnam is not owed to that enemy any longer, but to his own country, which trained him but wouldn't let him use that training. The continued use of the Vietnam War in martial-arts films well into the early 1990s (after the mainstream film had abandoned the topic around 1987) continues to show the uneasy attitude toward Asia: the hero skilled in Asian ways, betrayed by his own country. *Above the Law* begins in Vietnam; so, too, does *Universal Soldier*. Even an extremely marginal, low-budget effort like *Revenge of the Kickfighter* (1987) utilizes the corrupting legacy of the Vietnam War to set its action in motion.

If the hero's adoption of Asian martial arts may be seen as a legacy of the Vietnam War—an attempt at mastery, an effort to become one's enemy—that motif is carried even further by the persistent appearance of Asian masters who train the white (usually male) hero. Film after film shows this motif. This is seen as early as the original televisions series, *Kung Fu*. Kwai Chang Caine, the half-Chinese, half-Caucasian youth who desires to join the Shaolin Temple, is initially denied admission because he is not fully Chinese. But admitted he is and, as portrayed by Caucasian star David Carradine, he learns the secret, ancient wisdom of the Orient. Oftentimes, the Asian master's knowledge is put to use in the defeat of Asian opponents: Frank Dux in *Bloodsport* is taught karate by a Japanese master and he uses this skill later in life to defeat the fearsome Chong Li. The same motif is repeated in *Kickboxer*, in *Bloodfist*, in *Red Sun Rising*, in *The Karate Kid II*. In *Lady Dragon*, Cynthia Rothrock acquires greater skill from an aged master after she is raped and beaten by the villain, but this time her opponent is white. One cannot help but notice that the Asian martial arts are so often passed on to the Occidental hero, the white world (at least in Hollywood films), in order for this hero, this world, to master the Asian world whence these skills originally came.

Equally significant is the fact that these aging masters are, precisely, aging. Few of them are vital, strong, able to fight opponents on their own. It is as if Asia is no longer able to defend itself and must pass on its legacy to the West, which is better able to use Asia's skills and knowledge. This particular motif appears later in the genre, in the mid-'80s on occasion, and regularly by the late '80s. This coincides with an era of increased

"Japan-bashing," a time when American industry, especially the automobile industry, was losing ground both in the Asian and domestic market. But it was not simply automobiles where the United States had lost a technological edge: The Japanese domination of home video, television, and videocassette players was also a frequently noted phenomenon. The film industry was deeply affected by this transition; by the late '80s, home video income had, overall, equaled and then surpassed theatrical box-office revenues, meaning that the software (the film programming) was in virtually every case being played on imported hardware. This began to hit even closer to home for the film studios when Japanese electronic firms began to buy out Hollywood studios: Columbia's purchase by Sony was something of a traumatic moment itself. This was also seen in a culturewide context of Japanese purchase of other U.S. corporations and of U.S. real estate and landmarks. Though both Great Britain and the Netherlands had, and continue to have, more substantial real-estate and corporate holdings in the U.S. than do the Japanese, it was precisely the Japanese purchase of movie studios, American companies, American real estate (i.e., a sense that Japan was buying out America, that American may have won the war, but Japan had won the peace) that created an era of anti-Japanese fervor, of "yellow peril" discourse, not seen since the Second World War. This discourse appeared in such mainstream films as *Black Rain* (the version directed by Ridley Scott in 1989) or *Rising Sun* ([1993], from the controversial bestseller by Michael Crichton), among others.

It was in this atmosphere that Caucasian martial artists began to dominate a genre that was an Asian creation, that Asians often appeared as villains (Bolo Yeung's career is exemplary here), and that aging, weakened, usually sexless Asians helped transform these white protagonists into heroes capable of defeating these Asian villains. It did not matter what specific Asian nation, what national tradition, what martial art, was being utilized or represented. It no longer mattered whether the enemy was Japan, or Vietnam, or the Chinese (resurrecting the anti-Asian discourse of the Cold War and fears of the People's Republic of China). It no longer mattered whether the action took place in the Philippines, in Hong Kong, in Japan, on U.S. soil. All of Asia, including Asian-America, was homogenized into a combination of fearsome enemy and harmless helper. Steven Seagal could deliver a demonstration of aikido, while speaking passable Japanese, to Japanese martial arts masters in Japan in *Above the Law*; he speaks Chinese fluently and is a devout Buddhist in *The Glimmer Man*; he recovers his health and well-being while incense burns and Chinese antiques surround him in *Hard to Kill.* He becomes Asian, besting the Asians at their own game, their own culture, rendering them obsolete, a paradigm for the genre itself.

Still, one should not take an entirely dim view of the genre. It is one of the few genres where, though white, male heroes predominate, there is a space for nonwhite and female heroes. While neither Cynthia Rothrock nor Kathy Long has achieved anything like the stardom of a Michelle Yeoh or Brigitte Lin in Hong Kong, they led the way for action heroines in more mainstream films and, especially Cynthia Rothrock, have achieved a considerable success on their own. Bruce Lee and Jackie Chan have achieved a fame here previously denied any Asian star; Chow Yun-fat is also poised for mainstream stardom. Asian American actors like Russell Wong (in TV's *Vanishing Son* series, 1994–95), Phillip Rhee in the *Best of the Best* films, and, of course, Sho Kosugi, while not stars on the magnitude of Steven Seagal or Jean-Claude Van Damme, nevertheless represent an opening up of Hollywood's screens to a greater range of cultures and races. Ming-Na Wen, best known for more "serious" roles perhaps, has lent to Asian American actresses a presence in action films with her roles in *Street Fighter, Hong Kong 97* (1994) and as the heroine's voice in the Disney animated martial arts/musical, *Mulan* (1998). While we acknowledge that the Teenage Mutant Ninja Turtles are clearly coded as "white" teenagers, the multiracial, dual-gendered casts of *Street Fighter* and *Mortal Kombat* are a welcome sight on America's largely white, male screens. More than any other genre, it has been the martial-arts film, while co-opting an Asian genre and remaking it for white, mainstream cultural needs, that has nevertheless opened up a space for Chinese directors and Asian and Asian American stars. Troubling issues still remain as the genre works itself out as American culture continues to come to terms with Asia and Asian-America, but at least the genre provides a space where these struggles can include Asians and Asian Americans.

WORKS CITED

Clarke, Eric, and Matthew Henson. "Hot Damme! Reflections on Gay Publicity." *Boys: Masculinities in Contemporary Culture.* Ed. Paul Smith. Boulder, Colo.: Westview Press. 1996. 131–49.

Jeffords, Susan. *Hard Bodies.* New Brunswick, N.J.: Rutgers University Press, 1994.

Kinder, Marsha. *Playing with Power in Movies, Television and Video Games: From Muppet Babies to Teenage Mutant Ninja Turtles.* Berkeley: University of California Press, 1991.

Tasker, Yvonne. *Spectacular Bodies: Gender, Genre and the Action Cinema.* London: Routledge, 1993.

CHAPTER SEVEN

□

Same as It Ever Was: Innovation and Exhaustion in the Horror and Science Fiction Films of the 1990s

DAVID SANJEK

As the fin de siècle approaches, a common if not virtually knee-jerk tone of exhaustion permeates not only the bulk of the cultural production that inundates the public at large through the ever increasing profusion of media but also the commentary that endeavors to situate that body of materials. Much as one wishes to remain receptive to the transformative potential of cultural artifacts, a certain lassitude, bred of the feeling "been there, done that," proves unavoidable. This sensibility is reflected by the popular cinema in a striking fashion. While box-office figures reflect ever increasing levels of attendance, the material featured at the local multiplex paradoxically offers a multitude of opportunities and a minimum of alternatives. The profusion of sequels, remakes, and narratives that amalgamate familiar elements into various forms of pastiche results perhaps not in contempt on the part of consumers but a weariness bred of sensory overload and intellectual understimulation. At the same time, marketing campaigns continue to trumpet the novelty of ill-conceived narratives with a desperate intensity. That is not to say that stupefied audiences

111

reflexively succumb to any form of merchandising. For example, the recent touting of the multimillion-dollar remake of *Godzilla* (1998) with the tag line "Size Does Matter" met with resounding failure. Clearly, the intimation of penis envy conveyed by the phrase failed to arouse sufficient interest.

If one examines the current status of the horror and science-fiction genres in particular, reasons for this tone of ennui are numerous. For example, while the auteur theory has long fallen out of critical favor, it remains undebatable that a number of the most prolific and thought-provoking practitioners of these forms, the horror genre in particular, have either fallen by the commercial wayside or abandoned the field altogether. George Romero, writer-director of the "Living Dead Trilogy"—*Night of the Living Dead* (1968), *Dawn of the Dead* (1979), and *Day of the Dead* (1985)—has not produced a feature in a half-dozen years. Virtually every one of the narratives by Stuart Gordon subsequent to *Re-Animator* (1985) were released direct-to-video. Larry Cohen, creator of some of the most thematically sophisticated works in both genres, has ceased to direct and his scripts appear solely on video shelves. Tobe Hopper, best known for *Texas Chainsaw Massacre I* and *II* (1974, 1986), appears to have given up theatrical film for television. Clive Barker, writer-director of *Hellraiser* (1987), collided time and again with the MPAA ratings board, and, as a result, most of his work has been bowdlerized for the general public. *Hellraiser* brought up some genuinely troubling and provocative questions about the possibility of transcendence through pain and sadomasochism-driven relationships, yet the other three films in the series—*Hellbound: Hellraiser II* (1988), *III: Hell on Earth* (1992) and *Hellraiser: Bloodline* (1996)—abandoned thoughtful inquiry by and large for splatter and special effects, so far as the ratings board permitted. Barker was not the only victim of de facto censorship. The influence of the board's erratic and often indefensible decisions has inarguably affected the kinds of imagery and themes that reach the public. That is not to say that violent or excessive material does not continue to receive either an NC-17 or R rating, yet the manner of taboos broken in the process pale before the thematic and ideological rigor of some of the works produced by the aforementioned individuals.

At the same time, the public interest in the two genres is as pronounced as it has been for some time. The box-office domination by *Independence Day* during the summer of 1996 proved among other things that the fascination with the annihilation of antagonistic extraterrestrials has not gone out of fashion. During the same period, marketing of the horror film reached a new level of commercial sophistication with the advent of the work of scriptwriter Kevin Williamson. The films he wrote—*Scream* (1996), *Scream 2* (1997), and *I Know What You Did Last Summer* (1997)—illustrate that young adults prefer to watch their peers terrified or terminated, particularly when those individuals are played by performers they know from television series targeted at the same demographic model and the mayhem is scored to chart-topping popular music. For the historically savvy, these narratives and the manner with which they are marketed bears an uncanny resemblance to the "weirdies" of the 1950s that likewise targeted an adolescent audience; *Scream*, for example, might appropriately have been retitled "I Was a Teenage Sociopath." Nonetheless, the proliferation of ancillary marketing opportunities associated with these narratives puts the studios of the 1950s to shame. To wit, Williamson's 1998 film *The Faculty* (directed by Robert Rodriguez) not only clothes its young protagonists in Tommy Hilfiger products but also features them in an advertising campaign for the designer's jeans.

These practices do not so much vitiate the genre as incorporate its narratives in a web of other cultural materials, a practice not specific to either the horror or the science fiction film alone. Product placement and the creation of multimedia by-products constitute business as usual for the present-day media industries. What is more troublesome, and will focus the remainder of my comments on some of the key horror and science-fiction narratives of the current decade, is the degree to which their thematic and ideological underpinnings have undergone a less-than-subtle transformation. At one and the same time, the parameters within which the forms operate have become the object of public and corporate scrutiny and been virtually crippled by that very process. To some degree, this process provides yet another illustration of the kind of painful self-consciousness that permeates postmodern culture altogether, the manner in which it resembles a mirror-house of self-referentiality. The work of Williamson provides a virtual textbook instance of the phenomenon. His characters deliberately and repeatedly make reference to, mock, and model their behavior after parameters laid down in films familiar to the scriptwriter's target audience. The *Scream* sequence in particular depends upon the characters', and the audience's, willingness to abide by the rules of the game.

At the same time, neither Williamson nor very many of his contemporaries appear to be interested in critiquing or subverting those parameters. Instead, they merely call attention to them in the most blunt and obvious fashion. As a result, and unlike the work of those aforementioned directors and scriptwriters, the ideological dimension of much if not most of the horror and science-fiction narratives of the 1990s is paltry or pacified. These films either confirm the assumptions of the societies they represent or do little more than smirk at how laughable those assumptions are. Admittedly, genre cinema, if not motion pictures altogether, rarely if ever incorporates an overt radical or revolutionary agenda. More commonly, they reflect and respond to that body of common knowledge born of a lifetime of spectatorship possessed by their aficionados. That body of shared perceptions assists an audience either in making sense of the illogical or anticipating the twists and turns a generic narrative will take before they occur, thereby vitiating the potential shock effect. Increasingly, however, that knowledge resembles the experiential equivalent of insider trading in the financial markets, whereby audience members are more interested in observing the genre rearticulate itself rather than call attention to the social, cultural and ideological fissures and fault lines that the form represents. Jonathan Lake Crane argues that under the optimum circumstances, "*Watching a horror film is a reality check*" (8). Nowadays, that reality is merely reconfirmed in all its placid uniformity, time and time again.

That neutralization of the unusual or unsettling is not endemic to the horror genre alone, for the attempt to give form and substance to the oneiric or the otherworldly plays a role in science fiction, too. Each year, novel applications of effects technology assist in the effort to make concrete, if not always believable, whatever a scriptwriter or director might imagine. At the same time, the public has become saturated by this strategy of technological one-upsmanship. In addition to the films themselves, ancillary publications or other forms of publicity inundate one with professional discourse as can be found in publicity features shown on specialty cable channels, such as the Science Fiction Channel, or fan publications. Certain of these, most notably *Cinéfantastique*, can read like the cinematic equivalent of *Popular Mechanics*. More to the point, the articles as a rule address every conceivable question except whether an effect is necessary, interesting, or effective. This process has so reached the saturation point that the experience of watching an effects-laden feature with a representative body of the general public bears an uncanny resemblance to the famous remark of the Russian dance impresario Sergei Diaghilev: "Astonish me." Understandably, time and time again, that experience falls short of achieving a sense of wonder and, at best, delivers one of déjà vu.

Even the most popular and financially successful science-fiction films have been affected by this decimation of the experience of wonder and surprise. Among the most popular films of all time, the *Star Wars* trilogy—*Star Wars* (1977), *The Empire Strikes Back* (1980) and *Return Of the Jedi* (1983), each reissued in 1997 with updated special effects and some additional footage—at the time of their initial release touched a chord in the general public unlike any previous instance of the genre. Arguably, that strain of sympathy drew upon George Lucas's conservative and nostalgic ideological presuppositions but, at the same time, it is indisputable that the narratives achieved an otherworldly state of mind that became paradigmatic for a vast majority of the movie-going public. This has been the case as well with the *Star Trek* phenomenon, which encompasses the original television series (1966–69), its successor the syndicated *Star Trek: The Next Generation* (1987–) and the films *Star Trek: The Motion Picture* (1979), *II: The Wrath of Khan* (1982), *III: The Search for Spock* (1984), *IV: The Voyage Home* (1986), *V: The Final Frontier* (1989), *VI: The Undiscovered Country* (1991), *Star Trek Generations* (1994), and *Star Trek: First Contact* (1996). Like Lucas's films, these narratives embody a set of values that audiences have come to depend upon to deliver a sense of surety amidst a chaotic quotidian reality. The liberal assumptions of multicultural harmony, the desire to go where man has not gone before, and the sense that the universe possesses a tenuous but discernible order elicits an obvious appeal. What comes across to the critical consciousness as a simplistic one-worldism or the equivalent of a cosmic greeting card contrasts with the dominant cynicism of the age. These narratives, it can be argued, offer audiences a form of what Stephen Neale refers to as "epistemophilia," fulfilling the spectating subject's willingness if not eagerness to be "'satisfied,' to be given the answer to the riddle" (42). Having "the force" on one's side is better, it would appear, than having nothing on one's side at all.

To return to the horror genre, one of the most notable dimensions of the work of some of the aforementioned creators has been the degree to which the genre since the 1960s has situated the abject and the awful in the everyday whereas earlier cycles perpetuated a notion of the horrific as foreign and otherworldly. Central to that dynamic has been the frequency with which the genre has critiqued the family and the manner in which it perpetuates self-destructive or pathological tendencies. As Robin Wood notably argued, the contemporary horror film has been the primary vehicle for the replication of a family nightmare (Wood 1986). Wes Craven's initiation of the *Nightmare On Elm Street* series (1984) recapitulated this dynamic by making Freddy Krueger's lethal animosity an attack upon the family unit. The children he extinguished are the progeny of the adults who slew him for acts of molestation. As the series progressed,— *Part 2: Freddy's Revenge* (1985), *3: Dream Warriors* (1987), *4: The Dream Master* (1988), *5: The Dream Child* (1989), and *Freddy's Dead: The Final Nightmare* (1991)—the familial superstructure gave way to an emphasis upon the spectacularity of special effects and the effete manner with which Freddy savagely terminated the life of another individual. The familial superstructure reappears in *Wes Craven's New Nightmare* (1994), the latest and presumably the final installment in the series. It takes form not only in the "family" of actual individuals who created the series: director/writer Craven, producer Robert Shaye, and actors Robert England and Heather Langenkamp, as well as the family of consumers who made Freddy a ubiquitous piece of the cultural landscape. Craven cannily explores how that process of familiarization affects both those who create public imagery as well as those who consume it. The film argues with conviction that the influence of mass acceptance is not without its consequences or its costs. Such a broad-minded critique is absent in the writing of Kevin Williamson, who sells little beyond the ubiquity of horror other than its market dominance. Furthermore, the Williamson scripts, two of which were the *Scream* films directed by Craven, virtually abrogate any discussion of family. All three films focus primarily on the isolated and self-involved world of teenagers.

The other most successful and noteworthy horror film series of the period, *Friday the 13th*, (1980), began as a family-focused narrative, for the original antagonist was not the zombie-like killing machine Jason Vorhees but his mother. The subsequent narratives (1981, 1984, 1985, 1986, 1988, 1989) virtually recapitulate one another as if they were the cinematic equivalent of a serial killer. They provide a telling illustration of the process Bruce Kawin characterizes as "inappropriate repetition" whereby "a work or a life [is locked] into an unfulfillable compulsive cycle" (12). Again, the spectacularity of the murders takes precedent over any larger ideological or psychological dynamic. In the process, Jason becomes wholly "other." Behind his ubiquitous hockey mask lies nothing more or less than the embodiment of absolute evil, whose role in a Manichean universe is to exterminate those teenagers whose worst sin is the repeated transgression of socially defined sexual taboos. The self-negating circularity of these films is also reflected in the fact that they depend upon the audience's possession of what Isabel Cristina Pinedo calls "insider knowledge" about Jason's behavior but does nothing other than recapitulate that knowledge in film after film [44–45]. Nothing about Jason's behavior leads the audience to question very much about themselves or the subjects of the narratives; the audience assumes that these characters will inevitably expire in a manner that proves little more than the innumerable ways in which sharp objects can penetrate soft human tissue.

The perpetuation of the monster as an "other" existing in a Manichean universe was a mainstay of horror films prior to the 1960s and one of the principal characteristics of the genre that filmmakers heretofore enumerated, and others called into question. Eroding the former divisibility between the normal/abnormal or the logical/illogical forced audiences to establish their ethical or ideological internal gyroscopes each time they entered a movie theater. However, that unsettling but productive sense of instability no longer applies to most manifestations of either the horror or science-fiction genre. A self-satisfied complacency has taken its place. Audiences appear to like their monsters or aliens firmly established in a sphere unaligned to any segment of our quotidian existence. Two recent narratives that combine the visceral shocks of horror with the high-tech sophistication of science fiction epitomize this reinstallation of a Manichean worldview: *Species* (1995) and *The Relic* (1997). In the former, a group of scientists toy with strands of DNA only to produce a homicidal entity with the features of a seductive centerfold. The creature's insatiable compulsion to procreate and the lethal fate of her series of sexual partners reminds one that, the fecundity of female biology continues to possess a fearsome dimension to many people. If the film cannot understandably argue for obliteration of her progeny, it aggressively supports the creature's extermination.

In the case of *The Relic*, an embodiment of the social taboos and religious cosmology of a foreign, non-Western society wreaks havoc upon the architectural representation of Western empiricism: a natural history museum. The titular creature is exterminated by a female representative of that worldview, an evolutionary biologist, who identifies the entity's nature and origins not through any effort to comprehend the individuals who conjured it into being. Instead, she decodes its DNA with an elaborate computer program and discovers that the creature evolved from the physical matter of the self-regarding anthropologist who sought to obtain the secrets of the tribe for whom it acts as a protective entity. His fate may be viewed as punishment for the overweening aggression of Western rationalism, but the body of film vigilantly supports the strength of the intellect. It illustrates as well the manner in which the horror genre frequently manifests racial themes and, in this case, racist assumptions. "Race horror," Isabel Cristina Pinedo argues, endeavors to "estrange danger by introducing a dark and ancient religion, one associated with savagery and third-world peoples" (116). In the process, the form of agency possessed by the creature, and the society that created it, comes across as altogether aberrant and disposable. An elderly member of the museum's staff refers to the existence of such an entity as a manifestation of the "Calistos Effect," which is characterized by sudden, grotesque, and short-lived evolutionary changes. Rather than endeavor to comprehend such activity, *The Relic* advises that we dismiss these processes out of hand and exterminate their manifestations without compunction.

The voraciousness of contemporary audiences for time-honored generic modes like the nonhuman monster holds true with the familiar vampire figure as illustrated by *From Dusk To Dawn* (1996). As much a manifestation of the media's valorization of the male representatives of "Indie" cinema—the film is written by Quentin Tarantino (creator of *Reservoir Dogs* [1992] and *Pulp Fiction* [1994]) and directed by Robert Rodriguez (creator of *El Mariachi* [1992] and its "remake" *Desperado* [1995])—as an all-out, sensationalistic recapitulation of the vampire films of the past, *From Dusk To Dawn* posits its nonliving antagonists as wholly evil Hispanic "others" preying upon their Northern neighbors. The narrative admittedly dabbles in stirring up racial and gender stereotypes by including African American and Asian individuals among the protagonists as well as advocating agency on the part of the female lead. However, that effort at revisionism pales in comparison with the unexamined valorization of racial stereotypes, that are particularly troubling in light of recent legislative efforts to curb or eliminate foreign immigration, particularly from Mexico. We have not only to fear loss of our jobs, the film infers, but our lives. By comparison to the thoughtful and unsettling reinvigoration of the living dead illustrated by, for example, George Romero's *Martin* (1978) or Kathryn Bigelow's *Near Dark* (1987), *From Dusk To Dawn* bears closer resemblance to the classic texts such as Tod Browning's *Dracula* (1931) or F. W. Murnau's *Nosferatu* (1922). Its creatures are evil incarnate, and the audience so desires their extermination that we willingly valorize the actions of the narrative's hero, a trigger-happy thief and murderer.

A comparable process of simultaneous reinvigoration and deflation can be observed in those contemporary narratives the resurrect the BEMs (Bug-Eyed Monsters) of the 1950s and the simplistic ideologies that were reflected by them. Rather than the thoughtful appraisal of the complexity of extraterrestrial life and its intersection with humanity to be found in *2001: A Space Odyssey* (1968) and *The Man Who Fell to Earth* (1976); the childlike but still compelling narratives of Steven Spielberg, *Close Encounters of the Third Kind* (1977, 1980) and *E. T.* (1982), that celebrate interspecies communication; or the ground-breaking examination of the thin line that separates the human from the android exemplified by *Blade Runner* (1982; re-released in 1993), we have returned to the simplistic even reactionary notion that whatever or whomever dwells beyond our planet is radically different from us and wishes our extermination. For all the technical sophistication brought to bear upon special effects, "The vast majority of aliens," Kevin Jackson reminds us, "are still (approximately) humanoid bipeds with special features adopted from elsewhere in the food chain—most bluntly, guys in funny suits" (11). Those aforementioned films demanded that we reappraise our time-bound platitudes about the sanctity of human life and the superiority of Western intellectual tradition. The vast majority of contemporary science-fiction narratives defend those platitudes and all the ideological baggage that accompanies them. In the end, they constitute cheerleading for the corporate state if not recruiting campaigns for the military-industrial complex.

Independence Day epitomizes this crowd-pleasing if intellectually anaesthetizing form of cinema. In the aftermath of the national failure of military superiority in Vietnam, *ID4* (as it came to be known) consoled the public that our citizen warriors when called upon could still kick ass. Paradoxically, as Amy Taubin observes, this reaffirmation of the nation's sense of collective purpose occurred in "a feel-good picture about the end of the world, or rather about how the end of the world is averted by good men who put aside their racial and ethnic differences to come together in a common cause" (6–7). Little effort is made in *ID4* to question whether Western civilization deserves salvation. The smirky glee with which Tim Burton obliterates a society so corrupt and addle-headed as to deserve Armageddon in *Mars Attacks!* (1997) never arises in *ID4*. The saviors of our species furthermore constitute a ragtag approximation of Reverend Jesse Jackson's "rainbow coalition." As Taubin writes, "*Independence Day* is a film in which an African American, a Jew and a WASP band together to save the world (with a little help from a white-trash alcoholic who's fathered a bunch of ex-Tex-Mex brats). None of these people would make it on their own, but together they're inseparable" (8). Fighting against a common enemy breeds, it appears, not only national harmony but also a convenient respite from all insecurities about the perils of democracy. If the decimation of a number of the globe's capitals and their citizens needs to occur in order to bring about this putative sense of harmony, then so be it.

ID4 also illustrates the manner in which the once hidebound divisions between cinematic genres have fallen away. In particular, the patrol narrative one associates with the classic war picture, typified by *Objective, Burma!* (1945) or *Attack!* (1956), now takes extraterrestrials as the target of North American aggression and commitment to victory at any cost. James Cameron's *Aliens* (1986), the second in a tetrology of encounters between Sigourney Weaver's Ripley and the ravenous nonhumans, reflected the Reagan period's gung-ho encouragement of national strength and the suppression of "illegal aliens,' whether earthbound or otherwise. If the original 1979 film critiqued the borderline between human, extraterrestrial, and android, the protagonists in *Aliens* appeared to be devoid of uncertainty about their identity or their mission. In fact, their personalities seemed if anything amalgamated if not rendered identical with their tactical weapons. Even Ripley's grappling with the pregnant Queen at the film's conclusion required her use of a form of military equipment that bonded together human expertise with superior technology. Irony appeared in the process to be the furthest possible thing from Cameron's mind, whereas Paul Verhoeven's *Starship Troopers* (1997) is saturated with a ferocious but disturbing wit. Like *Aliens* and the patrol films that preceded it, this adaptation of Robert Heinlein's novel sympathetically endorses the fascistic military order that lies as society's sole bulwark between society as we know it and the brain-hungry bugs from beyond the stars. At the same time, Verhoeven calls attention to the denial of individuality and endorsement of the force of autocratically directed aggression that permits the terrestrial soldiers eventually to make their nonhuman enemy quake with fear. That willingness to commit to the will of the state might seem little different from the alien's literal emptying of their human enemy's brains except for Verhoeven's subtle critique—so subtle most of the audience chose to overlook it—of Heinlein's juvenile endorsement of a fascistic militarist state.

The interfusion of the patrol film with the BEM narrative occurs as well in *Event Horizon* (1998), a high-tech version of such extraterrestrial creatures-on-the-loose films as *It! The Terror from Beyond Space* (1958)—itself a precursor of *Alien* (1979). Furthermore, its notion of a dimensional gateway that creates a temporary black hole only to loose upon the ship's unsuspecting crew a malign force from beyond the galaxy's edge calls to mind other features, including a Roger Corman-produced film, *Galaxy of Terror* (1981). However, in that film the lethal anxiety-producing events turned out to be stage-managed by a benign entity whereas the forces at work in *Event Horizon* are altogether venomous. The attempt to delineate that force, characterized by the scientist who designed the eponymous vehicle in which it resides as "a dimension of pure chaos, pure evil," lacks sufficient imagination to engage one on other than the most visceral level. Even the means with which the power of the entity is illustrated bring to mind previous more successful films: the unexplained waves of blood conjured up in the late Stanley Kubrick's *The Shining* (1980), and the hallucinations of critical moments in the characters' past in Andrei Tarkovsky's *Solaris* (1972). Other than the opportunity the film affords African American actor Lawrence Fishburne to perform the heroic lead as the ship's captain, *Event Horizon* amounts to yet another instance of excessive pastiche taking the place of innovative filmmaking.

The failure in *Event Horizon* to give substance or credibility to a notion of the universe as a malign enterprise has its parallel in Robert Zemeckis's *Contact* (1997) wherein just the opposite is attempted. Jodie Foster plays a scientist whose conviction that there is other life attempting to contact mankind is filtered through a personal drama about the loss of her parents and the need for a spiritually inspired explanation for life's turmoil. What begins as an interesting if overly serious dramatization of C. P. Snow's landmark discussion of the "two cultures" descends to a soap opera about loss and redemption, a kind of space-jockey equivalent of *It's a Wonderful Life* (1946). The script's endeavor to provide a visual and thematic equivalent for an alternative cosmology comes across as treacly rather than thought provoking. Viewers have, in the end, as much difficulty swallowing the sentimentality of this sequence as Foster's scientist has explaining it to a government panel. One must assign credit to the filmmakers for the desire to give form and substance to the ineffable, but not the manner in which that endeavor eventuates.

More impressive and ultimately unsettling is *Mimic* (1998), directed by the Mexican director Guillermo De Toro who rethought the vampire mythos in the 1992 feature *Cronos*. *Mimic* brings together the fascination with the advances in DNA technology and the continuing fear and anxiety associated with the inner city. A female etymologist toys with insect DNA in order to avert a plague attacking young children. While the sickness subsides, the experiment backfires when the subjects begin to mutate underground, beneath the subway system, into an interspecies amalgamation of human and bug. In and of itself, the script breaks little new ground, but De Toro effectively depicts a phenomena that bears little resemblance to any previous celluloid creature. The moment in which an apparently human figure lets loose its outer garment and flies away into the tunnels with the female scientist under its wings provides one of the genuinely most eerie moments in recent genre cinema. Even more compelling is the capable manner with which *Mimic* combines the quotidian and the queasy, the thoroughly familiar and the thoroughly disquieting. It compares with Roman Polanski's *Rosemary's Baby* (1968) and *The Wolfen* (1981) in its transformation of New York City into a landscape rich with hidden lives and untold secrets.

The final film I wish to discuss ironically endeavors to create a world of the near future wholly other than the one we inhabit but succeeds in the end in manifesting some of the most problematic social tensions of our current time. *Gattaca* (1998) chronicles the efforts on the part of a young man born *in utero* during an age when parents routinely preselect the genetic characteristics with the greatest chance for the success of their progeny. Though the law prohibits any discrimination on the basis of body chemistry, he, and others like him, are subject to the practice of "genoism," whereby only the most select survive the turmoil of making a living. He avails himself of the illegal alternative, becoming a "borrowed ladder" by means of borrowing if not purchasing all elements of the identity of another individual, in this case a genetically superior but crippled former swimming star. What fascinates one about this film is not the technological mumbo jumbo or the murder-mystery subplot but the assignment of neither doubt nor prevarication on the part of the protagonist. At no point are his motivations or actions seen as other than valorized by the characters he encounters. Even the man whose identity he now possesses in order to fulfill his dream of space travel rationalizes all that he has done by the dubious statement "I only lent you my body. You lent me your dream." However, that dream comes across as self-involved and sanctimonious, its perpetuator a kind of futuristic Sammy Glick hustling for an open angle. *Gattaca* is redolent of the go-go boosterism of the yuppie '90s, when young men made themselves over through the stock market or on-line communications. Like them, the film presents the actions of its protagonist as self-evidently meritorious. *Gattaca* reinforces how the genre films of the 1990s, drawn from the domains of horror and science fiction offer audiences opportunities to imagine life beyond the confines of quotidian reality while simultaneously reinforcing the values we are forced to confront day after day.

WORKS CITED

Crane, Jonathan Lake. *Terror and Everyday Life. Singular Moments in the History of the Horror Film.* Thousand Oaks, Calif.: Sage, 1994.

Jackson, Kevin. "The Good, the Bad and the Ugly." *Sight & Sound* 2.3 (July 1992): 11–12.

Kawin, Bruce. *Telling It Again and Again, Repetition in Literature and Film.* University Press of Colorado, 1989.

Neale, Stephen. *Genre.* London: British Film Institute, 1990.

Pinedo, Isabel Cristina. *Recreational Terror: Women and the Pleasures of Horror Film Viewing.* Albany: State University of New York Press, 1997.

Roman, Monica. "Filmmakers get into designers' pants." *Variety* (September 7–13, 1998): 1, 86.

Sanjek, David. "Popular Music and the Synergy of Corporate Culture." *Mapping the Beat: Popular Music and Contemporary Theory.* Ed. Thomas Swiss, John Sloop, and Andrew Herman. London: Blackwell, 1998. 171–86.

Taubin, Amy. "Playing It Straight." *Sight & Sound* 6.8 (August 1996): 6–8.

Wood, Robin. *Hollywood from Vietnam to Reagan.* New York: Columbia University Press, 1986.

CHAPTER EIGHT

□

"Fighting and Violence and Everything, That's Always Cool":
Teen Films in the 1990s

WHEELER WINSTON DIXON

In the late 1990s, films aimed at a younger teenage audience, ages thirteen to nineteen, exploded on theatrical motion picture screens with a wave of productions that included Wes Craven's *Scream* (1996) and *Scream 2* (1997), Cameron Crowe's *Jerry Maguire* (1996), Baz Luhrmann's *William Shakespeare's Romeo + Juliet* (1997), Steven Spielberg's *The Lost World* (1997), Roland Emmerich's *Independence Day* (1997), Tom Shadyac's *Liar, Liar* (1997),Randall Wallace's *The Man in the Iron Mask* (1998), James Cameron's *Titanic* (1997), Jim Gillespie's *I Know What You Did Last Summer* (1997), Danny Cannon's *I Still Know What You Did Last Summer* (1998), John McNaughton's *Wild Things* (1998), and many others. Alfred Hitchcock's black-and-white masterpiece *Psycho* (1960) was remade nearly shot-by-shot by Gus Van Sant in 1998 with a more youthful cast (Vince Vaughn as Norman Bates, Anne Heche as Marion Crane) in color, to "update" this classic film for contemporary audiences. (In this case, however, the remake aroused a firestorm of critical protest, and despite a massive promotional campaign, the new *Psycho* failed at the box office.) These films might once have been labeled "gen-

125

eral audience films," suitable for all but the youngest members of the family, with casts comprising members of the entire adult-age spectrum. However, in the late 1990s, "teen presence" is essential in the enterprise of selling a motion picture, and so no matter what genre these individual films might belong to, their overriding audience appeal is to contemporary teenage filmgoers.

Kevin Smith's crude and brutally funny no-budget comedy *Clerks* (1994), shot in 16 mm black and white for a paltry $27,000, became a huge break-out hit for contemporary teenage audiences, who identified with its nihilistic and cheerfully coarse verbal humor. The relatively low-budgeted horror film *Scream 2*, directed by Wes Craven, had the largest weekend opening ever for a horror film, and the biggest December opening for a film of any genre, grossing $33 million in just two days versus a budget of $24 million. The film went on to generate box-office returns in the hundreds of millions, and ensure the creation of a sequel, *Scream 3*, which is already in preproduction. James Cameron's $200 million-plus *Titanic* has, to date, grossed more than one *billion* dollars in worldwide box-office rentals, exclusive of all possible merchandising tie-ins, soundtrack CDs, and other ancillary forms of commercial exploitation. Much of this revenue can be traced to the appeal of the two young stars of the film: Leonardo DiCaprio and Kate Winslet. The film instantly boosted Winslet to "A" list star status, and from a reported $2.5 million dollar price tag for his services as an actor in *Titanic*, DiCaprio's market value rose to an astounding $20.5 million per film.

Shortly after completing *Titanic*, but before that film was released, DiCaprio starred in Randall Wallace's teen-aimed remake of *The Man in the Iron Mask* (1998), which did not fare nearly so well at the box office. Yet for the time being, DiCaprio's value as a marketable asset in the realm of teendom remains unassailed, although, with the passing of months, and eventually years, he will undoubtedly be replaced in the affections of the teenage movie-going public by yet another earnest young swain. Indeed, in the current marketplace, a film such as Robert Benton's *Twilight* (1998), which stars a mostly over-sixty-five cast including Paul Newman, Gene Hackman, and James Garner, is a distinct anomaly. All of the above-mentioned teen, mass-market films had widely varying levels of technical sophistication, budget limitations (or the lack thereof), and operated within differing generic constraints. Yet all became substantial commercial hits, because more than ever before, teenage audiences dominate the global theatrical box office. One might thus argue that all films of the late 1990s might well be considered "teen" films for purposes of marketing alone, if for no other reason. Joe Roth, Chairman of Walt Disney Studios, notes that teenagers are the ideal movie audience: affluent, without responsibilities, and with plenty of time to kill. "They don't work. They don't have families to raise. They're available consumers with money" Roth summarizes (McGrath 30). And today's teenagers are more interested in going to the movies than in almost any other form of recreational spending.

A poll by the firm Teen Research Unlimited of more than two thousand teenagers throughout the United States revealed that "going to the movies" is the most popular leisure-time activity of contemporary teenagers, more popular than surfing the net, dating, playing sports, shopping, going to the beach, or participating in high school sports (Weeks D1). Mark Gill, president of Miramax/Dimension in Los Angeles, producers of *Scream* and *Scream 2*, notes that "there is a surge of teenagers coming our way. It's inevitable. And that, down the road, will be important" (Weeks D1). Who are these new teenage viewers? As Janet Weeks comments:

> Sometimes called Generation Y, these are the spawn of the huge population bulge known as the baby boom. These 77 million offspring born since 1978 started hitting their teen years in 1991, ending a 15–year cycle of declining teen ranks. Today, the teen population is accelerating at twice the rate of the rest of us. . . . By 2010, the teen population will crest at 30.8 million, the biggest in U.S. history. By comparison, the teen population of the baby boom crested in 1976 at 29.9 million. (Weeks D1)

As several industry observers have observed, this huge new audience requires entertainment specifically designed for its needs, unlike the big-budget spectacles that have recently dominated Hollywood's production schedule. Along with the modestly budgeted success of *Scream 2*, Quentin Tarantino's *Jackie Brown* (1997) was produced for a mere $12 million (Hirschberg 116), but proved a substantial hit at the box office. The producers banked on Tarantino's reputation as the foremost purveyor of contemporary cinematic brutality to lure audiences into theaters, and, at the least in this instance, it worked. In all these cases, the overall message to film producers seems clear. Genres aren't the crucial audience-producing factor they once were, and it really doesn't matter how much money one spends to produce a hit film. The only overriding question is simply this: *will the finished film appeal to teens?* Even a seemingly presold commodity such as Roland Emmerich's *Godzilla* (1998) needs Matthew Broderick to make the film more palatable to younger audiences; in addition, the new *Godzilla* opened at an unprecedented 7,000 theaters worldwide, as opposed to the usual wide break of 2,000 to 3,000 theaters. Wherever you are, the new *Godzilla* will seek you out; complete ubiquity and teen appeal are the hallmarks of the new megabudget action film.

David Davis, a Hollywood investment banker who specializes in predicting Hollywood trends, thinks that the current focus on teens as the dominant audience may represent a fundamental change in the way that the film industry does business in the future:

> "I've been watching films appear weekly for nine years, and this is the biggest change I've seen," he says. "It's the first real shifting in the 1990s. The idea has always been that if you can make your movie appeal to the widest audience you can succeed. Perhaps that isn't so anymore. Maybe the new idea is that if you can succeed in targeting to your core demographic, you can make a good gross." (qtd. in Weeks D2)

To Michael Woods, director of Teen Research International, this information comes as no surprise. "Teens are *so* into movies. Movies are really, really hot for teens" (Weeks D2). And these teens are very specific as to what sort of movies they want to view. One thirteen-year-old girl canvassed as part of the survey volunteered that "*Scream* was cool because . . . we were really scared one minute and laughing like crazy the next" (Weeks D2). An eighteen-year-old boy explained that "love stories and *90210* stuff [aren't] cool . . . [but] one of the greatest movies ever [is John Woo's] *Face/Off* [1997]. It had action right from the beginning. Fighting and violence and everything, that's always cool" (Weeks D2). And a fourteen-year-old girl from Bethesda, Maryland, noted that "Movies create a world that isn't our world. It puts you in another place and time, and everybody gets a kick out of that. Movie theaters are my favorite hangout to get away from my mom and dad" (Weeks D2).

In this respect, at least, little has changed in teenage viewing habits since the 1950s. The first American film company to specifically target the teenage audience realized that "getting away from mom and dad" was one of the key reasons that teenagers went to films in the first place.

Samuel Z. Arkoff, who founded American International Pictures (AIP) in the early 1950s with Jim Nicholson, instituted a policy of appealing *solely* to the teen market, making a series of violent, sensational films designed to lure teenagers out of the house and into the theaters, just as *Scream 2* does today. Although AIP sold out to Filmways in 1979, Samuel Arkoff retained, even in later years, a careful sense of why certain pictures clicked, and when. In the early 1960s, AIP moved into the *Beach Party* series (directed, for the most part, by William Asher), sensing that what teens of that era required more than anything else were escapist visions of a teenage life without adult supervision, but with plenty of money (and the things it buys) in evidence in every luxuriously appointed sequence. Thus such films as *Beach Party* (1963, dir. William Asher), *Bikini Beach* (1964, dir. William Asher), *How to Stuff a Wild Bikini* (1965, dir. William Asher), *The Ghost in the Invisible Bikini* (1966, dir. Don Weis) and *Ski Party* (1965, dir. Alan Rafkin) catered to a preexisting need for teen escapist fantasy during this era, following trends rather than trying to set them. AIP wanted to give the teenage public of the 1950s and early 1960s the spectacles they craved, the narrative plot lines and images they could obtain nowhere else. The audience, under this model, becomes the co-producer of the spectacle it witnesses and helps to create. That this phi-losophy was successful is self-evident; from 1956 until its absorption by Filmways, AIP effectively ruled the youth market by delivering to its audi-ences precisely those images branded as "outlaw" by the dominant cul-ture.

Jim Nicholson and Samuel Z. Arkoff's American International Pic-tures specifically targeted '50s teenagers with such films as Roger Cor-man's *Teenage Doll* (1957) and *Teenage Caveman* (1958), Burt Topper's *Diary of a High School Bride*, and the infamous 1950s teen programmer classics, Herbert L. Strock's *I Was a Teenage Frankenstein* (1957) and Gene Fowler Jr.'s *I Was a Teenage Werewolf* (1958). In the 1960s, as noted above, AIP moved on to such films as the enormously popular *Beach Party* (1963) and *Beach Blanket Bingo* (1965), both directed by William Asher, and Roger Corman's *The Wild Angels* (1966) and *The Trip* (1967). What all of these films had in common was their shared outlook on contempo-rary teenage culture, and the fact that all the films resembled one another to a striking degree. AIP was also one of the key companies that pioneered the "saturation hooking" method of distribution, in which a film is released in thousands of theaters simultaneously for maximum audience penetration, before any negative word of mouth can set in. Everyone gets the chance to participate in the newly released spectacle *together*, as a pre-constituted group; professional reviewers are thus reduced to the margins of critical discourse, and it is the public's appetite alone that ensures the success or failure of a given film.

Some thirty years ago American International Pictures also introduced the concept of releasing their biggest films (still only modestly budgeted at between $300,000 and $500,000 for a full-length color, Panavision feature) during the summer months, a period that studios had traditionally avoided until AIP demonstrated that even during supposed vacation periods, teenagers still went to the movies. Today, the "summer blockbuster" is a routine and cyclical part of the motion picture industry's annual output. When AIP merged with Filmways in late 1979, right after the release of Stuart Rosenberg's *The Amityville Horror*, the industry lost a studio that had been aggressively targeting the teen audience from the mid-1950s until the mid-1970s a studio that had demonstrated that it understood, more than any other, what teenagers of that era wanted to see on the screen.

AIP recognized up-and-coming talent and exploited it: Jack Nicholson, Francis Ford Coppola, Robert Vaughan, Michael Landon, Peter Fonda, Dennis Hopper, and numerous other teen stars of the '50s and '60s made key, early appearances in AIP films. Finally, AIP was one of the first studios to appreciate the fact that huge budgets and established stars weren't necessary to capture the teenage market. You needed an exploitable angle, an aggressive marketing campaign, and stars borrowed from television to make your film a success at the box office. And above all, the film must not partake of the real world, but rather of a construct having nothing to do with contemporary teen reality. AIP found this out when an early film, Burt Topper's *Diary of a High School Bride* (1959), unflinchingly depicted the endless grind of teenage marriage and pregnancy, and failed miserably at the box office as a result. The film hit too close to home, and fifties teens stayed away in droves. Significantly, AIP never made the same mistake again.

This seems remarkably in line with the findings of the researchers at Teen Research Unlimited; teens in the 1950s, as in the 1990s, want escapism without risk, and when it gets too close, they lose interest. Hyperreality is not the issue here; the key is *unreality*, unrelenting and unremitting. The movie viewer, ensconced in her/his seat in the darkness, seeks above all to *avoid* reality, to put off for as long as possible the return to normalcy, when they push past the upturned boxes of popcorn and spilled sodas and make their way through the doors into the world outside. But are they ever satisfied? The entire key behind contemporary genre films is to keep the viewer hooked, perpetually wanting more, to be satisfied yet still hungry for a return to the same world, the same characters, the same general plot line, with only minor variations. This explains why every cast member not killed in *Scream* (1996) is back for *Scream 2* (1997); contemporary, narrative-driven audiences want continuity and predictability in their entertainment above all other considerations. Today's genre films are really serials, in which formulaic thrills and entertainment are dispensed in two–hour bursts, with the promise of more to come held out in the final scenes of each episode. Tangentially, it is no surprise that the major television networks are increasingly targeting teenage women as a major portion of their audiences for daytime soap operas. As with film sequels, it is the *seriality* of the daytime soap opera, the mixture of the familiar with a slight plot twist to keep the narrative from becoming too predictable, that draws in younger audiences.

For a while in the 1970s and early 1980s, numerous *Saturday Night Live* alumni held sway at the box office, such as Bill Murray, Chevy Chase, Eddie Murphy, and Dan Aykroyd. Today, stars of teen films are drawn from such hit television shows as *Friends, Party of Five*, the teleseries version of *Buffy, the Vampire Slayer* and other teenage favorites. Former TV stars such as Drew Barrymore, Jada Pinkett, Neve Campbell, Courtney Cox, Sarah Michelle Gellar, along with popular teen theatrical film stars such as Helena Bonham Carter, Leonardo DiCaprio, Claire Danes, Kate Winslet, Robert Downey Jr., Keanu Reeves, Alicia Silverstone, Matt Damon, Ben Affleck, Jake Busey and many others, most of whom started out in series television or soap operas, have now become major studio box-office players. And even the most unapproachable classics are being remade for the new 1990s teen audience.

The company most identified with successful teenage product today is probably Dimension Pictures. Dimension (which, along with its parent company Miramax, is actually a Disney subsidiary) is following AIP's formula of low budgets, massive bookings, and canny exploitation to create a new wave of teen films for the next millennium. But the majors (Fox, Disney, Universal, Paramount, and the other big Hollywood studios) are jumping on the bandwagon as well, and in fact, have always been chasing the teenage audience. It just took a while for studios that were being run by women and men in their forties and fifties to wake up to the generational shift beyond "Gen X." But now that they've identified the basic principles of teenage appeal, what sort of "teen films" have the 1990s successfully spawned?

One of the most individual and accomplished teen films of the late 1990s was undoubtedly Richard Linklater's *Dazed and Confused* (1993), which followed Linklater's low-budget independent hit *Slacker* (1991). On the last day of school in 1976, a group of stoned and cheerfully nihilistic teens (Jason London, Adam Goldberg, Marissa Ribisi, and Michelle Burke) cut classes, get high, and stage a late-night kegger while listening to Black Sabbath, Ted Nugent, and Alice Cooper. Linklater's clear-eyed vision of this past Edenic time ends with a group of partying teens on a highway to nowhere as the sun comes up, blissfully unaware of the impending disasters of the 1980s: HIV, AIDS, the end of permissiveness toward recreational drugs. Kevin Smith shot his debut feature *Clerks* (1994) for $27,000, in black-and-white 16 mm, set in a convenience store where he worked. Working with a cast of unknowns, Smith created a convincingly foul-mouthed vision of the endless *ennui* of teenage existence, which led to his later films *Mallrats* (1996) and *Chasing Amy* (1997), further consolidating Smith's reputation as the voice of a new, iconoclastic, and disaffected generation. Jim Gillespie's *I Know What You Did Last Summer* (1997), with a script by Kevin Williamson, who also wrote both *Scream* films, pitted Jennifer Love Hewitt, Sarah Michelle Gellar, Freddie Prinze Jr., and Ryan Philippe against a vengeance-seeking fisherman from beyond the grave, and generated gratifying returns at the box office. Alicia Silverstone, who broke through to teen attention in Alan Shapiro's 1993 film *The Crush*, later starred in Marco Brambilla's *Excess Baggage*, a teens-on-the-run comedy also starring Benicio Del Toro. Baz Luhrmann's 1997 version of *William Shakespeare's Romeo + Juliet* transported Shakespeare's play into a series of rundown beachfront locations, and sketched the Montagues and Capulets as warring gangs, with Claire Danes and Leonardo DiCaprio as the "star cross'd lovers," set to a track of blasting rock and roll. The film was an enormous success at the box office, and became the definitive *Romeo and Juliet* for the contemporary teenage audience, even if it cut the original play to shreds, highlighted with Godardian intertitles to explicate key points in the text.

Tom Cruise and Cuba Gooding Jr. starred in Cameron Crowe's 1996 film *Jerry Maguire*. Ostensibly a film about a sports agent (Cruise) who discovers that he has a conscience after a career of underhanded business negotiations, *Jerry Maguire* is really a showcase for Cruise's somewhat fading teenage appeal, which traces all the way back to Paul Brickman's

FIGURE 8.1. Claire Danes and Leonardo DiCaprio in Baz Luhrmann's *Romeo + Juliet.* Courtesy: Jerry Ohlinger Archive.

1983 comedy *Risky Business*, the film that was Cruise's first big hit. Matthew Perry (from the TV series *Friends*) and Salma Hayek starred in Andy Tennant's *Fools Rush In* (1997), a romantic comedy about a one-night stand that turns into a long-term relationship. Mira Sorvino, Lisa Kudrow, and Jeanane Garofalo starred in David Mirkin's 1997 comedy *Romy and Michele's High School Reunion*, dealing with two young women, unsuccessful in their lives after high school, seeking to impress their former classmates at their tenth annual school reunion. The war film was updated with elaborate science-fiction trappings in Paul Verhoeven's 1997 *Starship Troopers*, based on the novel by Robert Heinlein, in a digital special-effects spectacular starring contemporary teen idols Casper Van Dien, Dina Meyer, Denise Richards, Jake Busey, and former *Doogie Howser* tele-series star Neil Patrick Harris in an ultra-violent tale of a group of paramilitary troopers who must attack and annihilate millions of gigantic "arachnid warriors" to restore order to the galaxy. The real stars of the film are Phil Tippett's elaborately point-plotted digital special effects, which raise the conceptualization and execution of science-fiction monsters to an entirely new level of verisimilitude. Viewed in comparison with Merian C. Cooper and Ernest B. Schoedsack's *King Kong* (1933), or even Ray Harryhausen's remarkable stop-motion films of the 1950s and 1960s, Tippett's computer-generated mastery is both remarkable and not a little frightening; for the first time, it seems, anything is now possible within the fictive realm of the cinema, both figuratively and literally. Then, too, Verhoeven's direction of the film borrows equal parts of Frank Capra's *Why We Fight* series of World War II documentaries, commingled in an unholy alliance with Leni Riefenstahl's Nazi propaganda films of the same era; the result is at once ultra-patriotic and hyper-fascist, and seemingly irresistible to contemporary teen audiences.

John McNaughton's *Wild Things* (1998) effectively brought film noir into teen territory, with a cast cagily comprised of "Gen X" stars Kevin Bacon, Neve Campbell, Matt Dillon, and Denise Richards (fresh from her breakthrough role in Verhoeven's *Starship Troopers*), along with the icons of two earlier generations, Bill Murray, the staple star of numerous adolescent comedies of the late 1970s and early 1980s, and Robert Wagner, a teen heartthrob of the 1950s. This casting benefits both the film's demographic, and the artists involved; the younger cast members get a taste of what film history has to offer in the way of sinuously contrived plotting, and the older members of the cast are associated with a high-profile "niche" project that may well rejuvenate their careers. Robert

FIGURE 8.2. The intergalactic bugs attack in Paul Verhoeven's *Starship Troopers*. Courtesy: Jerry Ohlinger Archive.

Wagner, indeed, recently appeared in a starring role in Jay Roach's down-and-dirty spy-film satire *Austin Powers: International Man of Mystery* (1997) alongside Mike Myers and Elizabeth Hurley; and 1950s glamour star Roger Moore (best known for his work in the teleseries *The Saint* and the 1970s James Bond films) was featured as the putative manager of the pop group The Spice Girls in Bob Spiers's *Spice World* (1997). In both cases, these stars of an earlier era are striving valiantly to remain contemporary in a business where the axiom "out of sight, out of mind" is not so much a concept as a certified fact of life.

On the less commercial but perhaps more artistically successful side, Peter Jackson's 1994 *Heavenly Creatures*, starring Melanie Lynskey and Kate Winslet, is a brilliant recreation of an actual New Zealand murder case in which two teenage girls conspire to murder one girl's mother, who threatens to end their friendship. In its depiction of teenage fantasy life and the bonds that can be so intensely formed in teen relationships, the film is both mesmerizing and aptly horrific. The film first introduced Winslet to international commercial audiences, and was instrumental in securing her role in James Cameron's *Titanic*. Other recent hit films aimed at contemporary teens include Donald Petrie's *The Favor* (1994), a romantic comedy starring Harley Jane Kozak and Elizabeth McGovern; Nicholas Kazan's *Dream Lover* (1994), a suspense thriller starring James Spader and Bess Armstrong; Ben Stiller's *Reality Bites* (1994), in which a group of friends (Winona Ryder, Ethan Hawke, and Ben Stiller) face the reality of life after college; Stephen Herek's 1994 version of *The Three Musketeers* (1993), in which Charlie Sheen, Kiefer Sutherland, Chris O'Donnell, and Rebecca De Mornay offer up a new telling of Dumas's classic tale; Joel Schumacher's 1990 *Flatliners*, featuring Kiefer Sutherland, Julia Roberts, Kevin Bacon and William Baldwin as a group of young medical students trespassing the frontiers of life and death in a series of perilous experiments; Cameron Crowe's *Singles* (1992), in which Bridget Fonda, Campbell Scott, Kyra Sedgwick, Sheila Kelley, Jim True, and Matt Dillon search for love and meaning in their lives in a frequently indifferent world; Jeremiah Chechik's *Benny and Joon* (1993), which features Johnny Depp, Aidan Quinn, and Mary Stuart Masterson in a screwball romantic comedy for the 1990s; and Tony Bill's 1993 *Untamed Heart*, in which Christian Slater, Marisa Tomei, and Rosie Perez struggle to find romance within the confines of a rundown diner.

No matter what their genre, these films have as their central focus that ineffable factor known as "teen appeal," something that shifts so rapidly as to be almost impossible to track. In the late 1990s, all films have become teen films, simply in order to gain some sort of toehold at the box office. Older stars latch onto younger up-and-coming talents to bolster their careers; at twenty-five, in today's cinematic landscape, you've practically become a character actor, consigned to playing parents, cops, teachers, or other marginal (and usually comic) "authority" figures. And if you're hot today, that's no guarantee that you won't be forgotten tomorrow. Remember Pauly Shore? Or Molly Ringwald? After a promising start on MTV as a VJ, an on-air personality, Shore got a series of starring movie roles, beginning with Les Mayfield's 1992 *Encino Man*, a slapstick comedy harking back to Mack Sennett, in which two high-school students unearth a frozen Neanderthal Man (Brendan Fraser) in their backyard, and attempt to integrate him into contemporary high-school society. Yet that film, and the Pauly Shore films that followed, including Steve Rash's *Son in Law* (1993), Daniel Petrie Jr.'s *In the Army Now* (1994), John Fortenberry's *Jury Duty* (1995), and Jason Bloom's *Bio-Dome* (1996) failed to secure him a berth in the new teen pantheon. Similarly, Molly Ringwald had a series of hits in teen films of the 1980s, including such films as David Anspaugh's *Fresh Horses* (1988), James Toback's *The Pick-Up Artist* (1987), Howard Deutch's *Pretty in Pink* (1986), and John Hughes's *The Breakfast Club* (1985) and *Sixteen Candles* (1984), but by 1990 it was clear that she'd fallen out of favor with the fickle movie-going public. Past fame is simply no guarantee of future popularity or employment.

Increasingly, as noted above, older stars feel the need to ensure the success of their films at the box office, and use younger up-and-coming teen stars to enhance their commercial appeal, as with the casting of Chris O'Donnell (Robin in the *Batman* films) alongside Al Pacino in Martin Brest's *Scent of A Woman* (1992), or the casting of the late River Phoenix to prop up Robert Redford and Sidney Poitier's audience clout in Phil Alden Robinson's *Sneakers* (1992). Teen stars are also used to breathe new life into supposedly moribund genres. Antonia Bird's *Mad Love* (1995) features Chris O'Donnell and Drew Barrymore on the run from unsympathetic parents who want to keep them apart; as the film develops, it becomes apparent that Barrymore has a chemical imbalance that renders her mentally unstable. The film's ending finds Barrymore back on medication, home with her family—a new nuclear family for the 1990s, based on coercive chemistry. Contemporary teen icons also feel the need to document their lives through films that selectively capture fragments of their highly staged existence. Madonna commissioned a documentary on her life and work in Alex Keshishian's 1991 *Truth or Dare*; Keshishian's crew, clad entirely in black for the duration of the shoot, follow Madonna through a grueling concert tour as she battles with fans, police, and censors in between offstage relationships with Warren Beatty and Sandra Bernhard.

John Hughes's 1991 *Weird Science* features one-time *Saturday Night Live* cast member Anthony Michael Hall in a rather conventional science-fiction comedy/fantasy in which two high-school students attempt to synthetically create the ideal woman; shortly after the film was released, Hall's career went into eclipse until he reemerged as a nearly unrecognizably beefed-up bully in such films as Tim Burton's *Edward Scissorhands* (1990). Brendan Fraser, Matt Damon, Chris O'Donnell, Ben Affleck, and Amy Locane starred in Robert Mandel's *School Ties*, set in the 1950s, in which a Jewish student in an exclusive boarding school finds prejudice holding him back both socially and scholastically; the film is essentially an update of Elia Kazan's 1947 film *Gentleman's Agreement*, which also dealt with anti-Semitism. More recently, Matt Damon has broken through to "A" star status in Gus Van Sant's most conventional and thus most commercially successful film, *Good Will Hunting* (1998), which documents the highly improbable life of a young janitor who is also a math prodigy. Using his gifts, the janitor is able to escape the rigors of this blue-collar upbringing in a formulaic (yet seemingly reassuring for most viewers) happy ending. Not surprisingly, the film was an enormous success at the box office, and Damon won an Oscar for his screenplay for the film, coauthored with Ben Affleck (and an uncredited William Goldman, an old hand at the screenplay game).

Indeed, in all these films what we see happening is a reworking of the same plots, themes, conflicts, and story structures that informed genre filmmaking since the dawn of the cinema. But with one essential difference: in the late 1990s, it's become an entirely teenage cinematic world, in which all the central roles are played by young men in their late teens or early twenties, no matter what genre a film ostensibly embraces. Older actors pop up in minor roles, their talents used to lend some solidity to what might otherwise seem an essentially ephemeral enterprise. Whether comedy, screwball comedy, drama, or horror film, the teen movies of the late 1990s are, for the most part, contemporary retellings of films that once starred adults. The new wave of thirteen- to nineteen-year-old viewers wants something that appeals directly to them, featuring stars that they know (from television) who are roughly their own age, rather than adults pretending to be teenagers. As critic Neal Gabler notes, there is no longer any "middle" in theatrical cinema audiences; mom and dad are home in the house, watching TV, and the kids will do anything to get out of the domestic sphere their parents have so assiduously created (76–78).

While reruns of Frank Capra's *It's a Wonderful Life* (1946) may please the entire family at Christmas in a grudging sort of way, and Disney films provide entertainment for the younger set, for the thirteen- to nineteen-year-old age group, the PG-13 to R set (depending on the laxity of rating enforcement), teen movies offer what they have always offered: action, escape, violence, drama, the simulacrum of personal involvement without actual presence or risk. The teen films of the 1990s are really just like the teen films of the '50s, '60s, and '70s, or the '20s, '30s, and '40s, for that matter. They mirror the hopes and dreams of young people who are just starting out in their lives, breaking away from family and friends, exploring sexual and emotional frontiers as every generation has before them. Before films and television, when radio held sway in America's households, teens went out dancing or cruising in their cars, parking in Lover's Lane, trying to get the same privacy they now find in shopping malls, friend's basements, or in the darkened womb of the movie theater.

But as the next generation of teenagers pauses before their entry into college, it is both sobering and distressing to find that of all possible avocations, the escapist act of "going out to the movies" is now the most popular teenage pastime by far. Today's world is so complex, so threatening, so demanding, with multiple sources of information assaulting us from all directions (via e-mail, faxes, web surfing, and the like) that, it seems, "time-outs" are more necessary than ever. Then, too, in a plague society, ravaged by the twin scourges of HIV and AIDS, perhaps more fantasy is required. Not everyone grows up to be an adult; today's teens can see disturbing evidence of their own mortality at every turn. If the teen films of the 1990s seem, perhaps, slightly more mechanical than their predecessors, perhaps it's because they are for the most part genre retreads. But in their embrace of the grandeur and sweep of fairy-tale romance (*William Shakespeare's Romeo + Juliet*) or the unstoppable serial frenzy of Jason, Freddy Krueger, or the masked killer in the *Scream* films, the teen films of the 1990s are at once more violent and less innocent, than their predecessors. Since contemporary audiences who view these films have rarely seen the numerous films they are based upon, most of the 1990s teen films discussed here benefit from an air of spurious novelty. From the vantage point of any sort of serious film scholarship, this seems lamentable.

But at the same time, new generations demand new versions of the classic genre tales that enthralled us in our youth, just as digital imagery has now become an integral and inescapable part of the fantasy filmmaking process, replacing stop-motion animation, moveable matter, and other photographic techniques, all of which were still fairly commonplace even at the start of the decade. As the millennium draws to a close, we will be seeing the same stories in slightly renewed versions with younger casts, for that is what the contemporary audience demands. In the dawn of the digital age, more teenagers are going to the movies than at any other time in recent memory, for instruction, amusement, and escapism, to hear and see for the first time the fables we adults know by heart. And the players will keep changing, for as long as new groups of teenagers flock to the movie theaters; Johnny Depp, Winona Ryder, and Brad Pitt may have ruled the 1990s box office, but as the recent ascendance of Claire Danes, Neve Campbell, Leonardo DiCaprio, and others aptly demonstrates, in the Hollywood zone of eternal commodification, there is always someone new waiting in the wings.

The stars discussed in this piece will inevitably be replaced by other, newer faces, who may or may not break through to "A" status as they toil their way through a series of forgettable program pictures on their hopeful way to the top. And having achieved the pinnacle of stardom, they will inevitably be knocked off their perches by the next crop of even younger stars. Given the speeded-up access afforded to today's teen audiences by the internet and the web, this process has taken on an increasingly hyped-up urgency; stardom is the currency of the moment, nothing more. Those who patronize, and appear in, the teen films of the 1990s are participating in a phantom zone whose rules are changing second-by-second, where today's success only guarantees itself, and nothing more.

WORKS CITED

Gabler, Neal. "The End of the Middle." *The New York Times Magazine* (November 16, 1997): 76–78.

Hirschberg, Lynn. "The Man Who Changed Everything." *The New York Times Magazine* (November 16, 1997): 112–16.

Lewis, Jon. *The Road to Romance and Ruin: Teen Films and Youth Culture.* New York: Routledge, 1992.

McGrath, Charles. "Being 13: It's Not the Way That It Used to Be—Except That It Is." *The New York Times Magazine* (May 17, 1998): 29–30.

O'Brien, Geoffrey. "What Does the Audience Want?" *The New York Times Magazine* (November 16, 1997): 110–11.

Redhead, Steve. *Unpopular Cultures: The Birth of Law and Popular Culture.* Manchester, UK: Manchester University Press, 1995.

Strawn, Linda May. "Interview with Samuel Z. Arkoff, February 11, 1974." *Kings of the Bs: Working within the Hollywood System.* Ed. Todd McCarthy and Charles Flynn. New York: Dutton, 1975. 255–66.

Weeks, Janet. "Hollywood Is Seeing Teen: Younger Set Favors Movies Above All." *USA Today* (December 22, 1997): D1, 2.

Weldon, Michael. *The Psychotronic Encyclopedia of Film.* New York: Ballantine, 1983.

CHAPTER NINE

◉

The Left-Handed Form of Human Endeavor: Crime Films during the 1990s

RON WILSON

The crime genre was revitalized during the 1990s, and in many ways represented a return to its original roots in both the press and literature. The 1990s showed an increased public interest in crime, not only in the film medium, but in television (the sensational trials of Rodney King and O. J. Simpson, as well as numerous police docudramas, to say nothing of the ubiquitousness of *Court TV*), and in the print media (true crime paperback "novels" and fictional murder mysteries being two of the more popular genres). With the effective demise of the western film genre (except for its sporadic revisionist texts), the crime film became the primary outlet for what Lawrence Alloway referred to as "covert culture of the United States" (11). Violence in the cinema becomes a part of the nation's covert culture, because it seems to be of greater interest to the mass audience "than is tolerable to elite critics of society" (11). Violence itself is an important convention in both westerns and crime film. Alloway goes on to suggest that "violence as motivation gives the maximum definition to a story, a principle common to magazine fiction and violent movies" (11). The connection to the pulp literature background is particularly important, in that both forms of the crime genre provide a popular "covert" culture, which is concurrent with the existing elitist culture. The recent criticism by some *literati* over the inclusion of Dashiell Hammett's *The Maltese Falcon* and James M. Cain's *The Postman Always Rings Twice* in the Modern Library's 100 Best Novels of the Twentieth Century list, illustrates the problem of the continuing marginalization of popular generic texts. Yet these books are among the most influential of the twentieth century. Mirroring the brutality of these source texts, and aided by a new relaxation in codes on the presentation of graphic violence, the crime film of the 1990s demonstrates an increased embrace of violence.

An important trait of '90s crime films, and one that distinguishes them from their '70s and '80s predecessors, is a return to original sources, both journalistic and literary. Crime writers such as Jim Thompson, Elmore Leonard, and James Ellroy are well represented in '90s crime films. Likewise, source material derived from true-crime nonfiction was adapted to the screen more frequently in the 1990s. True-crime docudramas, as well as police procedurals such as *Cops, Homicide, Law and Order*, and others are popular television shows. Martin Scorsese's two major crime films during the decade, *Goodfellas* (1990) and *Casino* (1995), were both adapted from nonfiction sources. Other successful screen adaptations of true-crime sources include Alexander Gregory Hippolyte's *Dead Man Walking* (1995) and Mike Newell's *Donnie Brasco* (1997). This return to source material is indicative of a return to the roots of the crime genre itself.

The crime film originated as a response to both topical events and sociological commentary. D. W. Griffith's *The Musketeers of Pig Alley* (1912) is generally regarded as one of the precursors to the modern crime film. According to the Biograph Catalogue entry, the film represented a "depiction of the gangster evil" that had "been a menace to the respectable citizen" (Clarens 15). Many of the gangster films of the early 1930s were based on incidents and persons pulled from newspaper headlines. Indeed, many of the screenwriters for these films, most notably Ben Hecht, were former journalists themselves. Tabloid journalism and newspaper circulation nearly doubled between 1900 and 1930. By reaching a mass audience, the popularity of the press became a font for stories that continually fed the violent imagination of its readers. The classic trio of early sound gangster films, Mervyn LeRoy's *Little Caesar* (1931), William Wellman's *The Public Enemy* (1931), and Howard Hawks's *Scarface* (1932), was popular because of its intertextual relationship with current events.

Another wellspring of source material for the crime film lay in its pulp-fiction background. This period of adaptation begins in the mid-thirties, and peaks during the forties. Film adaptations of Broadway plays, such as *The Petrified Forest* (1935) and *Dead End* (1937), contributed to the codification of the gangster/tough-guy persona. The successful adaptation of hard-boiled fiction begins with John Huston's *The Maltese Falcon* (1941). The majority of forties film noir had their literary basis in such diverse 'pulp' writers as Raymond Chandler, James M. Cain, W. R. Burnett, and Cornell Woolrich. The use of pulp-fiction sources clearly defines the target audience for these films. The hard-boiled tradition in American literature was a response against the English drawing-room detective fiction, exemplified by such writers as Agatha Christie and Dorothy Sayers. Hard-boiled fiction, for the most part, was concerned with the criminal element and the criminal act itself, in all its various and violent manifestations. According to writer/director Paul Schrader, "The hard-boiled writers had their roots in pulp fiction or journalism, and their protagonists lived out a narcissistic, defeatist code" (Silver 56). It is this strain of crime film that has flourished in the late 1990s, as it did in the early 1930s and late 1940s.

The primary focus of the majority of '90s crime films is on the criminal, which is indicative of a shift away from the detective/law-enforcer element in film. Charles Derry claims that "the popular work of art dealing with crime is composed of at least three major characters or elements: the criminal, the victim, and the detective." He goes on to state that in most popular works "one of the three elements takes precedence over the others" (57). Different subcategories of the crime-film genre quite often make it extremely clear as to which element is dominant. A film title such as H. Bruce Humberstone's *Charlie Chan at the Opera* (1936), for instance, clearly signifies the dominance of the detective figure in the narrative. However, in the case of most crime thrillers in the 1990s, the dominant figure is the victim. In many respects, the 1990s crime film is a self-conscious one, well aware of its cinematic, as well as its literary heritage.

The decade of the '90s began with the resurgence of the film noir, or more specifically, *neo-noir*. The year 1990 alone saw the release of two adaptations of Jim Thompson novels, Stephen Frears's *The Grifters* and James Foley's *After Dark, My Sweet*, as well as the sequel to Roman Polanski's *Chinatown* (1974), Jack Nicholson's *The Two Jakes*. These films contributed to the renewed interest in film noir in the early '90s, and the classification of neo-noir as a subgenre of the crime film. Todd Erickson, in his insightful essay "Kill Me Again: Movement becomes Genre," defines neo-noir as a new type of noir film "which effectively incorporates and projects the narrative and stylistic conventions of its progenitor onto a contemporary canvas. Neo-noir is . . . a contemporary rendering of the film noir sensibility" (Silver 321).

Erickson further claims that two significant factors contributed to this revival of noir: "the pervasiveness of crime and the public's fascination with sensational crime stories," as well as a "definitive noir sensibility among contemporary filmmakers" (316–19). The 1990s saw the extension of this interest in crime beyond the domain of the cinema—television, art, neo-noir crime fiction, and music, according to Erickson, "demonstrated, in some way or another, crime's influence in their creative efforts" (317). Two influential '90s noir films, Lee Tamahori's *Mulholland Falls* (1996) and Curtis Hanson's *L.A. Confidential* (1997), are indicative of this "noir sensibility" on the part of their filmmakers.

Mulholland Falls and *L.A. Confidential* are set in a nostalgic past, where hidden beneath the veneer of normalcy lies a world of vice and corruption. Both films are set in Los Angeles (the archetypal noir urban environment, thanks to Raymond Chandler), and placed in the late 1940s and early 1950s respectively. The films are also similar in that they focus on the activities of the Los Angeles police, and an initial murder investigation that proves to have wider implications than that of mere routine. Both films concern the tactics of a special antigangster police squad who attempt to "clean" L.A. county of any unwelcome organized criminal element.

In *Mulholland Falls*, Nick Nolte is part of the "Hat Squad," so named because of the wide-brimmed hats they wear throughout the film. The squad is a vigilante force empowered to keep L.A. county free of mobsters. The film's title refers to the cliff overlooking Los Angeles, which is the dropping-off point, so to speak, for any mobster strong-armed by the squad. The film's plot hinges on a murder investigation that ultimately leads to the exposure of graft, corruption, and government nuclear tests. The film's convoluted narrative involves a Chandleresque expedition into the environs of a corrupt community, exposing the dark underside of postwar America. John Malkovich's General Timms, in charge of the Atomic Energy Commission, who claims that "the cornerstone of civilization is human sacrifice," bears a distinct relationship to John Huston's portrayal of the corrupt Noah Cross in Polanski's *Chinatown*. Both characters represent the inherent evil that lies beneath the cloak of power and respectability.

Curtis Hanson's adaptation of James Ellroy's novel *L.A. Confidential*, revolves around a group of detectives in the Los Angeles police force.

The omnipresent corruption and graft in the film provide a link to its essential noir characteristics. Postwar Los Angeles provides the setting for the narrative, which reveals a labyrinthine world of menace and cynicism. The corrupt nature of the police department is demonstrated with the discovery of yet another vigilante-style squad, which attempts to prevent any organized criminal element from invading the city. The film's title refers to a trash tabloid monthly newspaper (edited by the appropriately leering Danny DeVito, in the role of Sid Hudgeons) that provided exposés of celebrity excesses, particularly of drugs and sex. Hudgeons's oft-quoted line from the film, "Off the record, on the QT, and very hush, hush," provides a thematic insight into the film noir environment, which is meant to celebrate the dark side of humanity. Whether it be a police chief responsible for murder, or a prostitute who is surgically altered to resemble a Hollywood celebrity, the artifice in *L.A. Confidential* ultimately reveals a world devoid of any moral value.

Although both films are original and contemporary as to their source material, they reflect a strong nostalgic element and noir sensibility that is reliant on the intertextuality of noir itself. As a historical genre or movement, classic film noir "peaked" in the period between 1945 and 1956. It was during this time that the disillusion of the post–World War II economy and social milieu came together to shape the mode of production and stylistic conventions that became known as film noir. Any crime film set within this period thus becomes self-consciously aware of its cinematic heritage. But the 1990s saw the emergence of original noir voices, who were cognizant of the noir heritage, but utilized it in new and revealing ways.

Perhaps the single most important and influential noir crime film of the decade was Quentin Tarantino's *Pulp Fiction* (1994), an epic crime thriller that encapsulted nearly forty years' worth of generic crime-narrative structures within the compass on one 154 minute film; Tarantino later reedited the film into an even longer director's cut, clocking in at a mammoth 168 minutes. Despite its length, the film is never boring, but instead becomes an extended, fascinating riff on the conventions of the crime-film, managing to incorporate nearly all the characteristics of the various crime film subgenres into one sprawling narrative. *Pulp Fiction* not only revitalized the crime genre, but can take credit "for putting the arcane term 'pulp fiction' back in the popular consciousness, and for making the term synonymous with pulp crime fiction" (Woods 101). The film opens with an *American Heritage Dictionary* definition:

Pulp (pulp) n. 1. A soft, moist, shapeless mass of matter.
2. A magazine or book containing lurid subject matter and being characteristically printed on rough, unfinished paper.

With a simple title, Tarantino refocuses the crime film back to its original roots in cheap, consumer-oriented material. Tarantino's film does not concern itself with the grandiose designs of a master criminal, or the rise and fall of a Mafioso, but rather with the eccentrics who live a mundane existence in the shadowland of crime, an existence that is sporadically highlighted by outbursts of senseless violence. As noted, the film is actually a combination of various subgenres of the crime film, a pastiche film that intercuts three different stories.

The film's prologue begins with two characters, Honey Bunny (Amanda Plummer) and Pumpkin (Tim Roth), who are conversing about a proposed robbery in a diner. Interestingly, Tarantino's shooting script emphasizes that the dialogue should be delivered with a Hawksian *His Girl Friday* pace. The conversation's subject, in typical Tarantino fashion, deals with the advantages of robbing a diner, as opposed to robbing a bank. The scene finishes with the two characters kissing passionately, and then suddenly pulling guns from underneath their shirts and declaring their intention to rob the diner.

Tarantino then switches to the next story, concerning Jules (Samuel J. Jackson) and Vincent (John Travolta), a pair of hit men working for Marsellus Wallace (Ving Rhames). The third narrative line involves a boxer, Butch Coolidge (Bruce Willis), who is ordered by Marsellus to throw a fight. This trio of narratives intersect at various points throughout the film. The nonlinear nature of the screenplay is one of the innovative aspects of the film. Tarantino opens with the prologue with Honey Bunny and Pumpkin, shifts with a freeze frame at the beginning of their heist of the diner, and at film's end returns to pick up the narrative thread with the inclusion of Jules and Vincent. Tarantino also kills off Vincent halfway through the film, and stills returns to the character at the end, in a flashback. As Douglas Brode points out, "Such a daring plot gamble would prove disastrous in most films, yet it's another wild narrative ride that Tarantino, in his endearingly goofy way, somehow manages to pull off" (239). Time in *Pulp Fiction* is convoluted, almost Joycean. The intentionally banal nature of the dialogue is another important element of the script, as well as Tarantino's emphasis on the pulp characteristics of his crime story. In Tarantino's films, dialogue is important in revealing the

FIGURE 9.1. John Travolta and Samuel L. Jackson in Quentin Tarantino's *Pulp Fiction*. Courtesy: Jerry Ohlinger Archive.

fatuous nature of crime and the absurdity of the criminal existence. This dialogue often turns on references to such mundane topics as McDonald's fast food, foot massages, milk shakes, and pork products. Tarantino's dialogue thus deconstructs the typical Hollywood concern with keeping the narrative focused on a single, linear subject, while moving forward in a clearly discernible manner.

Bryan Singer's *The Usual Suspects* (1995) is another neo-noir that takes a characteristic situation, in this case a police lineup and the subsequent interrogation of a suspect, and views it from an altogether different perspective. At the center of the film's narrative is Roger "Verbal" Kint (Kevin Spacey), a seemingly small-time hood who relates to patient detective Dave Kujan (Chazz Palminteri) the incidents surrounding an attempted truck hijacking. The story Verbal relates is intensely complex, centering on a mysterious figure known as Keyser Soze, a Hungarian master criminal who exerts such fearsome power that persons cower at the mere mention of his name. In many ways, the film resembles a Jacobean revenge tragedy, in which the mysterious Soze doles out vengeance to those who fail to live up to his expectations, or obey his draconian commands. Ultimately, the narrative drive of the film centers on the true identity of Soze, and the revelation that Soze is none other than Verbal Kint himself. Kint has been stringing Kujan along with a complicated narrative entirely of his own construction throughout the entire film, just to keep Kujan off track.

This equation of the ultimate evil as a criminal mastermind is not entirely new to neo-noir. Alan Parker's *Angel Heart* (1987) cast Robert De Niro as a Mephistophelian presence (Louis Cyphre) controlling events in a highly convoluted, often surrealistic narrative, while Mickey Rourke played the characrer of Harry Angel, a down-at-the-heels private detective trying to unravel a nearly impenetrable maze of deception and violent intrigue. In *The Usual Suspects*, Soze, though never seen, is the hidden power behind the criminal underworld. The film ultimately is a commentary on the elusive nature of truth itself, and utilizes the police interrogation to point out the absurdity of trying to separate fact from fiction. In his interrogation by Palminteri's character, Verbal basically constructs a "truth" from material he sees around him. He also constructs a truth concerning his own image as it is perceived by others. Distinguishing between the two within the context of the police investigation, which is meant to find out the truth, proves elusive to all involved, and particularly (by design) to the audience.

As can be seen, the neo-noir film, whether placed in the period of noir itself or in contemporary settings, provided a venue for filmmakers to explore different themes within the crime genre in the '90s. Todd Erickson claims that the late '80s and '90s saw a sociocultural development, similar to that of the postwar years, which helped the resurgence of the noir sensibility. Post-Vietnam disillusionment, the rise in international terrorism, and the growing disparity between the very rich and the very poor all fostered an environment for noir themes to once again reflect an image of the dark side of the American dream. Erickson states that "*film noir* and its contemporary descendant, *neo-noir,* offer some of the most fascinating insights the cinema has provided on topics such as including ambition, corruption, redemption, greed, lust and loyalty. . . . Most important, however, is the heightened level of co-experience with which the truly authentic noir grips its audience" (qtd. in Silver 326). The 1990s saw both audiences and filmmakers receptive to noir themes and stylistics.

The gangster film was another of the more influential crime subgenres during the 1990s. The early '90s saw such films produced as Francis Ford Coppola's *The Godfather, Part III* (1990), Martin Scorsese's *Goodfellas* (1990), Stephen Frears's *The Krays* (1990), Joel and Ethan Coen's *Miller's Crossing* (1990), Robert Benton's *Billy Bathgate* (1991), and Barry Levinson's *Bugsy* (1991). The gangster film during the 1990s, as it did from its inception, provided a social commentary on American business and the American success story. Commerce in gangster films is simply illegal, whether it be bootlegging, racketeering, or drugs, and the gangster in these films is only protecting his interests. Yet gangster films appeal to us on an aesthetic level, because their characters are driven by success within the *business* of crime itself. As an audience, we know that the gangster, in his many guises, is foredoomed from the first reel, but we take guilty pleasure in watching him pursue that ever elusive American dream. Robert Warshow was the first to point this out in his essay "The Gangster as Tragic Hero," when he noted that

> the importance of the gangster film, and the nature and intensity of its emotional and aesthetic impact, cannot be measured in terms of the place of the gangster himself or the importance of the problem of crime in American life. . . . What matters is that the experience of the gangster as an *experience of art* is universal to Americans. (130)

Warshow places the gangster subgenre on an aesthetic emotional level as an artistic experience, and connects the genre with what he refers to as the "ideology of cheerfulness" in American life. The classic gangster, Warshow claims, "speaks for us, expressing that part of the American psyche which rejects the qualities and demands of modern life, which rejects 'Americanism' itself" (130). This drive for success, which is emphasized by the gangsters' emphasis on wealth and power, is the ideological force of the gangster film. The stakes are always high, for failure means death. The 1990s gangster film is even more concerned with crime as a form of business—in many cases big business, and the world of incorporation and insolvency. The '90s interest in the gangster is also sparked by industrial growth, the booming economy, and the growth of big business at the expense of entrepreneurial interests. In many ways the gangster himself, as portrayed in the 1990s, mirrors the decline of individualism within a corporate society.

David E. Ruth suggests that "the fundamental business strategies explored by the inventors of the gangster were growth, consolidation, and organization. . . . As in legitimate business, growth was accompanied by successful efforts to limit competition" (43). The types of "business" change as the gangster genre addresses different generations: bootlegging and racketeering, armed car robbery, drugs, black market commodities, and gambling. The revisionist, nostalgic 1990s crime film posited Las Vegas as the Mecca of the underworld, prior to its domination by corporate business interests. The "classic" gangster-film narrative typically revolved around the rise and fall of the gangster hero, and highlighted the depiction of the gangster's drive toward success, which inevitably leads to failure. The gangster hero was often portrayed as an almost Shakespearean tragic figure, whose inevitable downfall was documented in near-Aristotelian terms.

The 1990s gangster film, in contrast, often looks at the lower echelons of the corporate ladder, at small-time hoods who also are striving for success but on a smaller perspective. As Ruth observes, "like most employees of any business, the majority of workers were near the bottom of the hierarchy" (53). The focus of films such as *Miller's Crossing*, Martin Scorsese's *Casino* (1995), and *Donnie Brasco* is thus on small-time, bottom-rung gangsters, attempting to climb the corporate ladder of criminal success, only to meet with failure because they reach beyond their level of competence. Coupled with this is the issue of misplaced trust in the criminal hierarchy; the gangster's tragic flaw is often being too trustworthy in a world where trust has no value. In film after film, both classic and contemporary, the gangster trusts an individual who ultimately betrays him.

Casino provides a good example of the crime-film's concern in the '90s with big-business strategies and the gangster as businessman. The film, based on Nicholas Pileggi's book, recounts the real-life story of gambler Sam "Ace" Rothstein (Robert De Niro), who is hired by the mob to manage the Tangiers Hotel and Casino in Las Vegas. Rothstein wants to operate the casino as a legitimate enterprise, but the trappings of wealth and power prove too tempting, and bring about his downfall within the organization. Joe Pesci (an icon of '90s crime films) plays the ruthless mobster Nicky Santoro who, in typical gangster fashion, wants to run things in his own violent way. The Las Vegas setting of the film becomes a metaphor for a decadent America, which is eventually engulfed, not by the syndicate, but by big business itself. *Casino* offers us a vision of Las Vegas in the pre-Disneyfication era; in the revisionist context of the 1990s, Disney has become one of the icons of corporate power and greed. Rothstein in the world of *Casino* is an outsider, "the Golden Jew," whose dreams of success are hopeless, because with the mob success comes only by being part of the group itself. Rothstein's business acumen is acceptable as long he is helping the syndicate, but they have no intention of bringing him into the "family."

Walter Hill's *Last Man Standing* (1996) illustrates another version of the gangster saga concerning two rival gangs and their attempts to take over a town. The film is an American version of Akira Kurosawa's *Yojimbo* (1961), which in turn owes a significant debt to Dashiell Hammett's 1929 novel *Red Harvest*. In Hill's version, the West Texas town of Jericho is the site for rival bootleggers in the 1930s, who are vying for control of the flow of illegal liquor from Mexico. Both gangs represent immigrant factions—the Italians are the Strozzi gang, and the Irish are the Doyle mob. An amoral loner, John Smith (Bruce Willis), enters the fray and begins playing each side against the other, in an attempt to profit from each. This entrepreneurial effort leaves an abundant body count in its wake. *Last Man Standing* contains all the trappings and icons of the classic gangster films of the thirties, but it fails to engender any sympathy for its characters, and instead becomes little more than a series of violent set pieces, something that director Hill is extremely adept at staging. Perhaps Hill should have attempted to make a film from *Red Harvest* itself (which has not been filmed to date); certainly this a novel that cries out for a filmic adaptation.

Donnie Brasco (1997) is an atypical character study of a minor gangster figure. Based on the experience of real-life FBI undercover agent Joseph D. Pistone, the film recounts Pistone's activities inside the Mafia from 1976 to 1981. During this time Pistone (a.k.a. Donnie Brasco) becomes the protégé of Lefty Ruggiero (Al Pacino in an uncharacteristic, yet refreshingly low-key performance), a hit man who aspires to bigger and better things. Lefty hopes for advancement through the ranks of the mob, but Donnie must betray Lefty as a function of his assignment, which leads to Lefty's dismissal by the Mafia, and ultimately his death. One of the many interesting qualities of the film is its portrayal of Lefty's family life, particularly his relationship with his wife and his son, as well as his acceptance of Donnie as part of that family unit. Thus Donnie's betrayal of Lefty is even more powerful when the criminal bond between the two men is finally broken.

The caper or heist film was another crime subgenre of the 1990s. This genre, too, has a long history. Phil Hardy defines the caper film as those "dramas in which professional crooks plan and execute a clever, daring but ultimately unsuccessful robbery. Often the thieves fall out, or make one fatal error that leads to their arrest" (70). Likewise, Charles Derry states that "the genre is composed of all those works which emphasize the efforts of a diverse group of criminals to pool their talents, generally under the guidance of a father figure, in order to commit a perfect crime which requires split-second timing. Since the crime is a robbery, one might consider the virtual victim the actual location that is to be violated (such as the bank vault, the racetrack receipts truck, the armored car, etc.)" (59). One of most influential modern templates for contemporary films is John Huston's *The Asphalt Jungle* (1950), which almost single-handedly popularized the genre for the mainstream cinema. *The Asphalt Jungle* brings together a disparate variety of characters in an attempt to commit a perfect robbery, which, of course, fails. Sterling Hayden plays Dix Handley, a plug-ugly who just wants to survive in the criminal jungle; Louis Calhern is the corrupt attorney, Alonzo D. Emmerich, who becomes involved in the heist in a last-ditch attempt to stave off bankruptcy. Sam Jaffe's Doc Riedenschneider, one of the most memorable characters in the film, is the brains of the outfit, who puts the entire plan for the robbery into motion. None of the characters in the film trust each other, with the exception of Doc and Dix, who form a strange symbiotic relationship as *The Asphalt Jungle* grinds toward its resolutely downbeat conclusion. The robbery itself, of course, ends in disaster, but director

Huston makes it clear that is the *personal* failings of these men that ultimately ensures their downfall. Other "caper" films that follow this formula include Richard Fleischer's *Armored Car Robbery* (1950), Stanley Kubrick's *The Killing* (1956), and Sam Peckinpah's *The Getaway* (1972). As with other genre crime films, one of the conventions of the caper film is the audience assumption that no matter what the plan, the heist will not succeed. The narrative in these films is generally quite linear and methodical, showing how the various members of the gang plan out and eventually commit the heist itself. The caper films of the 1990s experiment and play with these conventions, and continually stress the emphasis on character relationships within the genre, which often become more important than the crime being planned by the film's protagonists.

Quentin Tarantino's *Reservoir Dogs* (1992) utilizes a distinctly nonlinear narrative structure, in which flashbacks highlight moments of emphasis throughout the film. Tarantino does not allow the viewer to see the heist itself, but rather views the action *prior* to the event, and *after* the disastrous robbery attempt has taken place. The central characters, known only as Mr. White, Mr. Pink, Mr. Orange, Mr. Blue, and Mr. Brown in order to maintain their anonymity, become convinced that one of their number is an informer. Thus the film's narrative is essentially driven by the strained relationships between the characters, particularly that of Mr. White (Harvey Keitel) and Mr. Orange (Tim Roth). The audience is made aware of the fact that Mr. Orange is the undercover police operative during one of Tarantino's characteristic flashbacks. As with most generic gangster films, it is Mr. White's insistence on the reliability of Mr. Orange's character that leads to disaster. The mundane dialogue in the film evokes the banal life of the characters themselves, a characteristic that Tarantino was to further embellish in *Pulp Fiction*.

Michael Mann's 174-minute epic *Heat* (1995) is a combination heist film and police procedural, which highlights the relationship between criminal mastermind Neil McCauley (Robert De Niro) and detective Vincent Hanna (Al Pacino), who is investigating an armored car robbery. McCauley's crew of criminals specialize in high-tech professional jobs. Hanna becomes obsessed with bringing down McCauley. Verbal encounters between the two characters in the film ultimately reveal them to be complimentary types, although they function on different sides of the law, and embrace divergent codes of conduct. Neil's personal code is summed up in his oft-quoted dictum that one should "never have anything in your life that you can't walk out on in thirty seconds flat, if you spot the heat coming around the corner." When Neil forsakes this code, disaster inevitably follows. Hanna's code is equally obsessive and self-destructive, as he feels that "I gotta hold on to my angst. I preserve it because I need it. It keeps me sharp, on the edge, where I gotta be." Both maxims reflect the characters' unwillingness to open up, and commit to relationships that might prove long lasting. This dualistic formula is basic to many crime narratives—the relationship of the hunter and the hunted. In such a world, personalities cease to exist, and one's identity becomes wholly wrapped up in the chase. As Hanna confesses at one point in the film, "I am nothing but what I'm going after."

Another, somewhat more eccentric caper film is Barry Sonnenfeld's *Get Shorty* (1995), based on the novel by Elmore Leonard. John Travolta plays Chili Palmer, a loan shark, who goes to Las Vegas to track down a man who has faked his own death in order to avoid paying his debts. This leads to a confrontation with schlock filmmaker Harry Zimm (Gene Hackman), during which Chili pitches a film idea to Zimm, who becomes interested enough to collaborate on obtaining enough funds to back the project. The film directly equates Hollywood and filmmaking with the business of crime, as exemplified by the ease with which Chili is able to conduct business within the film community. Both industries rely on fear, greed, and intimidation in achieving results, and thus, by the film's end, Chili Palmer proves to be a "natural" as a Hollywood producer.

Many '90s crime films touched on the theme of corruption in high places. Public institutions, as well as persons of authority, were often targets of exposure to vice and corruption in the 1990s. Harold Becker's *City Hall* (1996) for example, dealt with corruption in big-city politics. Al Pacino played Mayor John Pappas as an over-the-top, Huey Long–type politician whose administration reveals itself to be rife with crime and corruption. Both Abel Ferrara's *Bad Lieutenant* (1992) and James Mangold's *Copland* (1997) are 1990s films that explore corruption and vice within law enforcement itself. These institutions prove to be as crime-ridden as the underworld itself. The figure of the corrupt law-enforcement officer, an icon of trust and public service, who is revealed to be a criminal, is a theme that appears again and again in classic and contemporary crime films. As another example of this subgenre, John Sayles *Lone Star* (1996) is a deconstructionist film whose multilayered texture reveals several versions of a series of events, centering around an investigation into the death of a corrupt and murderous sheriff of a Texas border town. The events surrounding the sheriff's initial disappearance and the discovery of his remains years later provide the skeletal plot of the film, whose deliberate pacing and style reveal the borderless boundaries between past and present, truth and fiction.

Alternative criminal viewpoints provided the subject matter for several '90s crime films. The drug subculture was well represented in the surrealistic British cult film *Trainspotting* (1996), directed by Danny Boyle. The film depicts the Edinburgh drug scene from the perspective of its users, and reveals the sordidly hilarious and contemptible lifestyles of heroin addicts in their day-to-day banal existence. The bleak fatalism of *Trainspotting* is best expressed in the words of the main character Mark Renton (Ewan McGregor) who confides to the audience, "I choose not to choose life. I choose something else. And the reasons? There are no reasons. Who needs reasons when you've got heroin?" *Trainspotting* is a brutal and often darkly hilarious film, which is at once despairing and triumphant in its celebration of a community of losers, united only in their quest for another fix, and the cash that will enable them to score.

Ernest R. Dickerson's *Bulletproof* (1996) provides an uneasy combination of the buddy crime/adventure film, although it is photographed with the style and panache one would expect of Spike Lee's former director of photography. In the style of Walter Hill's *48 Hours* (1982) and Richard Donner's *Lethal Weapon* (1987), the film is a showcase for two male stars. The two protagonists, Adam Sandler and Damon Wayans, both got their start in television comedy, and the film continually veers into slapstick at the least opportune moments. The mixture of comedy and police drama doesn't quite come off, and *Bulletproof* failed to connect with its intended audience.

The prison drama also had a brief resurgence in the mid-'90s, with films such as Frank Darabont's *The Shawshank Redemption* (1994), *Dead Man Walking* (1995), and Marc Rocco's *Murder in the First* (1995). Like the gangster film of the early 1930s, the prison film was a response to topical events in newspaper headlines. American penal-reform issues were first opened up in this century during the early 1930s, due to prison riots in Dannemora and Auburn during the summer of 1929, and the resultant generic response, the prison film, is a sporadic subgenre extending from films such as George W. Hill's *The Big House* (1930) to John Frankenheimer's *The Birdman of Alcatraz* (1962). The basic themes explored in this subgenre are the need for prison reform, and the inherent corruption of the penal institution itself.

Dead Man Walking, for example, explores the issue of death-penalty ethics. The film, based on the memoirs of Sister Helen Prejean, revolves around the efforts of a nun, Sister Helen (Susan Sarandon), who tries to appeal the death sentence of Matthew Poncelet (Sean Penn), a convicted killer awaiting execution. The sister truly believes that all men are redeemable. The film hinges not on the issue of guilt, but on the hope of redemption. The film is thus both sentimental and rather calculating in its relationship to the audience. Indeed, both *The Shawshank Redemption* and *Murder in the First* respond to the traditional conventions of the prison film by addressing issues within a nostalgic framework, thus reassuring audiences that what they are seeing is a reflection of a different time and place.

The thriller, unlike the crime film, seeks to create an emotional response on the part of the viewer due to the element of suspense inherent in the genre. According to Charles Derry, two of the most salient characteristics of the suspense thriller are that it is a "genre which uses thrills— which are on one level a simple depiction of danger and violence, and on a second level a vicarious psychological experience" and it is a genre that uses suspense not only as a "simple structural device" but as a psychological "device which directly engages the spectator by causing anxiety" (19). This use of suspense is what distinguishes the thriller from crime films previously cited in this essay. Films such as Jonathan Demme's *Silence of the Lambs* (1991), Danny Boyle's *Shallow Grave* (1994), Jeremiah Chechik's *Diabolique* (1996), and Brian Gibson's *The Juror* (1996) are concerned with the manipulation of suspense and the emotional response of the viewer. A subgenre of the psychological thriller is the serial-killer film, which became increasingly popular as a cinematic staple in the 1990s. The serial-killer film deals almost exclusively with the pursuit of a serial killer whose motivations remain unclear throughout the film. The term "serial killer" was first coined in 1978 by FBI agent Robert Ressler in order to distinguish "the growing number of sexually motivated repeat killers from mass murderers who kill for profit" (Hardy 297). Although several films have dealt with serial killers in the past, most notably Alfred Hitchcock's *Psycho* (1960), which can be seen as the progenitor of the subgenre, and Richard Fleischer's *The Boston Strangler* (1968) based on Gerold Franks's book concerning the murderer Albert De Salvo, filmmakers in the '90s generally portrayed the serial killer in a far more compassionate light. The treatment of the character of Hannibal Lector (Anthony Hopkins) in *Silence of the Lambs* provides the best example. Although he is seen throughout the film as unspeakably evil and depraved, the film's narrative structure goes so far as to allow Hannibal to escape unharmed at film's end, promising future killings to agent Clarice Starling (Jodie Foster), who has been interviewing him throughout the film to extract information on the activities of yet another psychopathic killer.

Crime films and crime thrillers of the 1990s rejuvenated the genre by responding to sources responsible for the genre's origins in pulp literature and popular literature, as well as to journalistic sources in the press, magazines, and television. Violence, as a way of life, is indigenous to the crime genre. And it is the covert culture of violence, as it is presented not only in the crime film, but in other arts as well, that allows a society to address both its cultural past and its present. What form the crime film will take in the coming century is open to debate, but one can assume that many of the same generic derivations discussed here will find new life in the decades to come, where they will continue to entertain and thrill audiences in the next millennium.

WORKS CITED

Alloway, Lawrence. *Violent America: The Movies 1946–1964.* New York: Museum of Modern Art, 1971.

Brode, Douglas. *Money, Women, and Guns: Crime Movies from Bonnie and Clyde to the Present.* New York: Citadel Press, 1995.

Clarens, Carlos. *Crime Movies: An Illustrated History.* New York: W.W. Norton, 1980.

Derry, Charles. *The Suspense Thriller: Films in the Shadow of Alfred Hitchcock.* Jefferson, N.C.: McFarland & Company, 1988.

Hardy, Phil. *BFI Companion to Crime.* Berkeley: University of California Press, 1997.

Ruth, David E. *Inventing the Public Enemy: The Gangster in American Culture, 1918–1934.* Chicago: University of Chicago Press, 1996.

Silver, Alain, and James Ursini. *Film Noir Reader.* New York: Limelight Editions, 1996.

Warshow, Robert. *The Immediate Experience.* Garden City, N.Y.: Doubleday, 1962.

Woods, Paul A. *King Pulp: The World of Quentin Tarantino.* New York: Thunder's Mouth Press, 1996.

CHAPTER TEN

Action Films: The Serious, the Ironic, the Postmodern

JAMES M. WELSH

They are usually big and often brainless and they are extraordinarily popular. They may or may not constitute a genre, though a case can certainly be made for a particular variant, the action-adventure film. Action films fall into at least two larger categories: pure action and action-adventure. The former usually involves a minimal plot leading to some impending disaster or catastrophe that will introduce spectacular special effects constituting the film's major selling point; the latter involves a rather more complicated plot involving more flamboyant and colorful characters, malignant villainy, dastardly deeds, and larger-than-life characters who will ultimately save the day. Action-adventure comes closer toward meeting the definition of a film genre that requires a recognizable iconography, coded characters designed to respond to dangerous situations in predictable ways, and clearly defined formula filmmaking. Pure action movies are more broadly defined. But in the postmodern 1990s the genre was still evolving.

Jan De Bont's *Twister* (1996), for example, scripted by Michael Crichton and his wife, Anne-Marie Martin, is a good example of the pure-action spectacle. The plot involves two competing groups of "scientific" thrill seekers who chase tornadoes and are chased by them. Bill

Harding (Bill Paxton) and his wife Jo (Helen Hunt) are about to be divorced, mainly because Bill intends to pursue a boring career as a television weatherman and marry his therapist, Melissa (Jami Gertz). The competing group, headed by Dr. Jonas Miller, has state-of-the-art, corporate-funded technology and are profit seekers, in comparison to Harding's ragtag university team of idealists who are driven only by scientific curiosity to unlock the mysteries of weather prediction for the benefit of humankind. *Twister* grossed over $240 million at the box office and therefore was nominated for two Academy Awards for Best Visual Effects and Best Sound. It sucked thrill-seeking viewers into its awesome spectacle, but it was certainly disappointing in terms of human drama. The backstory of Jo's childhood tornado-trauma, a storm that killed her father, is the picture's most touching episode, but this constitutes little more than sentimental manipulation.

James Cameron's *Titanic* (1997) was a far better and more successful variation on the disaster motif than *Twister* because it devoted far more time and attention to character development. The film begins as a sort of documentary. The historical facts are established. The "unsinkable" *Titanic*, sailing from England to the United States under Captain Edward Smith, spotted an iceberg in the North Atlantic at 11:40 p.m. on April 14, 1912, collided with it, and sent out its first distress call shortly after midnight. The ship carried only enough lifeboats to accommodate about half of the passengers, and fifteen hundred people perished. In 1986 Robert Ballard and Martin Bowen rediscovered the *Titanic*, seventy-four years after it had sunk, using an ARVIN submarine and a robot camera. The film begins with a fictional replication of these excavating efforts. The approach seems "authentic" and "realistic."

Writer-director Cameron used the sinking of the *Titanic* as a backdrop for his main story, involving the romance between socialite Rose DeWitt Bukater (Kate Winslet), engaged to marry the arrogant, controlling, and possessive Cal Hockley (Billy Zane) , and the poor but artistic and sensitive Jack Dawson (Leonardo DiCaprio). Trapped in an arranged-marriage engagement, desperately unhappy Rose is saved from a half-hearted suicide attempt by Jack, who wins her heart. Rose plans to elope with Jack when the ship docks, but, since they are on board the *Titanic*, disaster intervenes. She is fated to be rescued, while he perishes, after saving her life as the ship sinks ever so slowly after striking the iceburg. This is obviously Rose's story, as the film makes clear from its framing apparatus, involving treasure hunters excavating the sunken *Titanic* years later in search of a fabulous lost diamond called "The Heart of the Ocean," a jewel old Rose has kept all these years, and pitches into the sea at the end of the film as a tribute to Jack.

Cameron's *Titanic* was the most expensive film ever made and certainly qualifies as an action-disaster picture, but it became a huge international hit and swept the Academy Awards in 1997 (including Best Picture and Best Director) because it was character-driven and not simply because of its impressive action spectacle. Cameron's *Titanic* gamble raised the stakes for blockbuster epic filmmaking to unprecedented budget levels (over $200 million) and demonstrated that huge initial investments of cash and resources could reap unprecedented returns at the box office ($554 million by May of 1988), while also demonstrating that a three-hour film could be immensely popular. Of course, such a long film could be shown fewer times during the day, but abroad, in Romania, for example, the price of admission was doubled to compensate for the more limited number of screenings possible.

Many of the biggest and most popular films of the 1990s fall into the action-adventure category, starting with *Jurassic Park* (1993), adapted by David Koepp and Michael Crichton from his own bestselling novel, an adventure story about cloned dinosaurs running amok, disguised as a cautionary fable about presumptive science and the potential danger of fooling with Mother Nature, and directed with aplomb and splendid special effects by Steven Spielberg. Jeff Goldblum's character, mathematician Ian Malcolm, makes the point in the film that nature is unpredictable, but, of course, this Spielberg monster movie is not primarily concerned with the moral and ethical issues of DNA experimentation.

This monster-movie blockbuster begins with the discovery of the remains of a poisonous lizard that has attacked people and is suspected of being a sort of dinosaur. Whereas the novel was mainly a cautionary allegory that updated the Frankenstein motif, Spielberg's film is more concerned with the spectacle of dinosaurs running loose than with the dangers of cloning them. The characters of the film are altered somewhat from their original design, especially Dr. John Hammond, an eccentric billionaire whose insane notion it is to create "Jurassic Park" as a theme park on an isolated island off the coast of Costa Rica, combining the Disneyworld approach with genetically cloned dinosaurs. In the novel, Hammond was a merely a mad scientist and a raving egomaniac who was eaten by chicken-sized dinosaurs and deserved to be; in the film he is a sweet, slightly befuddled, grandfatherly old gentleman (Richard Attenborough) who deserves to be spared, and is. The film was a tribute to technological wizardry that overpowered the characterizations of scientists Alan Grant (Sam Neill) and Ellie Sattler (Laura Dern), whose function is to be victimized. The film was enormously successful, the highest-grossing film to date, with earnings of over $800 million worldwide.

Action-adventure movies could be considered a director's genre that depends on the talents of a number of specialists. *Superman: The Movie* (1978), for example, was Richard Donner's first major hit, followed by the hugely successful *Lethal Weapon* series that spawned three sequels during the 1990s. Other talents include the cult sensation John Woo, who was born in China but made his reputation in Hong Kong, starting in 1975 and covering twenty-two films, including *The Killer* (1989), featuring the actor Chow Yung-Fat as a hit man coerced into doing one last job, and *Bullet in the Head* (1990); his American debut picture was *Hard Target* (1993), with Jean-Claude Van Damme, followed by *Broken Arrow* (1996) and *Face/Off* (1997). Tony Scott became a box-office sensation with *Top Gun* (1986), followed by *True Romance* (1993, based on a Quentin Tarantino script) and the nuclear-submarine thriller *Crimson Tide* (1995). James Cameron, born in Ontario, first made his mark as an action director with *The Terminator* (1984), followed by *Aliens* (1986), The *Abyss* (1989), *Terminator 2: Judgment Day* (1991), and his biggest project to date, *Titanic* (1997).

Certainly, it takes a competent filmmaker to make an effective action-adventure film, and a case could be made for John Woo or Richard Donner as action auteurs; but the role of the producer might be considered even more important, as demonstrated by the highly lucrative James Bond series, starting with *Dr. No*, produced by Harry Saltzman and Albert R. Broccoli in 1962. In 1975 Saltzman cashed in his Bonds after a fifteen-year partnership, but Albert "Cubby" Broccoli carried on the Bond formula, the style, and the tradition for another twenty years. Actors playing Bond would come and go over the years. Sean Connery defined the screen character in the first five films; he was followed by George Lazenby, who was soon replaced by Roger Moore, who played Agent 007 in thirteen films before the mantle passed to Timothy Dalton for two films, then to Pierce Brosnan, the Bond of the 1990s. Directors such as Terence Young, who started the series, Guy Hamilton, and Lewis Gilbert, would vary, but the influence of Broccoli as the producer of these entertainments remained constant.

After Broccoli's death in 1996 and after the end of the Cold War, the future became uncertain. *GoldenEye* (1995), named for writer Ian

Fleming's Jamaican cottage rather than for any actual Bond novel, introduced Pierce Brosnan as Bond gave New Zealander Martin Campbell his first action directorial assignment. *Tomorrow Never Dies* (1997), directed by Roger Spottiswoode also starred Pierce Brosnan as Bond. Both films were produced by Michael G. Wilson and Barbara Broccoli. Could the series keep going after thirty-five years? *GoldenEye*, the first Eon Productions Bond film produced without "Cubby" Broccoli, grossed $350 million worldwide. *Tomorrow Never Dies* initially grossed $73 million and was likely to gross over $200 million worldwide, which would seem to indicate that gadgetry never dies. The Bond pictures have been critic-proof genre vehicles and remain popular.

Another influential producer, Gene Roddenberry, created and shaped the *Star Trek* formula, which, although belonging to science fiction, also involved action-adventure. After developing the space opera for television, Roddenberry later was able to bridge the media gap to the large screen with *Star Trek: The Motion Picture* (1979), under the able direction of Hollywood veteran Robert Wise, a film primarily designed to appeal to Trekkies long deprived of their favorite series. The *Star Trek* series sustained itself through five sequels into the 1990s with *Star Trek VI: The Undiscovered Country* (1991), directed by Nicholas Meyer, but whether the series could survive after the death of Gene Roddenberry and the aging of the *Enterprise* crew seemed less certain. As will be demonstrated, the action-adventure genre should be considered a producer's medium, if one considers the blockbuster hits of that genre.

Action-adventure pictures are about money, investing huge budgets in order to realize huge returns if the product is successful. The producer is the gambler whose job it is to hedge the bets. The producer will naturally have the authority to assign directors and to cast oversized talents for these oversized pictures in order to assure box-office drawing power. Modifications to the original concept are not uncommon. For example, *The Negotiator* (1998) was originally designed as a Sylvester Stallone vehicle, but Samuel L. Jackson ended up in the Stallone role opposite Kevin Spacey in the finished film. Likewise, *The Mask of Zorro* (1998) originally was to have starred Sean Connery and Andy Garcia under the direction of Roberto Rodriguez, but the completed film was directed by Martin Campbell and starred Anthony Hopkins and Antonio Banderas. Regardless, star power drives the genre.

It would be difficult, for example, to imagine how the *Lethal Weapon* series might have worked without the talents of Mel Gibson and

Danny Glover, or *The Terminator* series without Arnold Schwarzenegger, or the *Die Hard* series without Bruce Willis. *Die Hard* (1988), and *Die Hard with a Vengeance* (1995) were directed by John McTiernan; *Die Hard 2* (1990) was directed by Renny Harlin; but all three pictures had Bruce Willis in the lead, and all three were produced by Joel Silver, who developed the concept and whose signature imprint is on the series.

The action-adventure formula, fine-tuned and sophisticated by such directors as Richard Donner and Steven Spielberg during the 1980s was perfected after a fashion that set the style during the 1990s by producers Jerry Bruckheimer and his partner Don Simpson, who died of a drug overdose in 1996. Together they made hits such as *Beverly Hills Cop* (1984), *Top Gun* (1986), *Crimson Tide* (1995), *The Rock* (1996), and *Con Air* (1997) that were tremendously popular and created stars (Tom Cruise, Eddie Murphy, Nicolas Cage, and Will Smith, e.g.). Those pictures went on to generate huge profits—$335 million worldwide for *The Rock*, for example, and $222 million for *Con Air*. So when Jerry Bruckheimer mounted *Armageddon* (1998) on a budget of $140 million, with Disney willing to spend another $60 million to promote the picture, the film was designed as the biggest summer blockbuster of 1998.

The Bruckheimer-Simpson approach begins, then, with an oversized budget to support a picture that will be "high on concept" and "long on action," featuring "macho heroes backed by amped-up rock music," with "edge-of-your-seat special effects" to power the "breakneck pace" (Puig D1) Such pictures require competent directors capable of harnessing nervous intensity, such as Tony Scott or Michael Bay, who helmed *Armageddon*, but not necessarily auteurs, since the producer is calling the shots. Such films also require action heroes, of course, but Bruckheimer will also cast against type "for maximum effect," as he told Claudia Puig of *USA Today.* "Everyone has to be careful about not getting stale," he explained. "You see characters on the screen playing the same role many times either on television or in the movies. So you've got to keep changing it up because there is nothing new under the sun. It's all been done. It's how you change it, turn it on its ear" (Puig D2) In this way Nicolas Cage was transformed into a superstar action hero in *The Rock*. Bruce Willis led the cast of *Armageddon*, but Bruckheimer also factored in some surprises, such as Ben Affleck before he got recognition as the cowriter and costar of *Good Will Hunting*, one of the most highly regarded films of 1997. The freakish star of *Fargo* (1996), Steve Buscemi, is a part of the film's heroic A-Team, and Billy Bob Thornton, the creator of *Slingblade*

FIGURE 10.1. Destruction as spectacle in Michael Bay's *Armageddon*. Courtesy: Jerry Ohlinger Archive.

(1996), is cast against type as the scientist in charge of NASA.

The Bruckheimer approach has not always yielded spectacular results, as will be obvious if one remembers the Tom Cruise blunder *Days of Thunder* (1990), about redneck racing, with its idiotic romantic coupling of Cruise's race driver and a brain surgeon played by Nicole Kidman. But most of what Bruckheimer has touched has turned to gold, and he has a track record for making movies that are critic-proof. Reviewers heaped contempt on *Armageddon*, for example, ridiculing the scale, the self-importance, the sentimentality, and what Janet Maslin of *The New York Times* called the "jingoistic, overblown spectacle," of this action potboiler "with a nasty political agenda that takes cheap shots at Greenpeace, antin-uclear protesters, and an inept Russian Cosmonaut played by Peter Star-mare" (Maslin B1). But if Bruckheimer's boom-and-doom spectacle did not perform up to its expectations, it was not because of the stupidity and vulgarity of the script, but because of its massive budget and because its was the second asteroid movie of the summer season of 1998, following Mimi Leder's *Deep Impact*, which had a whole lot more to say about the human consequences of a catastrophe that could destroy the planet. *Armageddon* opened big, as it was expected to do, and earned nearly $100 million during its first two weeks, big returns, but not enough to cover its costs; by that time *Deep Impact* had earned nearly $138 million.

Genre vehicles are successful when they satisfy audience expecta-tions by following predictable formulas. But all genre pictures walk the line between predictability and variance, since eventually audiences begin to tire of similar stories told and retold in similar ways. As filmmakers attempt to integrate new ideas and characters and dilemmas, they risk the danger of tampering with the original formula, for if this is twisted too far and bent out of shape, the audience is also likely to be bent out of shape. Too much originality, then can be risky and dangerous, once a successful formula has been established. Theme and variation are essential but not *too* much variation, because as sequels are generated, the original concept will begin to break down. That is why some action series may fail after three to five sequels. Audiences will eventually tire of the cartoon villains of *Batman* (1989) or *Superman* (1978), for example, regardless of how flamboyantly they may be presented.

In the case of *Lethal Weapon*, on the other hand, which began in 1987 and was still being reworked eleven years later, there was a clear attempt to change and update the formula as the actors who played Roger Murtaugh and Martin Riggs grew older. As the fate of the *Star Trek* series gave evidence, it is difficult to follow action heroes into middle age and beyond, and changing the formula to accommodate a "new generation" can only cause problems as the older generation marches toward retirement. Richard Donner's solution in *Lethal Weapon 4* (1998) was to stress family values. Riggs becomes a father and Murtaugh becomes a grandfather at the end of the film, which could mark the end of the line for the series. If another sequel were to follow, Murtaugh could retire, moving Danny Glover into the background and replacing him with his hyperactive, motormouthed son-in-law played by Chris Rock, who might be in line to become Riggs's new partner, maintaining the black-white balance. But the Mel Gibson character could never return to its on-the-edge craziness that originally defined it. In the original *Lethal Weapon* Riggs was a whacked Vietnam veteran who was grieving the death of his wife, a man who would take impossible chances because he seemed not to care whether he lived or died. By marrying Lorna (Rene Russo) at the hospital just before she delivers his child, Riggs takes a giant step toward domesticity and in future sequels would have a reason for living, which would have to moderate his defining recklessness. Presumably the series will end with this sequel. If it is revived, it will have to be drastically redesigned.

Action-adventure spectacles are testosterone movies designed to match the interest of juvenile audiences—far-fetched, overstated, male-driven, often cartoonish, depending mainly on special-effects wizardry and hyped-up soundtracks. At best, such films are "movies"; at worst, they are products designed by committees of writers and armies of technicians with one goal in mind: building a bigger spectacle in order to generate millions of box-office dollars. They thrive on hyperbole intended to convince viewers that such movies must be seen because of the promised spectacle. They are formula films that might be considered genre vehicles populated by wild but predictable characters, laconic heroes sometime supported by prop partners, male or female, and designing, inhuman villains motivated by evil intent and a lust for power, always posing a threat to civilization or order. Catastrophic danger looms large and in the disaster scenario of the action-adventure genre can be inanimate—comets, meteors, asteroids, tornadoes, earthquakes, fires, or floods. In such scenarios the challenge is to save the planet or the country or one's neighbors from impending disaster, man-made or otherwise.

The iconography of the action-adventure thriller depends on massively budgeted production values. Settings are often borrowed from the film noir tradition involving an atmosphere of menace and a corrupt or corrupting city, past, present, or future. In addition the urban landscape provides freeways, highways, or waterways, providing opportunities for some manner of chase. Add to this images of demolition or destruction and the technology for sophisticated weaponry or explosive devices, digital ticking devices for time bombs or computers controlling doomsday devices.

Clearly, then, viewers know and understand what action-adventure movies involve: a tough, potentially brutal, sometimes cynical, often laconic, preferably muscular, oversized hero, an action-packed spectacle involving car chases (or some equivalent—motorcycles, boats, busses, trains, speed and recklessness being necessary to quicken the pace), explosive devices and demolition, impending disaster caused by either natural causes (fires, floods, earthquakes, meteors, tornadoes, hurricanes, and the like) or the evil machinations of wicked villains, terrorists, mad bombers, anarchists, power-hungry despots, or crime lords. The task is always to avert the disaster, disarm the bomb, control the situation, thwart the villain, and save the day. Such films depend largely on special effects and an army of stuntmen willing to take spectacular chances; these films are not usually character-driven, though the hero will probably be defined by distinctive idiosyncrasies and signature quirks, phobias, or phrases such as Clint Eastwood's "Go ahead, make my day," or Arnold Schwarzenegger's "Hasta la vista, baby," and "I'll be back," tag lines created by dialogue doctor William Wisher, who also worked on *Eraser* (1996).

Schwarzenegger is the perfect action hero. In *Eraser*, as Federal Marshal John Kruger, his specialty was making people disappear. He is in a familiar role as "protector" of Lee Cullen (Vanessa Williams), a problem witness who knows too much about a scheme devised by defense experts to sell top-secret weaponry to the Russian Mafia. The imagined technology arms Arnold with "rail guns," hyper-velocity weapons that fire aluminum rounds at just below the speed of light. The star's deadpan delivery is constantly amusing, and his stylization saves the film from being just another thriller. And that made *Eraser* a better film than *Mission: Impossible* (1996), which it resembled in its "MacGuffin" (its motivating gimmick), a computer disk with sensitive evidence that will incriminate highly placed government officials; *Mission: Impossible* took itself far too seriously.

One problem with defining the genre is that action films often interface with other genres—disaster films such as *Armageddon* and *Deep*

Impact, on the one hand, and Cameron's *Titanic*, on the other, ranging from natural disasters to man-made disasters, ecological, or nuclear, for example, science fiction (the *Terminator* series), espionage (the James Bond thrillers, or *Mission: Impossible* [1997]) and conspiracy, caper films, or detective and police-buddy movies—which makes it difficult to define them as clearly belonging to a single free-standing genre. The examples that follow may help to demonstrate the problem.

Costing up to $100 million to produce, *Terminator 2: Judgment Day* turned out to be *the* blockbuster of the summer of 1991. It was a sequel to James Cameron's first blockbuster, *The Terminator* (1984), in which a time-traveling cyborg had been sent back in time to murder Sarah Connor (Linda Hamilton) before she could give birth to the son who would one day lead human resistance against machines of the future; another cyborg Terminator (Arnold Schwarzenegger) was sent to protect her. In the sequel, another Terminator (Robert Patrick) is sent back to kill Sarah's son John while he is still a child, and Schwarzenegger's Terminator is also sent back to protect him. Cameron, who had cowritten the first film with Gale Anne Hurd, returned to direct and cowrite the sequel with William Wisher, and Gale Anne Hurd returned as executive producer. Together, they created an inventive sequel that in many respects could be considered superior to the original film.

Poor Sarah Connor has been in the looney bin since 1984 since her story about the cyborg Terminator from the future understandably sounded to doctors like a paranoid fantasy. She is unable to get released through regular channels, but when an improved model, a chrome-plated Terminator is sent back in time in order to murder her son John (Edward Furlong), she has a powerful motive for escaping. Fortunately for John, Schwarzenegger's Terminator is also sent back to protect him. Both Terminators have superior tracking skills and it's a race against time to see which one will reach John first. Both androids are improved models: Patrick's Terminator is an upgraded Model T-1000; Schwarzenegger's Terminator Model T-800 is a robot with a human exterior, reprogrammed to be a protector rather than an assassin. John and his protector rescue Mom from the insane asylum, then try to change the future by destroying the technology that will shape it. The design of this picture, offering a brutally tough mother determined to protect her child from a mysterious killing force, will remind some viewers of *Aliens* (1986), which was also written by the Canadian-born Cameron, and directed in his signature, unrelenting style.

According to David Sterritt, *Terminator 2* was "the most expensive picture in history" (Sterritt 10), setting a precedent for super-expensive budgets for future summer blockbusters. Cameron's track record, established by this film no doubt gave him bargaining power in budgeting *Titanic*, which set another record for over-the-top budgets. This was extraordinarily well-crafted escapist entertainment, but one might wonder, along with sensible David Sterritt, if the result is something twentieth-century civilization can or should be proud of. Stuart Klawans defended the film, however, by suggesting that Cameron "offers an education of the emotions," first by cranking up "the audience's desire for bloodshed," then by attempting to purge the audience of that desire "in the act of satisfying it" (Klawans 278). When John Connor orders the Protector to stop killing people, he maims them instead. By the end of the film, Schwarzenegger is destroying a great deal of property, "but the casualty count is zero" (Klawans 279); Klawans finds this reassuring, because, given the tremendous cost of producing such a movie, it "had *better* seem important." This is not the case with most summer blockbusters.

A more typically brainless futuristic action-adventure thriller is writer/director John Carpenter's *Escape from L.A.* (1996), a cult action/dystopian fantasy set in the near future (2013 is the year), with a demented backstory. An evangelical nazi (Cliff Robertson) was elected president in 1998 (which was not an election year, by the way), the story goes, and an earthquake in the year 2000 separated Los Angeles from the mainland. All manner of criminals, misfits, and undesirables have been transported there by the right-wing government. The president's daughter, laughably named Utopia (A. J. Langer), has somehow stolen her father's Doomsday Machine for Cuervo Jones (George Carraface), a Che Guevara–type revolutionary who rules over chaotic L.A. Renegade hero Snake Plissken (Kurt Russell), famous for his exploits in *Escape from New York* (1981), is ordered to "rescue" Utopia, but, in fact, the president mainly wants to recover his Doomsday Machine, and Snake's real mission is to kill Utopia. To seal the deal, the president has Snake infected with a virus that will destroy him if his mission fails. Snake gets help from a crazy surfer named Pipeline (Peter Fonda) and a transsexual named Hershe (Pam Grier). The style of this film is as scrambled as its crazy plot, alternating between self-conscious parody and heroic but unconvincing action-adventure.

The villains of Joel Schumacher's *Batman Forever* (1995), Harvey "Two-Face" Dent (Tommy Lee Jones) and E. Nigma, also known as the

Riddler (Jim Carrey) threatened to steal the show, though Carrey's Riddler was the more dynamic of the two. To keep the relationship between Bruce Wayne (Val Kilmer) and Robin (Chris O'Donnell) from looking too kinky, the script factored in criminal psychologist Chase Meridan (Nicole Kidman) as a heterosexual love interest for the Caped Crusader. Critics missed the "dark vision" of Tim Burton, who directed the first two Batman epics in his own eccentric way. In Schumacher's sequel Bob Kane's Dark Knight becomes dark lite, though reviewers agreed that Val Kilmer made a better Batman than Michael Keaton. The film set a box-office record (over $53 million) its opening weekend. The half-cocked story was saved by Carrey's antics and the tilt-a-whirl camera techniques. At least it had a sense of humor. Humor gave *Batman Forever* the edge over another comic-inspired epic, Tim Pope's *The Crow: City of Angels* (1996), a sequel to the 1994 film that starred Brandon Lee, derived from the popular James O'Barr comic books, a film that interfaced with gothic fantasy and film noir, dismissed by mainstream critics as an "occult junkyard" and a "stunningly awful sequel" (Welsh/Mulford 115).

The ultimate conspiracy film is Richard Donner's *Conspiracy Theory* (1997), in which Donner reinvented Martin Riggs from the *Lethal Weapon* series as the apparently paranoid Jerry Fletcher (Mel Gibson), a New York cabbie who thinks the government is out to get him, Jerry has a huge crush on a Justice Department lawyer (Julia Roberts), whom he seems to be stalking. As one reviewer noted, Gibson excels when "playing damaged goods" (Burr 75), and Jerry Fletcher is the sort of role Gibson was born to play. Donner knows how to channel his crazed, manic energy, once it becomes clear that the government *is* after Jerry because the conspiracy newsletter he publishes has touched sensitive material, and his half-dozen subscribers start turning up dead. In keeping with the genre, the plot is as schizoid and illogical as Fletcher himself, but the nonstop action is very well orchestrated. On the other hand, John Woo's *Broken Arrow* (1996) was a disappointment, given its star actors, Christian Slater and John Travolta. It was helmed by the cult Hong Kong action director John Woo, but hampered by a mediocre screenplay by Graham Yost, who struck box-office gold with *Speed* (1994), a nonstop action picture about a bomb chasing a bus, directed by Jan DeBont. Woo made his Hollywood debut directing Jean-Claude Van Damme in *Hard Target* (1993), but was disappointed to learn that he would not control the final-cut privileges he had been used to in Hong Kong. At least he was able to negotiate more control for *Broken Arrow*.

"Broken Arrow" is military jargon for a lost nuclear weapon. In this fast-paced, stylishly goofy movie, hot pilot Major Vic Deakins (John Travolta) intends to steal two nuclear bombs. His hotshot copilot, Captain Riley Hale (Christian Slater), intends to stop him before Vic can blackmail the government out of $250 million. The plot hangs on the conflict between these two hotshots duking it out, first in the boxing ring, then in the cockpit of their B-1 Stealth Bomber, then in a coppermine, then on a freight train headed for Denver—duking it out, then nuking it out. The plot ought to work better than it does.

The two are assigned to fly a night mission over the desert with armed nuclear bombs. Deakins ejects his copilot, releases the bombs that parachute harmlessly to earth, then ejects himself and ditches his plane. A gang of cohorts is waiting to truck the bombs away, but his copilot keeps turning up to complicate things and keep the plot rolling. Riley is unable to face these killer terrorists on his own, so the screenplay gives him an unlikely sidekick, plucky park ranger Terry Carmichael (Samantha Mathis), who is miscast as an action heroine. An American director might have sensed the problem, but Woo, who has a knack for filming spectacular action sequences, seems not to notice. Slater is competent as the hero but not very charismatic in comparison to the flamboyant, smart-alec, psycho villain played by Travolta. The film offers some eye-catching stunts but makes little sense, though it does capture some typical Woo themes: betrayal, friendship, abandoned honor, and lost loyalty (Buehrer 67).

In 1997 Travolta joined forces with Woo again for *Face/Off* to play FBI agent Sean Archer against Nicolas Cage as terrorist-assassin Castor Troy, his evil twin, who is captured and wounded in an airport face-off. But Castor has planted a bomb in Los Angeles timed to explode within seventy-two hours, releasing chemical nerve gas that will kill millions. In order to discover where the bomb is planted, Sean assumes Castor's identity through ghastly plastic surgery that takes Castor's "face off." Castor later awakens and forces the surgeon to give him Sean's face, then kills the doctor and torches the clinic. Each actor is therefore forced to assume the other's identity, style, and mannerisms. Thanks to an all-too-speedy recovery, Castor (as Sean) manages to get his mythic brother Pollux (Alessandro Nivola), an explosives expert who has been captured, released from the prison where Sean (as Castor) has gone in disguise to get information about the bomb. After the switch, Cage has the larger challenge, playing the tortured Archer, trapped in Troy's body, wearing the face of the man he hates most, and knowing that his mortal enemy is sleeping with his wife, who does not seem to notice the difference, except that she finds him more romantic and sexually active than he used to be.

The screenplay by Micke Werb and Michael Colleary is pretty far-fetched and as over the top as Woo's direction, but the talent is impressive and the film was favorably reviewed as Woo's best American effort to date. Reviewing this film for *The New Yorker*, Terrence Rafferty puzzled over the absurdity of the plot and concluded that "credibility has ceased to be any kind of criterion for this genre, that audiences expected comedy as much as suspense, and that the best action movies are those that excel in the ingenuity and the audacity of their effects" (Rafferty 84). Thus *Face/Off*, directed by a master antic stylist of action filmmaking, "is a giddy, violent live-action cartoon" that owes more to Chuck Jones and Buster Keaton than to Steven Spielberg or Alfred Hitchcock. The film succeeds *because* the plot is absurd and the acting overstated, not despite it.

Of course, Rafferty is on target here. John Woo and Jackie Chan helped to set the high comic style that slowly insinuated itself into Hollywood filmmaking. It began to surface at least as early as the Bruce Willis caper film *Hudson Hawk* (1991), then become dominant during the 1990s in such pictures as Arnold Schwarzenegger's *Last Action Hero* (1993), directed by John McTiernan, featuring at one point in a fantasy sequence Arnold playing Hamlet in black-and-white, transforming the Dane into something he never could be, an action hero. Nicolas Cage is the perfect postmodern action hero, an ironic antihero who becomes heroic despite his nature. His brilliance is the mechanism that drives *Con Air* (1997) and Brian DePalma's *Snake Eyes* (1998). And therein lies the future of action/adventure filmmaking. Audiences may eventually tire of endless car chases and explosive potboilers, but not of the antics of Jackie Chan or the humorous stylings of Schwarzenegger or Cage or Gibson. Such trend modifications will persist in the postmodern era, setting new expectations for action amusement.

WORKS CITED

Brosnan, John. *James Bond in the Cinema*. 2nd ed. San Diego, Calif.: A. S. Barnes, 1981.

Buehrer, Beverley Bare. *Broken Arrow. Magill's Cinema Annual 1997*. Ed. Beth A. Fhaner. Detroit: Gale Research Press/VideoHound Reference, 1997. 67–68.

Burr, Ty. "Mel-adjusted." *Entertainment Weekly* 413 (January 9, 1998): 75–76.

Klawans, Stuart. "Summer Celluloid Meltdown II: The Sequel." *The Nation* (September 9, 1991): 276–79.

Maslin, Janet. "Henny Penny Gets the President's Ear." *The New York Times* (July 1, 1998): B1, B6.

Puig, Claudia. "The Bruckheimer Touch." *USA Today* (July 1, 1998): D1, D2.

Rafferty, Terrence. "Self-Reflections." *The New Yorker* (July 14, 1997): 84–85.

Sterritt, David. "Sci-Fi Movies Kick into Gear." *The Christian Science Monitor* (July 5, 1998): 10.

Welsh, James M., and Liz Mulford. *The Crow: City of Angels. Magill's Cinema Annual 1997.* Ed. Beth A. Fhaner. Detroit: Gale Research Press/Video-Hound Reference, 1998. 113–15.

CHAPTER ELEVEN

◨

Children's Films in the 1990s

HEATHER ADDISON

What, in the late 1990s, constitutes a children's film? Essentially, it is a film made by adults for children, a film that "deal[s] with the interests, fears, misapprehensions and concerns of children in their own terms" (Bazalgette and Staples 96). (Here, a "child" is anyone age twelve or under.) In the United States, most children's films are actually family films that are intended to appeal to adults as well as to children. According to Cary Bazalgette and Terry Staples,

> In a family movie, there normally have to be well-known adult stars to help bring in the audience. . . . Naturally, the producer wants to get full value out of an expensive star, so the part has to be a meaty one, with commensurate production values. The focus therefore tends to be on the problems of coping with kids. Such problems, big or small, are often presented in adult terms and in ways that are inaccessible to children. (95)

Examples of such inaccessibility are widespread. In the G-rated *Muppet Treasure Island* (1996), for instance, Benjamina Gunn (Miss Piggy) greets the pirate Long John Silver (Tim Curry), a former boyfriend, by exclaiming, "Well, hello, Loooooong John!" and flashing him a coy look. Bazalgette and Staples cite a scene from *Home Alone 2: Lost in New York*

177

(1992). Ten-year-old Kevin (Macauley Culkin) is told to put on his tie in preparation for a Christmas pageant. "My tie's in the bathroom. I can't go in there," Kevin tells his father, "because Uncle Frank is taking a shower. He says if I walked in there and saw him naked, I'd grow up never feeling like a real man—whatever that means." "In short," say Bazalgette and Staples, "the overall viewpoint of a family film is summed up by the title *Honey, I Shrunk the Kids*, whereas in a children's film it would be *Sis, Dad Shrunk Us*" (96).

In this chapter the term "family film" will refer to any Hollywood film whose plot, characters, and style are intended to appeal to children under the age of approximately twelve years. Generally, this includes all G- and PG-rated animated features and all G- and PG-rated live-action features with child protagonists. The adult appeal of such films ranges from the slight to the substantial, but because children constitute the core target audience of family films, adult material complements rather than excludes or replaces the material intended to appeal to children.

The second major question confronting a discussion of family films is whether or not they constitute a film genre. In his classic study on film genres, *Hollywood Genres: Formulas, Filmmaking, and the Studio System*, Thomas Schatz defines a film genre as a system of rules, a "tacit 'contract' between filmmakers and audience," whose fundamental structural components (plot, character, setting, thematics, style, etc.) address basic social conflicts (16). *Genres of order* involve physical and ideological struggle in a contested environment/space (examples: westerns, war films), while *genres of integration* involve conflicts of values between characters who inhabit an ideologically stable setting (examples: musicals, family melodramas; 26). It can be argued that the label "1990s American family films" applies not to a specific genre but to a broad category of films intended to appeal to children. Within this category, there are at least four distinct genres: the musical, the rite of passage film, the buddy film, and the sports film.

Family-film musicals consist mostly of animated Disney films. The mise-en-scène of such films varies, but their exuberant lyrics and dance help them convey a "utopian" attitude. Musicals are a genre of integration; protagonists must confront social and familial tradition and find their place within it. To a great degree, Disney musicals pattern themselves after Hollywood musicals of the 1930s–1960s, although they have specific characteristics of their own, such as mischievous incidental characters. Disney's 1990s animated musical renaissance is often said to have begun with 1988's *Oliver and Company*. Disney musicals of the 1990s include *Beauty and the Beast* (1991), *Aladdin* (1992), *The Muppet Christmas Carol* (1992), *The Lion King* (1994), *Pocahontas* (1995), *The Hunchback of Notre Dame* (1996), *Muppet Treasure Island* (1996), *James and the Giant Peach* (1996) and *Hercules* (1997). Non-Disney animated musicals include such films as *All Dogs Go to Heaven* (1989) and *All Dogs Go to Heaven II* (1996).

Interestingly, though Hollywood musicals foreground heterosexual happiness and marriage, such is *not* the case in many family-film musicals of the 1990s. Only in Disney fairy-tale films is romance the central focus of the narrative. *Beauty and the Beast* (1991, dir. Gary Trousdale and Kirk Wise), for example, follows the romantic tradition of such classics as *Snow White* (1937), *Cinderella* (1950), and *Sleeping Beauty* (1959). Each thread of the narrative is a part of the tapestry that eventually unites Belle (voice by Paige O'Hara) and the Beast (voice by Robby Benson). In contrast, *Pocahontas* (1995, dir. Mike Gabriel and Eric Goldberg) and *The Hunchback of Notre Dame* (1996, dir. Gary Trousdale and Kirk Wise) are "message" films. Though both offer romance, they also attempt to convey the arbitrariness and cruelty of prejudice. *Pocahontas* was inspired by the true tale of a young Algonquin girl who saved the life of seventeenth-century English soldier John Smith. Disney's Pocahontas (voice by Irene Bedard), who has been aged to her early twenties, intercedes when her father, Chief Powhatan (voice by Russell Means) is about to execute Captain John Smith, an Englishman with whom she has fallen in love. The film is a homage to a kind of prelapsarian Indian life, a life that is compromised when a shipload of Englishmen led by a greedy, manipulative governor arrives with the intent of "improving" the land (and finding gold). As Betsey Sharkey notes in "Beyond Tepees and Totem Poles":

> A core difficulty studios face today is how to create animated characters without using stereotypes that will offend. . . . British males seem to be one of the few safe villains in these politically correct times. . . . "Nowadays the ultimate villain . . . would be a fat, white male terrorist who ran a Fortune 500 company on the side," says Terry Rossio, a Disney screenwriter. (1, 22)

In *The Hunchback of Notre Dame*, as well, the only thoroughly evil character is a white male—Minister Frollo (voice by Tony Jay). Based on Victor Hugo's novel *Notre Dame de Paris*, *Hunchback* is a sophisticated animated film that questions the nature of religious hypocrisy, prejudice, cruelty, beauty, and ugliness in subtle, yet intense terms. Quasimodo (voice by Tom Hulce) is a hunchback raised by Minister Frollo, a physically withered but powerful man whose life is defined by his hatred of gypsies. Quasimodo yearns for the beautiful gypsy girl Esmeralda (voice by Demi Moore), but she falls in love with the attractive, golden-haired Phoebus (voice by Kevin Kline). *Hunchback* offers a multi-layered treatment of difficult issues that will be most fully appreciated by adults. For example, adults can recognize Minister Frollo's lust for Esmeralda as particularly ironic, given his role in the church and his supposed "disgust" for gypsies.

Aladdin (1992, dir. John Musker and Ron Clements) and *Hercules* (1997, dir. John Musker and Ron Clements) avoid the somber messages of *Pocahontas* and *The Hunchback of Notre Dame*. Loaded with zany characters and hip popular-culture references, these are self-reflexive Disney musicals, providing evidence for the "baroque" phase of a genre's development (Schatz 37–38). In *Hercules*, for example, Disney comments on its own hucksterism. In what Janet Maslin describes as "happily bastardized mythology" ("Hero" 1) the film follows Hercules' (Tate Donovan's) attempts to prove himself a hero so he can be readmitted to Olympus. After Hercules kills a many-headed hydra in the city of Thebes, he is acclaimed as a hero. Five Muses sing "Zero to Hero" in girl-group Gospel style while we see a montage of the perks of fame. Hercules does a commercial for the "Grecian Express" charge card; he produces a "Buns of Bronze" workout scroll; and his name is featured on "Air-Herc" sandals.

Though *Hercules* features a romantic coupling when Hercules eventually foregoes his status as a god to be with Megara, the woman with whom he has fallen in love, their romance plays a marginal role in most of the film. Indeed, the 1990s might be characterized as the decade of romantic decline for family-film musicals. In addition to the dilution of romantic focus in those films that *do* conclude with a "heterosexual clinch," a significant portion of family-film musicals offer nonromantic conflicts. Such musicals still involve social integration, however, as characters develop affection or respect for others and find their place in the social order.

Family-film musicals adapted from novels are nonromantic films, presumably because novels involving romance are considered too "adult" to adapt for children. In *Oliver and Company* (1988, dir. George Scribner), inspired by Dickens's novel *Oliver Twist*, orphaned kitty Oliver (voice by Joey Lawrence) searches for a home in New York City. He is taken in by the scruffy Fagin (voice by Dom DeLuise), whose larcenous canine gang, led by the streetwise Dodger (voice by Billy Joel), tries to help him pay his debt to the sinister Mr. Sykes (voice by Robert Loggia). In this "Disneyfied" version of Dickens's story, Fagin is a sweet man who is down on his luck instead of a self-interested criminal who exploits children. The film emphasizes the importance of family; Oliver finds his with a little girl named Jenny (voice by Natalie Gregory), while Dodger and his pals find theirs with Fagin.

Oliver and Company presents its story in a simple, straightforward fashion, avoiding pop-culture allusions or sexual innuendo intended for adults. Another musical that is admirable in this and many other regards is *James and the Giant Peach* (1996, dir. Henry Selick), an adaptation of a Roald Dahl novel of the same name. Incorporating live action as well as 3-D stop-motion and 2-D animation (during a dream sequence), *James and the Giant Peach* creates a striking storybook world in 1940s England and New York City. James (Paul Terry) and his parents have plans to go to New York City, but before that can happen his parents are killed by a rhinoceros and he is sent to live with his cruel aunts, the skeletal Spiker (Joanna Lumley) and the rotund Sponge (Miriam Margolyes). One day, a peddler (Pete Postlethwaite) gives James a bag of green crocodile tongues that cause a giant peach to grow. James burrows inside, where he meets a group of insects who have been magically enlarged. Together, they embark on a journey to New York, battling a fierce mechanical shark and skeletal pirates along the way. Like *Oliver and Company*, *James and the Giant Peach* foregrounds the development of familial bonds. James has no family other than his despicable aunts; the personable bugs he meets inside the magical peach comfort and inspire him and eventually become his adopted family.

The *Muppet Christmas Carol* (1992) and *Muppet Treasure Island* (1996) are also based on classic novels: Charles Dickens's *A Christmas Carol* and Robert Louis Stevenson's *Treasure Island*. Both films were directed by Brian Henson, son of Jim Henson, whose productions have been praised as a direct challenge to the "hegemony" of Disney storytelling (Zipes 112). Though Henson Productions now distributes their films under the Disney name, *The Muppet Christmas Carol* and *Muppet Treasure Island* continue the tradition of using the "Muppet" puppets to create challenging, amusing narratives. *The Muppet Christmas Carol* stars Michael Caine as Ebenezer Scrooge, Kermit the Frog as Bob Cratchit, and

Miss Piggy as his wife Emily. Dickens's tale about the redemption of a selfish man is secondary to the film's central focus on the constructed nature of storytelling. The Great Gonzo narrates, claiming to be Charles Dickens. His sidekick, Rizzo the Rat, is skeptical: "A blue, furry Charles Dickens who hangs out with a rat?" he asks. "Absolutely!" says Gonzo. *Muppet Treasure Island* offers more of the same. When a pirate character dies from an apparent heart attack, Rizzo the Rat cries, "He died?! And this is supposed to be a kids' movie!" At the end of the film, when all of the pirates have been imprisoned, one of them moralizes, "I feel better about myself and I believe I have learned a valuable lesson." The other pirates groan and start hitting him. This is the charm as well as the strength of these Muppet films: they create participatory narratives while making fun of their own status as narratives.

All Dogs Go to Heaven (1989) and *All Dogs Go to Heaven II* (1996) are two animated musicals that are not literary adaptations. *All Dogs Go to Heaven* is based on a story directed and conceived by Don Bluth, who left Disney to establish his own studio. Like *Oliver and Company, All Dogs Go to Heaven* features animal characters who are trying to eke out a living in an urban setting. Charlie Barkin (voice by Burt Reynolds) is a street-wise mongrel who escapes from prison with the aid of his loyal beagle pal Itchy (voice by Dom DeLuise) in 1939 Louisiana. One of his partners in crime runs him down with a car, but Charlie returns to earth for a brief, second life. The chief conflict in the film revolves around Charlie's unreliability; his paternalistic relationship with a little orphan girl, Anne-Marie (voice by Judith Barsi), finally makes him become "responsible." In *All Dogs Go to Heaven II* (directed by Paul Sabella), Charlie is overjoyed when Itchy finally joins him in heaven, but then the two are dispatched to San Francisco to recover Gabriel's Horn when it is stolen by Carface (voice by Ernest Borgnine). To facilitate the antics of this film, all of the character development Charlie achieves in the first film is discarded. In addition, this G-rated film resorts to crude humor to keep its audience's interest. For example, when the police have Gabriel's Horn in a storage area, a policeman blows the horn and his fly unzips.

The Lion King (1994, dir. Roger Allers and Rob Minkoff) is a more impressive example of a nonliterary, nonromantic family-film musical. As the film opens, the song "Circle of Life" boldly dramatizes the birth of the new lion king, Simba (voice by Jonathan Taylor Thomas; adult voice by Matthew Broderick). Simba's idyllic childhood is interrupted when Scar, his ambitious uncle (voice by Jeremy Irons) murders Mufasa, Simba's father (voice by Earl Jones). Eventually, Simba must battle Scar for his rightful place in the Circle of Life. *The Lion King* features an eco-friendly message about all life existing in a "delicate balance," but has been criticized for its racism—in particular, its portrayal of hyenas, who are the outcasts of the Pride Land. These lower-class hyenas are given African American and Hispanic characteristics (voices Whoopi Goldberg, Cheech Marin, and Jim Cummings). When Scar does become king, his hyena supporters at his side, the Pride Land soon becomes a wasteland that is revitalized only when the golden-haired Simba overthrows the dark-maned Scar.

The second major genre of family films is more loosely defined than the musical category. "Rite of passage" films focus on the central character's integration into the adult world. Sample titles include: *Home Alone* (1990), *Home Alone 2: Lost in New York* (1992), *Home Alone 3* (1997), *The Indian in the Cupboard* (1995), *Harriet the Spy* (1996), *Homeward Bound: The Incredible Journey* (1993), *Homeward Bound II: Lost in San Francisco* (1996), *Babe* (1995), and *Fly Away Home* (1996). A cursory examination of these films makes their inclusion in the same genre seem unlikely. Yet in attitude, structure, and development, these films have much in common. All present a central character who passes through a crisis or performs an act that allows him/her to become more "adult": more self-sufficient, more considerate, more respectful, and so forth. Adulthood and its attributes are presented as highly desirable, and allowing the protagonist to become more adult is the ultimate goal of the story. The protagonist's discovery of the adult world is facilitated by an encounter with a wise, sensitive, adult character who functions as a mentor.

Certainly the most lucrative films in this genre are the *Home Alone* films. In the first film, *Home Alone* (1990, dir. John Hughes), eight-year-old Kevin (Macauley Culkin) is accidentally left behind when his family flies to France for Christmas and must fend for himself for a few days. Much of the humor of the film is associated with Kevin's comical attempts both to copy adult behavior and to outwit adults at their own game(s). When Kevin goes grocery shopping and a clerk questions whether he is alone, he responds, "Ma'am, I'm eight years old. Do you think I'd be here by myself?" She is suspicious and asks him where he lives but he points out that he can't tell her because she's a stranger. After he has finally begun to miss his absent family, Kevin meets Mr. Marley (Roberts Blossom), the elderly man known locally as the "snow-shovel killer." At first Kevin is afraid, but Mr. Marley assures him that none of the rumors about him are true. Mr. Marley is quiet and nonthreatening; he is the first adult who treats Kevin with respect. Mr. Marley's nonjudgmental attitude prompts Kevin to confess, "I've been kind of a pain lately. . . . I really like my family, even though sometimes I say I don't." After this meeting, Kevin not only recognizes his need for his family, but also summons the resolve he needs to foil the burglars who plan to ransack his home.

The structure of *Home Alone 2: Lost in New York* (1992, dir. Chris Columbus) precisely mirrors that of the first film, although this time Kevin is marooned in New York City. Mr. Marley's function as a model of adulthood is fulfilled by the Pigeon Lady of Central Park (Brenda Fricker), a figure whom Kevin initially fears and eventually befriends. *Home Alone 3* (1997, dir. Raja Gosnell) features child actor Alex D. Linz in lieu of the "aging" Macauley Culkin. In many ways, *Home Alone 3* is an inverted rite-of-passage film. Alex's character remains unchanged as he battles criminals who threaten to invade his home, but the adults around him begin to recognize just how much they've been ignoring him. Ultimately, the film questions whether the beautiful home Alex's parents maintain is worth the isolation their child must endure while they pursue their careers.

Just as separation episodes provide opportunities for maturation in the *Home Alone* films, the journeys in *Homeward Bound: The Incredible Journey* (1993, dir. Duwayne Dunham) and *Homeward Bound II: Lost in San Francisco* (1996, dir. David R. Ellis) prompt a recalcitrant young canine to recognize his duties to others. In the first film, Shadow, a wise, loyal golden retriever (voice by Don Ameche); Sassy, a Himalayan cat (voice by Sally Field); and Chance, an adventurous young bulldog (voice by Michael J. Fox), must travel across a mountain range to return to their masters. This journey becomes a rite of passage for Chance, who lives only for himself and doesn't trust or depend upon others. Eventually, as he witnesses Shadow's steadfast devotion to humans and to animals, Chance begins to have a change of heart. In a memorable scene in which Shadow is silhouetted by the setting sun, Chance comments, "Looking at him that night, he seemed so wise and ancient, like the first dog that ever walked the earth. I just hoped that one day I could be like him." Unfortunately, *Homeward Bound II* jettisons the character development Chance achieves in the first film. When the pets become separated from their masters in San Francisco, Shadow (voice by Ralph Waite) must again try to curb Chance's irresponsible rambunctiousness as they meet up with a group of street dogs, rescue a boy from a burning house, and foil dog-nappers. Like *All Dogs II*, *Homeward Bound II* is little more than a collection of anthropomorphic antics.

In contrast, *Babe* (1995, dir. Chris Noonan) is a family film so unique that it may not be proper to refer to it as a genre film. Based on a book by Dick King Smith, *Babe* is a live-action film that tells the story of Babe, a young pig (voice by Christine Cavanaugh) who, by chance, is taken from the mechanized pig farm where he is born and becomes a prize at a fair. He is won by Farmer Hoggett. Adjusting to life on Hoggett's sheep farm becomes Babe's rite of passage. He learns about "The Way Things Are": Dogs herd sheep and lead the barnyard; only dogs and cats can go into the house; and humans sometimes eat farm animals. Babe is befriended by Fly (voice by Miriam Margolyes), a sheep dog who supports and guides him when he demonstrates a talent for sheepherding. Beneath the charm of the film's setting lies a serious consideration of the violence that is part of the order of things; Babe will eventually be consumed by the Hoggetts unless he can prove that he is "special."

The Indian in the Cupboard (1995, dir. Frank Oz) is another noteworthy rite-of-passage film. Based on a novel by Lynne Reid Banks, the film tells the story of Omri (Hal Scardino), a sincere, thoughtful boy of nine who is given a battered cupboard for his birthday. When he obtains an old key that will open it, he discovers that placing his toys inside the cupboard will bring them to life. At first, Omri is charmed and excited by his new power, treating Little Bear (Litefoot), a small Indian figure whom he brings to life, as an object. Omri must learn that with power comes responsibility, and Little Bear slowly guides him to this realization. In a vision they share at the end of the film, Little Bear becomes full adult size and towers over Omri, dramatizing the symbolic mentor-child relationship between them.

Harriet the Spy (1996, dir. Bronwen Hughes), in which aspiring writer Harriet (Michelle Trachtenberg), with her nanny's (Rosie O'Donnell's) guidance, learns to consider other's feelings as well as the facts of their lives, and *Fly Away Home* (1996, dir. Carroll Ballard), in which Amy Alden (Anna Paquin) learns to respect her father as they help a family of orphaned geese, mark a new trend in rite-of-passage films because their protagonists are female. Until the 1990s, female heroines were virtually absent from family or children's films, largely because, as journalist Beth Pinsker has noted, Hollywood has had a long-standing marketing philosophy that "little boys won't go to see little girl movies, thus dooming them to failure." The 1990s have brought an outpouring of female-oriented films, including the above titles as well as *The Little Princess* (1996), *Matilda* (1997), *Mulan* (1998), and *Madeline* (1998). According to Pinsker, "What's bringing women into the fore is that Hollywood continues to put less and less stock in kid-oriented films, creating a kind of ghetto where girls have capitalized on the lack of interference and interest." Less money is being poured into most G and PG productions, while studios pin their blockbuster hopes on "nonoffensive" PG-13 films with family appeal. Unfortunately, the "girl's films" that have been released have not performed well at the box office, despite full-blown marketing campaigns—suggesting that boys have not yet learned that "just as girls pinned their dreams to male heroes throughout the ages . . . women can serve as role models for them [boys]" (Pinsker).

A genre that is closely related to but discernible from the rite-of-passage genre is the "buddy" genre. Both are genres of integration in which central characters try to adapt to an ideologically stable adult world. The crucial difference between the two is that, while rite-of-passage films promote maturity through adult mentorship, buddy films feature protagonists who mature through a close friendship with an equal. This friendship allows both characters to evolve. Sample buddy films include: *Free Willy* (1993), *The Secret Garden* (1993), *Toy Story* (1995), and *Dragonheart* (1996).

In *Free Willy* (dir. Simon Wincer), Jesse (Jason James Richter), a troubled adolescent, meets a killer whale when he and a friend vandalize its tank. Forced to clean up the damage, Jesse slowly develops a friendship with the young, newly captured whale (played by Keiko the Whale). Through his relationship with Willy, Jesse learns to trust others, while the forlorn Willy is able to return to his orca family with Jesse's help. The mutuality of the relationship between the protagonists is an important marker of a buddy film. *Fly Away Home* (1996), for example, is not a buddy film even though the main character, Amy (Anna Paquin), forms a close attachment to a group of orphaned geese. Willy is able to interact with Jesse in a sophisticated fashion, responding to his moods as well as to his language. In *Fly Away Home*, Anna's father is the one who provides her with key feedback and advice. Though both *Free Willy 2: The Adventure Home* (1995, dir. Dwight Little) and *Free Willy 3: The Rescue* (1997, dir. Sam Pillsbury) feature friendships between Willy (Keiko) and adolescent males, such friendships receive comparatively little attention. These films foreground their "save the whales" message and are more properly called whale-advocacy films than buddy films.

The Secret Garden (1993, dir. Agnieszka Holland) is based on a book by Frances Hodgson Burnett and tells the story of Mary Lennox (Kate Maberly), a sullen, imperious orphan who must go to live with her uncle and her cousin, a sickly, selfish boy named Colin (Heydon Prowse). Through the friendship that Mary and Colin develop, they are able to overcome their self-centeredness and reawaken their uncle from the gloom that has surrounded him since his wife's untimely death. In *Toy Story* (1995), an animated film from Disney and Pixar generated entirely by computer, two toys must compete for "favorite" status in "Andy's room." Woody (voice by Tom Hanks), a cowboy, initially tries to sabotage Buzz Lightyear (voice by Tim Allen), but they learn to depend on one another when they find themselves outside the house. Interestingly, though an animated film, *Toy Story* is not a musical. Its characters do not spontaneously break into song and dance, and most of the music in the film is non-diegetic.

Finally, in *Dragonheart* (1996, dir. Rob Cohen), Bowen (Dennis Quaid), a knight, and Draco (voice by Sean Connery), a dragon, come to have mutual respect for one another's species as they become friends. *Dragonheart* is rated PG-13 and has no child protagonists, yet it merits discussion here because reviewers have identified it as a film intended for children. Janet Maslin describes it as "a film geared to extra-patient 8–year-old viewers" ("Buddies") while a review in *Rolling Stone* claims, "*Dragonheart* delivers the goods—if you're about 5 years old" ("Dragonheart"). Both reviewers find fault with the disjointed structure and inadequate character development of the film, and it is unfortunate that they imply that the film's flaws make it better suited for child audiences—as if children won't be perceptive enough to recognize a "bad film." Though children may admire Draco, a limber, personable dragon who is the digital creation of Industrial Light and Magic, they will not appreciate the film's uneven tone any more than adults.

Sports films are unique among family films because they constitute a genre of order. Unlike musicals, rite-of-passage films, and buddy films, which encourage their characters to find a place in an ideologically stable setting, sports films (like war films and westerns) involve a physical struggle for control. Typically, two teams confront one another in a championship game. Sports films diffuse class conflict by demonstrating how a diverse team with "heart" can defeat a snobbish (usually all-white) team with unlimited economic resources.

For example, in *The Mighty Ducks* (1992, dir. Stephen Herek), hot-shot lawyer Gordon Bombay (Emilio Estevez) must coach the hopeless

FIGURE 11.1. Dennis Quaid makes friends with the dragon (voiced by Sean Connery) in Rob Cohen's *Dragonheart*. Courtesy: Jerry Ohlinger Archive.

"District 5" hockey team when he is sentenced to community service after being apprehended while driving drunk. His team must contend with the "Hawks," the intimidating championship team from the wealthy area of town. After some urging, the owner of Gordon's law firm, Mr. Ducksworth, agrees to sponsor the team if it is named after him, and the "Mighty Ducks" emerge. Their chant of "quack, quack, quack, quack" soon becomes a rallying cry against prejudice and other injustices. In *D2: The Mighty Ducks* (1994, dir. Sam Weisman), a promoter from Hendrix Sports asks Gordon to take his Mighty Ducks to the Junior Goodwill Games. As Team USA, the Mighty Ducks are able to defeat the ultra-trained, all-male, all-white Iceland team after a heckling fan takes them into the 'hood, where a street hockey team teaches them "real" hockey. In *D3: The Mighty Ducks* (1996, dir. Robert Lieberman), the Mighty Ducks receive full athletic scholarships to Eden Hall Academy, an exclusive prep school, where they become the junior-varsity hockey team. The Mighty Ducks don't perform as well as the school had hoped, and their scholarships are revoked. Gordon, representing the team as their lawyer, convinces the board to renew their scholarships, and the Ducks soundly defeat the all-male, all-white varsity team in the annual junior-varsity versus varsity game. The *Ducks* films feature well-developed main characters and dynamic shots of hockey play. Unfortunately, *The Big Green* (1995), a sports film obviously patterned after *The Mighty Ducks*, lacks such key ingredients. The clichéd plot involves a group of Texas children from the small town of Elma who form a diverse soccer team that eventually defeats the "big city" team from Austin. One pleasant surprise is that *The Big Green* offers a central role to a woman—Olivia d'Abo, who plays Anna Montgomery, the exchange teacher from England who introduces the town to soccer.

Musicals, rite-of-passage films, buddy films, and sports films do not constitute an exhaustive catalog of contemporary films for children, but identifying such genres is a convenient and meaningful way to analyze films intended for young audiences. Clearly, a majority of family films emphasize the importance of social integration, either through romantic coupling or personal maturation. If the films adults make for children are a good marker of their expectations of children, it would seem that adults' main expectation of children is that they become productive, law-abiding citizens who do not disturb the status quo.

As the 1990s draw to a close, it appears that G- and PG-rated family films are a species on the decline. At the beginning of the decade, family-film box-office receipts were high and film critic Richard Corliss declared, "Kid Power Conquers Hollywood." By the latter half of the decade, however, critics were noting the disappointing box-office returns for family films: "in the past few years, studios have been straining to make child-friendly films without wholesale slaughter. The problem is that in most cases audiences have stayed away" (Masters). And in November 1997, a *New York Times* article remarked,

> It wasn't so long ago that the business of making movies for children looked like the easiest way to earn a fortune in Hollywood. Films like *E. T.* and *The Lion King* earned hundreds of millions at the box office, and hundreds of millions of dollars more on video release. . . . In the last several years, the children's movie market has proved one of the . . . toughest niches in the business. (Sterngold)

Perhaps the decline in family-film receipts can be partially attributed to the fact that many recent family films have had female protagonists, and young male audiences are not yet willing to embrace such "girl's films." Or it may be that, as the president of Disney's family-fare division, David Vogel suggests, kids "want what's slightly illicit" (qtd. in Masters). In a culture where children become media savvy almost as soon as they can speak, G- or PG-rated films may be dismissed as too tame. In lieu of such films, children seem to be turning to PG-13 films such as *Jurassic Park* (1993), *Independence Day* (1996), and *Men In Black* (1996). Although some family films *can* still reap huge box-office and video returns (*The Lion King, Home Alone,* etc.), the uncertainty of the market has prompted some executives to scale down their budgets or move their family-film projects to television. A trend toward smaller theatrical budgets and more television productions may not be detrimental to the future of family films, however. Bazalgette and Staples argue that more modest budgets usually dictate less adult-oriented content and more focus on children's interests and perspectives. More low-budget family films may not mean big box office, but it may mean a steady outpouring of quality films that address children's concerns.

WORKS CITED

Bazalgette, Cary and Terry Staples. "Unshrinking the Kids: Children's Cinema and the Family Film." *In Front of the Children: Screen Entertainment and Young Audiences.* Ed. Cary Bazalgette and David Buckingham. London: British Film Institute Publishing, 1995. 92–108.

Corliss, Richard. "Kid Power Conquers Hollywood." *Time* (January 7, 1991): 81–82.

"Dragonheart." *Rolling Stone* (June 27, 1996): 62.

Maslin, Janet. "A Couple of Buddies (One Breathes Fire)." *New York Times* (May 31, 1996): C10.

———. "Oh, Heavens! What a Hero!" *New York Times* (June 13, 1997): C1, 22.

Masters, Kim. "Dole's Bomb Squad: Virtuecrats Notwithstanding, It's Been a Tough Summer for Kid-Friendly Movies." *Time* (August 12, 1996): 64.

Pinsker, Beth. "Girls Are Taking Over the G- and PG-rated Summer Movie Screens." *Detroit Free Press* (June 19, 1998): C3.

Schatz, Thomas. *Hollywood Genres: Formulas, Filmmaking, and the Studio System.* New York: McGraw-Hill, 1981.

Sharkey, Betsey. "Beyond Tepees and Totem Poles." *New York Times* (June 11, 1995), sec. 2: 1, 22.

Sterngold, James. "Children's Movies, Facing a Tough Market, Find a Home on a Revived Disney Series." *New York Times* (November 17 1997): D9.

Zipes, Jack. "Once Upon a Time beyond Disney: Contemporary Fairy-tale Films for Children." *In Front of the Children: Screen Entertainment and Young Audiences.* Ed. Cary Bazalgette and David Buckingham. London: British Film Institute Publishing, 1995. 109–26.

CHAPTER TWELVE

◼

Noir in the Red and the Nineties in the Black

TOM CONLEY

Saving Private Ryan (1998) might rank among the more unlikely proper names inaugurating a study of film noir in the 1990s. Steven Spielberg's war film revives a genre and is publicized as a movie at the end of the twentieth century to end all filmed depictions of war "as we know them." In its treatment of the Allied invasion of France it has the misfortune, because of its genre, of establishing a relation between its making and broader issues concerning the writing of history. We know that by and large any history returns to the past in order to state what it cannot avow about the present; in its inadmissiveness it utters secretively, in simulation of the past, a wish for something it would prefer to fulfill in the future (Certeau, *L'écriture* 63–64).

A history is "akin to a car produced by a factory" and is "bound to the complex of a specific and collective fabrication more than it is the effect merely of a personal philosophy or the resurgence of a past 'reality.' It is the *product* of a *place*" (72/64). A history is always organized around a silence or a camouflage cloaked over its making (63). In this light any history film invariably reveals its crush on allegory. In Steven Spielberg's blockbusting epic, the depiction of D day and its aftermath is less about the event of 1944 than a carefully crafted trope in which, in the guise of a "good fight" commemorating heroic times, the film declares a new war on Europe, in this instance, on the European Economic Union and, by extension, the foreign film industry. The Europeans destined to be "saved" in the film are represented as vile. The protagonist (Tom Hanks) reports that the English have done "nothing" for the Allied advance; the camera records a French family huddling in the wreckage of their home and precipitating the death of one of the Americans' few good men; the Germans are blatantly inhuman bastards, if they are not shot right off, who return, like the repressed, to haunt and maim the American soldiers. The rhetorical machinery of *Saving Private Ryan* mobilizes and enacts unstated violence on the geographical world in which it takes place.

By inverse means the same might be pondered about the newly established category of cinema called neo-noir, but with the difference that an unstated relation with history endows the genre with a stronger critical dimension. The spate of films that fall under this rubric bear the attributes that spelled out the defining traits of film noir in the 1940s, but only by virtue of an ostensive return and revival over a lapse of fifty years. Like the war film conquering the Cineplex, neo-noir arches back to what it calls paradigmatic traits in order to gain an affiliation before it puts forward other agendas designed to signify, unlike the dazzle of *Private Ryan*, a failed recurrence of the past. More than in other genres, in neo-noir the present remains silent, unuttered, or muted by virtue of an aura given in the name of history guaranteed by studious labors of cinephiles. To enjoy neo-noir is tantamount to celebrating something taken to be the condescending pleasure of knowing what noir "really" was. The very prevalence of the moniker in current journals and histories betrays efforts to stabilize circumstances bearing on its conception and execution. The *neo* of neo-noir is a symptom of an effort to make the genre a variant of history-writing. According to the logic of its relation, it would not be wrong to say that neo-noir exhumes noir in order better to inter and embalm it. Noir is dead, long live neo-noir.

I would like to follow the loops and folds of history in neo-noir because, at its seeming origins, film noir already displays a troubled relation with its past and present. The argument that follows contends that the starkly obvious erasure of history in the works of the 1940s tends to be obliterated in the ostensive "return" by neo-noir to the earlier origins of its style. The most salient feature of neo-noir, then, can be formulated as its erasure of the rubbings of historical erasure. Before attention is drawn to *The Last Seduction* (1994), the dynamics can be illustrated by reference to the presentation of history in two seminal feature films. Crucial to the development of classical noir, Billy Wilder's *Double Indemnity* (1943) and Robert Siodmak's *The Killers* (1946) make their historicity clear through visual and narrative means. In the former a depiction of everyday life in Los Angeles appears to take place outside of any palpable time. In the latter an embroiled narrative almost overtly avows that it cannot obfuscate the history on which its tortuous construction is based.

A city street in crepuscule, viscous dabs of light emanating from distant street lamps, and traffic signals in soft focus: liquid illumination of ordinary spaces conveys an urban landscape in the opening sequence of *Double Indemnity* before Fred MacMurray's voice-over spools the story back to the time of its occurrence. The image track, a reconstruction simultaneous to the confession spoken into a Dictaphone, offers several daylight shots of Los Angeles seen from the surrounding hills. At one point MacMurray drives his car uphill, in bright sunlight, to the mansion where his future lover and accomplice resides. A splash of day—and of geographical and historical precision—in the ominous intrigue anchors history in luminous contradiction. "Life as usual" comes with sunshine. A visual accent is put on the nonplace of an everyplace, Beverly Hills, in which the plot unfolds. MacMurray is presumed to embody the age and stature of a man who would be a soldier fighting for the Allied cause in September 1943, the date of the first showing of the feature.

His excursions about contemporary Los Angeles throw the time and place into a dappled milieu displayed to eradicate its moorings. Yet the make and model of his car assigns a signature, a date, and a serial number to the film. Automotive evidence invites the spectator to participate in what Joan Copjec (163–200) calls the "detective function" in *Double Indemnity*, a celebration of numeration. In the midst of the coding and numbering of things, the voice of MacMurray that tells the story is absent "from the narrative," the latter being what Copjec equates with social space (190). The prevalence of private worlds in noir in the immediate context of the Second World War, it can be inferred, clearly underscores the denial of an encounter with history.

In the daylight sequence where MacMurray and Stanwyck meet in Jerry's Market (minuscule by today's standards) their plot unwinds. They will murder her husband and collect a whopping sum from the insurance company where MacMurray is a leading salesman. Suddenly, however, sight and sound explode into an image. MacMurray gruffly whispers into Stanwyck's ear, "I love ya, baby," adjacent to the aisle where serial rows of boxes of baby cereal display a proto-Warholian picture of replicated baby-faces staring at the viewer. The emblem of pabulum provides an origin for the future public of movie-going "baby-boomers" who will return, years later, to the type of film being crafted: the same infants will mature as cinephiles purchasing rereleases of early noir (say, the new prints of Anthony Mann's noir phase as an *auteur* of the late 1940s) or adepts of neo-noir in Cineplexes and video-rental outlets.

Double Indemnity does not mirror or "reflect" its time. Like the war movie, it remains the paradigm of a logistics of perception (Virilio), a film paradigm that exploits the allure of its narrative conflict to map out future reality. The film generates *perceptions* that fascinate or immobilize the spectator all the while they are diagrams made to control collective behavior. The concept bears uncanny resemblance to the distinction that Gilles Deleuze (*Foucault* 51), in dialogue with the writings of Michel Foucault, draws between an *archive* (what sums up or reflects the past) and a *diagram* (the imposition of a strategic model, like a map, that will order future behavior). It will be shown that both classical and neo-noir can be read through this filter, the diagrammatical area of the latter serving the future by way of the curtsies it makes to the former. When neo-noir alludes to the past, whether innocuously or obsequiously, unlike commemorative genres, it invites a critical and an interpretive relation.

A shift from an unlocatable narrative time and space to another, of uncanny specificity, marks the imbroglio of *The Killers*. Siodmak's feature tacks onto a terse sequence of ten minutes, a nearly verbatim rendering of Ernest Hemingway's story of the same name, the classical noir scenario resembling what takes place in Fritz Lang's *Scarlet Street* (1945), Robert Siodmak's *Criss Cross* (1949), Tay Garnett's *The Postman Always Rings Twice* (1946), and other films of the 1940s. A man falls hopelessly in love with the spouse of a man engaged in illicit activity. Out of love and devotion he buys his way into sleaze in order to gain the services of the woman who eventually doublecrosses him in fidelity to herself and to her husband. The innovation of Siodmak's film lay in the way Hemingway's piece of spare but highminded "literature" becomes an expressionistic movie trailer both initiating and dissolving into a more pervasive cinematic convention. The present time of the encounter in the café and the assassination (by William Conrad and Charles McGraw) of the hapless hero are consigned to provisional oblivion in the medley of flashbacks that develop the narrative.

The repressed moment "returns" when the bulky hitman and his svelte companion shadow the rival protagonist of the film, the sleuth

(Edmond O'Brien) en route to the Green Cat Restaurant with the dou-
ble-crossing spouse (Ava Gardner). The return of the killers mirrors the
return of history. Their sudden appearance becomes, as it were, Stendhal's
"pistol shot in an opera," the novelist's formula (in *La chartreuse de Parme*
[*The Charterhouse of Parma*]) that awakens a political and historical animal. Their return is underlined by that of *real dates*, in the final sequence
in the office of the president of the insurance company where the sleuth
has summed up his findings. The event that unlocked hermetically sealed
enclosure was a shard of color invisible on the black-and-white film stock,
a green scarf worn by one of the men in the robbery of a payroll delivery
at the Prentice Hat Company in Hackensack, New Jersey, in 1941. But
the time of the telling, notes the president with sardonic glee, is 1946,
which the spectator quickly realizes matches the date of its release in
North America. Implied is that the time of the noir scenario took up the
duration of the years 1941–45, the entire duration of the Second World
War. The conventional plot is equated to be identical to the grim and
bloody history of the European and Pacific campaign (Conley "Stages").
The film thus does not elide or silence the events in its midst but, rather,
colors them into its form. It cues events by transmuting them into an
oblivion of traumatic presence.

It suffices to define neo-noir in the televisual glare of its own histo-
riographical operation. In the fall of 1995 on an ABC version of *Good
Morning America* Sam Rubin, the network's entertainment correspondent
in Hollywood, delivered an up-to-date report on new developments of a
new genre. It was labeled neo-noir and based on a what was assumed to
be a common ambiance of many new features harking back to films of the
1940s and 1950s. The immaculately groomed hostess, her cheeks without wrinkle and lips painted with aloe varnish mirroring the studio lights,
initially defined classical noir as a mode that "reflected the times." "Everything old again is new again." Turning to the television monitor emitting
a frontal view of Rubin, she and her spectators learned, in Rubin's on-the-
spot report, that "out of the dashed dreams of the Depression, Hollywood's B movies of the '40s and Æ50s created a new mythology, not of
hope, but of despair." The films were about "dreamers and drifters"
(accompanying the words were shots from the bottom of the swimming
pool of Billy Wilder's *Sunset Boulevard* [1950] and of Charlton Heston
hustling under an arcade in Venice-cum-Tijuana in Orson Welles's *Touch
of Evil* [1958]), "grifters and schemers . . . characters who talk with a certain tough-guy poetry" (a cut was made to dialogue between MacMurray

and Stanwyck in *Double Indemnity*, in staccato quid pro quo, about speeding cars and speeding lines). The ten-second history lesson served as a segue to a list of films scrolled over citations of recent noir features of the new order: first and foremost, Quentin Tarantino's *Pulp Fiction* (1994); then, in second place, Gary Fleder's *Things to Do in Denver When You're Dead* (1995); third, Bryan Singer's *The Usual Suspects* (1995); also worthy, Mike Figgis's *Leaving Las Vegas* (1995) and Gus Van Sant's *To Die For* (1995) before, *ad seriatum*, Kathryn Bigelow's *Strange Days* (1995), Carl Franklin's *Devil in a Blue Dress* (1995), Abel Ferrara's *The Addiction* (1995), Gregg Araki's *The Doom Generation* (1995), David Fincher's *Se7en* (1995), Michael Keusch's *Double Cross* (1994), Roberto Rodriguez's *El Mariachi* (1992), Lee Tamahori's *Mulholland Falls* (1996), Danny Boyle's *Shallow Grave* (1994), Wes Anderson's *Bottle Rocket* (1994), and Steven Soderbergh's *Underneath*.

The list completed, there followed a recorded interview with John Dahl, dressed in black and cowering with delight in front of a backlit screen. The director was heralded as author of four neo-noir features that included *Unforgettable* (1996), *Red Rock West* (1992), and *The Last Seduction* (1994); this last film was originally shot as a TV movie. Dahl's words fleshed out the definition of the new breed of old film. It treated, he said, of "morally ambiguous characters doing morally ambiguous things. There's a line that people are willing to cross that seems to be awfully murky in noir characters, morally corrupt people . . . [in] deliberate and harsh lightings, and [*sic*] other techniques." The interviewer led Dahl to affirm that the films take place in "sleazy hotel rooms" and "isolated landscapes, even in big cities." Venetian blinds were the rule of the decorative game. "It would seem like we really don't know what is right and what's wrong. We seem to have a tremendous appetite for ambiguity, and lo and behold, it's 1995."

In the review, *Pulp Fiction* was taken to be a point of departure for neo-noir on the grounds that the *série noire*, hard-boiled fiction printed on sulphite paper in the early postwar years, stood at the origin of the French adjective soon imported to America. The editors did not have time enough to mention that it came, too, with Sartre, whose trenchcoat—that Bogart also sported in Michael Curtiz's *Casablanca* (1942)—emblazoned existentialism, the intellectual staff of life of French curricula in America before massive imports of Bordeaux wine and camembert cheese. Unmentioned were Etienne Laborde and Raymond Chaumeton (1957/1984), who offered a complex view richer than etymology or borrowed finery. Their

FIGURE 12.1. Lara Flynn Boyle and Nicolas Cage in John Dahl's *Red Rock West.* Courtesy: Jerry Ohlinger Archive.

work was issued by Editions de Minuit, a press begun in the night of the French resistance (hence "Midnight" editions). In search of precursors the two authors invoked Fritz Lang's *M* (1931), the German street-movie, and expressionistic decor; the French tradition of poetic realism, including, it can be added, proto-noir scenarios and effects in works such as Marcel Carné's *Le jour se lève* [*Daybreak*] of 1937 and the well-named Jean Renoir's *La bête humaine* (1938) [*The Human Beast*]. Also unmentioned on the television broadcast was the ferment of neo-Hegelian existentialism, in which subjectivity was assumed predetermined and selected by fate. In 1995 classic noir was thus conveyed in a postmodern, do-it-yourself aura that cherished the ease with which citations could be invoked for play and pleasure or fun and profit. The interview and the report were meant to suture the quotations from masterworks of the past (given to be available on video, within reach of those ready to buy or rent cassettes) to the new features of here-and-now (either in circulation at major theaters or soon to be released by major distributors).

Film, video, and contemporary reporting, indeed the raw material of the sequences shown on the morning television show, were imbricated in the very substance of neo-noir. The existential closure of the noir plot-line of the 1940s was transposed from narrative to space infused with mood and moral ambivalence. Pregiven destiny of the type that Sartre schematized in the noir-like drama of *Huis-clos* [*No Exit*], was dissolved in favor of a giddy pleasure of a choice of one's evil. Dahl's words betrayed a return of free will and chic "lifestyle." Characters were taken to be as such—not as pawns of perception—and were granted the right to choose their fates as cinephiles might rent classic features. They were ambiguous by nature but in positions that allowed them to cross "murky" ethical lines as they might pass through the surveillance barriers at video stores.

Two recent essays on neo-noir provide ample evidence of the evolution implied by the television report. Todd Erickson (308–30) notes that a time of gestation, spent in the interim between the early postwar years and the 1980s, was needed to gain a perspective on the movement. Rehearsing historical studies that show how a "movement" becomes objectified (Certeau, Julia, and Revel; Certeau *La fable*), he argues that a distance had to be established before a name and a definition could be applied to neo-noir. According to this approach noir was especially oper-ative when it was a "convention," a "tendency," or a "style," but at the point it turned into a historical object bearing the substantive film noir (that is, at the time of Laborde and Chaumeton's study in 1957, just prior to Godard's *A bout de souffle*, a parody of both American and European currents of noir), it went underground. As a result it could only scatter into other fragmentary forms and places.

Symptomatic of neo-noir, insofar as it does not own substantive status, is a Baroque self-consciousness imbuing it with an allusive force of citation, one of the building blocks of auteur cinema in the years 1950–70. As a consequence the evocative force of the new movement can be said to depend on its capacity to sift out degrees of cinematic consciousness among the viewing public. Two recent films not falling under the purview of Erickson's analysis are noteworthy. In Steven Soderbergh's *Out of Sight* (1998), the success of George Clooney's escape from prison with Jennifer Lopez in a car trunk is found not in the chiaroscuro of two attractive bodies laced together amidst jacks and spare tires but, rather, in their own dialogue of cinematic quotation. They exchange notes about former movies, clearly forgetting—any moderately informed viewer recalls—the famous sequence of Raoul Walsh's *White Heat* (1949) in which James Cagney confined a stool pigeon in a car trunk in a getaway from a high-security prison. After enduring a long and bumpy ride, suffocating, he thumps on the inner wall of the trunk and begs for air: "It's stuffy in here." Cagney, crazed leader of the Jarret gang, chewing on a fried chicken wing, responds by casually shooting bullets into the trunk. *Out of Sight* obviously edulcorates the frame of reference in the moment of love born of entwined bodies and cinephilia. The same situation of an excluded or latent term prevails, too, in Curtis Hanson's *L.A. Confidential* (1997), but in that film reference is clearly *not* made to the oedipal psychopathology of Broderick Crawford in Russell Rouse's *New York Confidential* (1955). In sharp contrast, *Out of Sight* manages to offer a structural reflection on its historicity by restaging the dilemma of the attraction of good and evil (the female policewoman loves the man she must incarcerate) that draws into its realm the strengths of Fritz Lang's work from *M* up through *Human Desire* (1954). As the excursive itinerary of this paragraph shows, the seduction of citation in neo-noir is one of its composite elements.

Erickson concludes that certain lines of demarcation can be drawn between noir and neo-noir. The advent of color cinema required a different tonal register and a spatial coding that realigned contrasts and symbolic effects originally mobilized by backlighting and contrasts between black and white. Low-budget photographers obtained immediate psychological effects through appeal to the close-up, especially in the period of the growth of television, in which it is the rule and the long shot the exception. The medium shot, what played on daring effects of light and the narrative of action, was reduced to a minimum (310).

Along a more thematic line he notes that "nostalgic exercises" convey aesthetic choices (312) that allow form to negotiate political and ethical malaise. The latter, that comes with global spatiotemporal compression, the advent of global flexible capitalism, and the impending sense of an accruing loss of agency on the part of both individual and collective subjects (Lefebvre *Production* and *Critique*; Harvey; Conley "Creative") is inferred to be a fittingly dark background for the new genre. In this light, neo-noir would not concern free will in situations and plot lines that had earlier denied its condition of possibility but, we can extrapolate from Erickson's careful account, what it cannot state. At stake, in other words, is the inverse, but to such a new and depressing degree that the only solution on the horizon is for viewers to take grim pleasure in *consuming* the massive number of films produced in the reflective gloss recalling films of "simpler times past." Preferring to avoid issues of ideology (which means, paradoxically, that appeal is made to Marxian criteria), Erickson returns to technology, concluding that the conditions of possibility for neo-noir owe to advances in the production of faster color-film stock, the convergence of growing quanta of crime seen and reported in America, a tendency on the part of screenwriters to reflect the changes in the style of their scenario, and the presence of a "noir sensibility" among younger filmmakers, who are implied to have studied the earlier films in institutional or formative settings. Stated is that at its inception noir was "an innocent, unconscious cinematic reaction to the popular culture of its time" (323), whereas the three hundred neo-noir films completed since 1971 are "self-conscious" and are more than cognizant of their heritage (323). The historical appraisal depends on the inscription of an immaculate origin: an innocent paradise garden of formative film noir, in vital and unmediated contact with ambient culture, preceded a lapsarian moment, a fall into history.

The analysis begs us to wonder where the unconscious migrates in the history of the genre. It cannot merely disappear in commercialization or else be so easily located in the exponential increase of on-screen violence in films associated with the revival. Alain Silver (331–38) offers some viable answers. For Silver the history of noir begins from a classic period that "encompasses several hundred motion pictures from John Huston's *The Maltese Falcon* (1941) to Orson Welles's *Touch of Evil*

(1958) before disappearing for about a decade and resurging into view from the late 1970s up to the present." The rebirth has to do with economy, reflecting André Gide's dictum that "art is born of constraint and dies of liberty." Original noir films were shot on low budgets and in tight shooting schedules and were shown as second features in double bills. The directors used the limits of production to obtain maximal effects. In a similar vein, nowadays "[t]he low-budget feature, made at a cost ranging from less than $500,000 to $3–$4 million cannot be financed based on U.S. theatrical prospects alone but must follow the dictates of the foreign, video, and cable markets" (332). To be understood among audiences over the world and to insure adequate remuneration narratives need to be "spare," and "violence and compulsive sexual behavior" made rampant.

A Baroque aspect of neo-noir is explained by a "return to its roots" (333) in "violence and unsavory themes" cultivated at its beginnings. William Lustig's *Hit List* and *Relentless* (both 1989), adds Silver, cast actors known for their work in big-budget features at once to camouflage the constraints facing the director and to sell his wares. Return to the plot lines of original noir assures efficient transposition of time-held conflicts, but with the bonus of offering sordid settings and gratuitous or "offhanded" violence reflective of "the videotapes of real events [seen] from surveillance cameras" (337). Money, a new network of distribution, competition, the exponential growth of recording apparatus in everyday life, and increased pace of production are the unstated but ubiquitous influences that account for the revival. Silver adduces his points by allusion to "movies-of-the-week and cable originals" that return to the locale and the constraints of noir, that include John Dahl's aforementioned films *Red Rock West* and *The Last Seduction*. Silver's coda is taken, unconsciously perhaps, from a prophetic epigraph in Stendhal's *Le rouge et le noir* [*The Red and the Black*] in which the post-Enlightenment novelist affirmed that a realistic novel is a mirror erected by an author walking along an open road. Silver concludes that no cinematic movement has yet replaced the originality of noir, and that "until filmmakers discover another mirror to hold up to American society, none ever will" (338).

Something red taints Silver's history of films black: he may indeed be recalling the prevailing color in the two neo-noir films that cap his analysis. Insofar as color stock is the medium of the new genre, it almost goes without saying that the blood and guts of neo-noir derives from a palette of reds over matte and somber backgrounds. The conflict of colors might serve to typify both the visual allure and the allegorical traits of noir in the nineties.

If the title of Stendhal's realistic novel—which shares many noir traits in its mix of chronicle, preciosity, study of male and female psychologies, and its depictions of sudden spurts of self-destructive passion—still defies reduction to allegory, it can serve as a threshold for analysis of neo-noir. Scholars have argued that *Le rouge et le noir* is a chromatic emblem of the struggle between the ecclesiastical robe (black) and military uniform (red); the *damier* pattern of a chessboard on which less-than-heroic protagonists try to master their fates and win agency; the contrast of the black ink—alluding to the newspaper and its relation to the new and gritty style of "realism" in the serial narratives purveyed by the new medium—and the red blood of romantic pulp fiction in the line of Sir Walter Scott.

Less important than the confusions of meaning in these and other glosses are the constancy of the tension they generate and, above all, the persisting vivacity of the color field. The tensions apply to the stakes of history and its relation to neo-noir. Red and black bear on the struggle a subject encounters in "making it" through sex and money in the cloth of belief and war. *The Last Seduction*, a film endowed with a serial title, is not far from Stendhal's model. A low-budget essay on values red and black, the film can be likened to a "mirror" held before contemporary American society. The plot, engineered by a spare shooting style, straight cuts, and dialogue in quid pro quo, is easily remembered and translated into other languages for worldwide distribution. Linda Fiorentino's long, lithe, svelte, sinewy legs, displayed in manneristic counter-tilted pans that follow her across streets or through apartments or insurance offices, carry the narrative of a man-woman—a hyperphallic female exceeding all expectations about the doublecrossing *uxor*—who makes her mark in an international center of deregulated capitalism.

The story tells of her stealing the booty her husband obtains from a pharmaceutical drug deal made with black street hoodlums. In their apartment he slaps her when she shows no compassion for the deadly risks he took (the blacks held a gun to his head before letting him go). While he showers she grabs the money and a pair of condoms, leaves the apartment, runs to a car and drives west. She gases up at a town called Beston, enters a bar, meets a gullible admirer, and quickly makes love with him ("you're my designated fuck," she later states about their developing relation). To evade pursuit she nestles in the town by obtaining employment in the telephonic arm of an insurance company. She takes a pseudonym, a mirrored spelling of the city of her origin (Wendy Kroy after New York, plus "dy" or "yd"). She convinces her lover, employed at the same firm, that professional murder can be arranged by telephone and that she has gumption enough to commit the crimes she fantasizes in conversation with long-distance interlocutors. She takes a taxi from Beston to Buffalo to meet her lover's former "wife," a transvestite named "Trish." She baffles a private detective hired out by her husband who had recently deciphered her whereabouts. (While delivering baked cookies, she hides a board of nails beneath her apron before putting it under the tires of the dick's car.) She and her lover return to New York in a scheme by which the latter will murder the husband and thus bring freedom to their future. She sets up a change of names that soon entraps the lover in the hands of the police and allows her to be driven away, scot-free, in a dark limousine that rolls along one of the major avenues of Manhattan.

The plot leads almost unilaterally, in peripatetics obvious to viewers familiar with classic noir, from the deal and the marital skirmish to the lover's botched but bloody murder of the husband. Unless it is the transvestite, of whom a brief image confirms what the lover could not admit earlier, little returns from the beginning of the narrative to the conclusion in the shape of an element forgotten or repressed. The noir paradigm is made obvious everywhere, but nowhere better, paradoxically, than in the seemingly natural play of light and color. Daylight photography captures the deal made under either the Williamsburg or Manhattan Bridge; the protagonist's getaway is taken in crepuscule at the same site, evincing at best a simulated indifference about narrative loci. Repeated shots of cars moving away from the frame betray the pleasure of dotting the image with red flashes of light. The ostensibly classic moment of the tradition, the meeting of the gullible lover and the phallic female, referring to—but a far cry from—a defining moment when Burt Lancaster set his eyes on Ava Gardner to the piano notes of "Lou Tingle" in the Mafia club in *The Killers*, takes place in a nondescript bar ("Ray's") in Beston. Inside the area, adjacent to a couple of pool tables, neon backlighting and flecks of red on signboards animate the dark space in which the instincts are assumed to awaken. Close-ups of the protagonist's bare legs in amorous combat bring forward the sanguine feel of flesh on white sheets beneath windows equipped with venetian blinds. Red mediates striking oppositions of spaces in daylight and in darkness. Unlike classical avatars in black and white, Dahl brings color into the field of the image with economy that conflates the spectrum of natural tones and realistic representation so directly that the attendant allegories of red and black reach back to the title of Stendhal's classic.

In anticipation of a conclusion, can we say that Dahl, the author of *Red Rock West*, is defining neo-noir through an unlikely namesake? Is Pierre Beyle, alias Stendhal, a key to the aesthetics of John Dahl? The film provides evidence enough to respond in the affirmative and, as a result, to bring us to the hypothesis that the new genre is marked by a troubled relation with different frames of history. The only enigma in the film that bears resemblance to a psychic play of the repressed occurs in its depiction of writing. In the sequence in which the husband and wife meet at the end of their respective days of work the wife writes—in blue ink—a playful note to her husband that, as it is scripted, every spectator is hard put to decipher. Instants later, after her departure from the apartment, as if the note were a parting shot, the husband displays the card before a mirror. Her words ("how are we supposed to celebrate?") are suddenly legible, revealing a quirk or odd talent of writing in reverse. Her trait is put aside until the husband surmises that his wife has renamed herself by using the palinym of New York, the city to which she holds unswerving dedication. It becomes her proper name; she is mirrored in and by New York. Backwards and forwards, she thus personifies an international economic space. The connection is established by an affiliation with deeply rooted traditions common to classic film noir (the mirror being a symbolic prop defining real and imaginary space in Fritz Lang's "New York" avatars *Scarlet Street* and *Woman in the Window* [1944]), the realistic novel (as Stendhal typified in its specularity in *Le rouge et le noir*) and, no less, the historical tradition that inscribes *secrets* within discourses heralding veracity.

The latter, tied to Dahl's work in the historical register of *The Last Seduction*, reach back to early modern "theaters" and "mirrors" of history. Scriptural inversions inhabit historiography, "as in all cryptographies, in children's games, or in counterfeiters' imitations of coins, fictions forging deceit and secrets, tracing the sign of a silence through the inversion of a normative practice and its social coding" (Certeau, *L'écriture* 87). The works conceal a relation to history that is today "political and commercial; but in using a past in order to deny the present that they repeat, they set apart something foreign to current social relations, they *produce secrets* within language" (87). The author calls mirror writing "serious because of what it does—it states something other through the inversion of the code of practice; it is illusory only insofar as, not realizing what it is doing," we take "its secret to be what it puts into language, and not what it subtracts from it" (87). The public secret in Dahl's film would be the money emblematized in the figure of the golden condoms ("Max" is the brand) the protagonist extracts from a drawer in a chest in the bedroom of the apartment, a "mirrored" figure that alludes to the equivalence of money and sex conventionalized in films of the 1990s, especially in the condom coins seen in a man's hand in the first shot of Garry Marshall's *Pretty Woman* (1990), the Cinderella counterpart to Dahl's feature. In this light *The Last Seduction* mixes the ingredients of classic noir by becoming an inversion of the fairy tale in which the "bad" Linda Fiorentino is the mirrored counterpart of the "good" Julia Roberts.

In *The Last Seduction* a telling secret is found in the difference drawn between the tradition of sleazy zones, "non-places" or "places-of-any-kind-whatsoever" (Deleuze, *Cinéma 1* 283 and *Cinéma 2* 16–17) that defined classic film noir and those of Dahl's New York in the 1990s, the *locus amoenus* and paradise garden of international capitalism. The difference between "Brentwood" and the implied contiguity of the Hollywood back lots of *The Killers* has a doublet in what holds between Dahl's "Beston" near Buffalo and the topless towers of Manhattan. Here we glimpse reflections of a secret relation with history and money. On cursory view it spells out what Alain Silver noted about the bottom (but hardly "murky") line of neo-noir narratives. The success of Dahl's film can be measured by a failure either to erase present time in its return to earlier films or to obfuscate the historical dilemmas they themselves had evinced. An intensified historical presence results through its invitation to make comparative analysis. Dahl's film clearly depends on its forebears, including *Double Indemnity* and *The Killers*, and thus revives the conditions of the relation they could not name. It does so in order to embody the traits of an abyssally mirrored signature.

Dahl's cinematic paraph is seen in the first shot of *The Last Seduction*. Therein is inscribed a secret later reflected in the protagonist's writing and in the shape of her borrowed name. The film moves from a fade-in, out of the black background of the credits, into an uncanny establishing shot. A close-up of a sculpted eagle looking over a street below submits to focus-pull that puts a street far below into view. A yellow taxicab moves upward from the point defined by the bird's beak, the camera following its course along a city block hatched with a double-x'ed crosswalk, until it draws up and captures a view of the entirety of Manhattan seen from the north to the south over a slightly polluted haze. In deep focus and in a downward plunge, the shot captures the aspect of a narrow street. But it begins with a close-up of a mediating object. The eagle is perched on the corner of a building before the camera seems to soar high enough to offer a three-quarter or "bird's-eye" view of a cityscape. The eagle resembles a gargoyle, watching over Gotham in bright daylight, its wings extending on a plane defining the almost—but only almost—omniscient point of view of the camera. The shot that follows is an extreme close-up of a black telephone and heteroclite objects in a telephone-sales office where males and females of First, Second, and Third World origin are working in a neo-Tayloristic sweatshop.

From the start the eagle is a duplicitous emblem, a summary icon, referring to American money on which its image is stamped and printed. It also—but perhaps in a more wily, intensely secretive fashion—alludes to what emblazons the aspirations of ambitious subjects of moderate or mediocre means, notably the hero of *Le rouge et le noir*, in the post-Napoleonic age. The eagle is the totem of power and money, seen not from below but from above, like the camera itself, that looks over New York. In the second and third shots the protagonist enters. A pan begins from a point of reference, a black telephone, designated in close-up. Her torso is visible across the desk on which the receiver is placed. Soon we see her face. She is wired to a mechanism by which she monitors employees hawking fake commemorative coins in telephone sales. A framed set of commemorative coins, placed on the desks of the men under her own aquiline eye, now alludes to the eagle in the establishing shot that preceded. The female is the raptor, the men its prey. Yet, as a logical consequence the exchange value of the entire film becomes equivalent to the worthless commemorative objects being scammed. The harried salespeople, residents and immigrants alike, are at odds with the "system" that canvasses the population in search of dumb consumers all the while they sit below the bionic female who stands over them.

It would be wrong to conclude that the aggressive cynicism of the protagonist or the association of the film with counterfeit money in the image of American patrimony reflects a deregulated economy of the 1980s and 1990s. We would be shortchanging interpretation if it were said that neo-noir merely mirrors degradation on a worldwide scale. To entertain a different and more cinematic conclusion, we can affirm that the secret of the film reveals more than the admission of an economic relation with the tradition of noir, now recycled and intensified, to sell and to depict violence on an international scale. In homage to what grew out of the reception of classical film noir, it is licit invoke to another concealed dimension, that of the auteur and its politics, that had prompted close analysis of the convention and later inspired its transmutation into later genres and styles.

We have noted that the eagle, set at the most underdetermined moment in the film (at its first sighting nothing yet in the image field or on the soundtrack can be compared to it) can allude to the totem emblem of *Le rouge et le noir*, in which the bird that captured Napoleon's aspirations was the volatile of ambition and dialectical flight. In *The Last Seduction* the bird is caught in a middle field, between bourgeois vision (as it would be in Hegel, the philosophical eagle of the Napoleonic era) and its inversion, as a form materialized in stone and money, in the urban space of the conflict of classes (as it would in Marx). In John Dahl's feature the potency of struggle, where different stakes and multifarious conflicts are put forward, returns through the dialogue of noir with what is at once red and black and old and new. It arches back, as in new-wave cinema of the 1950s and 1960s, to a world of *auteurs* and literature that includes the political dimension of Stendhal.

Our essay opened by noting how Steven Spielberg has brought to the American public a commemorative work of historical erasure. We can end by observing that as long as a historical relation is inscribed and is reinvented, be it through citational, specular, or other means, in the tradition of film noir smudges of erasure tend to be visible and, as a result, they are marked with political and ethical valence. Those very smudges betray a historical relation that needs to be elucidated when we reinvent the fables and fortunes of film noir. As nonconsumers it is up to us, not to an industry of commemoration, to make selective and forceful use of neo-noir.

WORKS CITED

Certeau, Michel de. *La fable mystique. XVIe-XVIIe siècle.* Paris: Gallimard, 1982.

———. *L'écriture de l'histoire.* Paris: Gallimard. English translation (1992): *The Writing of History.* Trans. Tom Conley. New York: Columbia University Press, 1982/1992.

Certeau, Michel de, Dominique Julia, and Jacques Revel. *Une politique de la langue.* Paris: Gallimard, 1975.

Chaumeton, Etienne, and Raymond Borde. *Panorama du film noir américain.* Paris: Editions de Minuit, 1957. Reprinted 1984.

Conley, Tom. "A Creative Swarm." Afterword to English translation of Michel de Certeau's *Culture in the Plural.* Minneapolis: University of Minnesota Press, 1997. 149–61.

———. "Stages of *Film noir.*" *Theatre Journal* 39.3 (October 1987): 347–63.

Copjec, Joan. "Locked Room/Lonely Room: Private Space in Film Noir." *Read My Desire: Lacan against the Historicists.* Cambridge: MIT Press, 1994. 163–200.

Deleuze, Gilles. *Cinéma 1: L'image-mouvement.* Paris: Editions de Minuit, 1983.

———. *Cinéma 2: L'image-temps.* Paris: Editions de Minuit, 1985.

———. *Foucault.* Paris: Editions de Minuit, 1986.

Erickson, Todd. "Kill Me Again: Movement Becomes Genre." *Film Noir Reader.* Ed. Alain Silver and James Ursini. New York: Limelight Editions, 1996. 307–30.

Harvey, David. *The Condition of Postmodernity.* London: Basil Blackwell, 1991.

Lefebvre, Henri. *Critique of Everyday Life.* Trans. John Moore. London: Verso, 1991.

———. *The Production of Space.* Trans. Donald Nicholson-Smith. London: Basil Blackwell, 1989.

Silver, Alain. "Son of Noir: The Emergence of Neo-Film Noir and the Neo-B Picture." *Film Noir Reader.* Ed. Alain Silver and James Ursini. New York: Limelight Editions, 1996. 331–38.

Ursini, James. "Film noir: A Modest Proposal." *Film Noir Reader.* Ed. Alain Silver and James Ursini. 1978. New York: Limelight Editions, 1996. 95–106.

Virilio, Paul. *Guerre et cinéma: Logistique de la perception.* Paris: Gallimard/Cahiers du Cinéma, 1982.

CHAPTER THIRTEEN

◉

Fade-Out in the West:
The Western's Last Stand?

CHUCK BERG

The western is one of the first genres to have established itself at the onset of the film age. Today, however, after a long and storied history, the western seems to have lost much of the punch of its classical antecedents, in particular the landmark westerns of directors such as John Ford and Howard Hawks. At the end of the 1990s, then, it seems reasonable to ask if we are witnessing a fade-out on the western as a truly viable and vibrant genre? Will Clint Eastwood's *Unforgiven* (1992), at some point in the not-too-distant future, be looked at as the western's last stand?

In order to better assess the status of the contemporary western, this essay will offer a brief sketch of the genre's evolution, noting its basic thematic concerns and its unique ideological role in American history. Against this backdrop, key westerns of the 1990s will be discussed in terms of the genre's traditional ideological moorings, the various attempts to make westerns relevant to 1990s audiences through the incorporation of contemporary gender, minority and cultural issues, and, finally, the impact of stylistic and thematic issues grounded in the postmodern critique.

When films first began to hint at their capacity to entertain by provoking brief moments of laughter or melodramatic suspense, the movies' pioneers soon came to realize that there was more to filmmaking than merely shooting "scenic views" or "topicals." Yes, scenic views did take audiences to distant and exotic locales such as the Grand Canyon. And, yes, topicals did put spectators in the midst of newsworthy events such as the coronations of European heads of state. Significantly, the attractions inherent in scenic views and topicals began to merge, a phenomenon given impetus in the rush to produce titles designed to capitalize on the "war fever" heated up by the intense newspaper coverage of the Spanish-American War of 1898.

Indeed, in the wake of the sinking of the American battleship Maine in Havana Harbor on February 15, 1898, the Spanish-American War became hot copy for newsmen and filmmakers alike. The day's major film companies—Edison, Biograph, and Vitagraph—all released films depicting scenes of American troops in training, disembarking for combat, or on the front lines in Cuba. Every war needs a hero and the cameras soon found one in the dashing figure of the politically astute Teddy Roosevelt. Most famously, Vitagraph followed Roosevelt to Cuba and photographed scenes of his assault with the Rough Riders on San Juan Hill (Fielding 31). Here, in this brief Vitagraph short, and in its reenacted or "faked" imitations, were the seeds of the movie western: the off-beat scenic view of a faraway place (San Juan Hill, Cuba), the topical interest of a highly publicized current-event war (the Spanish-American War), the spectacle of men on horseback (the Rough Riders) charging to the rescue, and, finally, in the figure of Roosevelt, a larger-than-life hero embodying truth, justice, courage, and the propagation of the American Way.

With the coming of a new millennium, and without a war to cover, the press increasingly turned to the West for action-packed stories peppered with murder and dastardly deeds designed to derail the expansion of Eastern law and order. At the same time, dime novels (perhaps better described as "docu-novels") by writers such as Ned Buntline and Prentice Ingraham puffed up putative "heroes" such as Wyatt Earp and Doc Holliday. In major cities, audiences could glimpse well-promoted Western heroes through "live" extravaganzas such as Buffalo Bill's Wild West Show. On Broadway, David Belasco offered the "Western dramas" *The Girl I Left Behind Me* (1893) and *The Girl of the Golden West* (1905), the second of which was transformed into a grand opera by Giacomo Puccini in 1910.

Undergirding these varied cultural phenomena that reflected the public's abiding fascination with all things Western, was a largely tacit but nonetheless firmly rooted ideology. Promulgated in the decades preceding the American Civil War, the notion of Manifest Destiny suggested that U.S. expansion to the Pacific was not only inevitable, but, indeed, divinely sanctioned. Horace Greeley, fabled founder-editor of the *New York Herald Tribune*, reduced it to its epigrammatic essence in urging "Go West, young man, go West." For Americans entering a new century with a sense of growing responsibly as an emerging world power by dint of its victory in the Spanish-American War (and, with it, U.S. control of Cuba, Puerto Rico, Guam, and the Philippines), the burgeoning discourse on the American West provided an ideal site for elaborating on the ideological implications of Manifest Destiny. In what many historians have now labeled "The American Century," the American motion picture, especially the western, became a key in the mythologizing process that helped rationalize central aspects of American domestic and foreign policy. Westerns were also important in helping define the very nature of the American character.

The first westerns, like all early films, were humble affairs. *Cripple Creek Barroom* (1898), for instance, provided a brief one-minute look at western life, as did a number of other early Edison films. There were also snippets of cowboys twirling lassos and punching cattle. That all changed in 1903, when Edwin S. Porter released his twelve-minute "epic," *The Great Train Robbery* for Edison. Hyperbolically hailed as "the first story film" (which it manifestly was not) and "the first Western," Porter's opus was nonetheless pivotal in telling a genuinely dramatic tale through visual means without intertitles. According to film historian Lewis Jacobs, it was "the Bible for all film makers until Griffith's films further developed Porter's editing principle" (Jacobs 43). An enthused public responded by making *The Great Train Robbery* the nascent American film industry's first "blockbuster."

And for several years, each time a new Nickelodeon opened, at the head of the bill, more often than not, was *The Great Train Robbery*. In the aftermath of World War I, which resulted in Hollywood's domination of the international film market, westerns became powerful tropes for Manifest Destiny. At one level, stories of westward expansion further legitimized U.S. postwar political and economic imperialism. Just as significantly, westerns provided Americans with positive images keyed to the period's idealized profile of the American character, that is, a rugged individual at once courageous and caring, an inner-directed man of principle who although a loner, when the chips were down, always came to the rescue of the downtrodden. Interestingly, the westerner was sometimes even a visionary, part dreamer, part entrepreneur, and, therefore, a romantic builder whose visions of taming the West tallied with the businessman's governments of Harding, Coolidge, and Hoover and the doctrine of laissez-faire capitalism. These themes found ample and direct play in the decade's two large-scale Westerns, James Cruze's *The Covered Wagon* (1923) and John Ford's *The Iron Horse* (1924), whose heroes and heroines struggle to carve empires from the Western wilderness through epic battles with nature, greedy villains, and hostile "Indians." In reference to the latter, a note is in order. It was not until the 1960s that Native Americans began to receive at least some faint recognition in the cinema as American citizens with cultures and civilizations unique to their own experience. Still, in terms of the classical Western, which had always been written by whites, "Indians," although at times briefly idealized in the tradition of Rousseau's "natural man," primarily served the genre's narrative needs by dramatically embodying an obstacle to be overcome—through annihilation, subjugation or "civilization"—by whites presumably blessed by the divine aura inherent in the nation-building rationale of Manifest Destiny.

With the coming of sound, most westerns became a mostly low budget, B film affair. There were cliff-hanging serials featuring such mythical characters as The Lone Ranger, and similarly kid-oriented feature films of "good guy" heroes like Hopalong Cassidy. And, there were the commercially successful B films of singing cowboys Gene Autry and Roy Rogers. In 1939, however, that changed with the appearance of two "A" epics, John Ford's *Stagecoach* and Cecil B. DeMille's *Union Pacific*. The western, once again, was something worthy of adult attention and serious criticism. In fact, the highly regarded *Stagecoach* still stands as an exemplar of the classical western, and therefore a yardstick against which all westerns have been subsequently measured (Fenin and Everson 239–40).

In the intervening decades since *Stagecoach*, the fate of the movie western has waxed and waned. While basically adhering to the genre's tacit agreements between filmmakers and audiences as to basic themes and conventions, the western has at times also reflected more topical concerns. The most celebrated example of a western taking aim at an immediate societal controversy is *High Noon* (1952), a cautionary tale warning of the destructive forces of McCarthyism as seen through the prism of the classical western. The genre has also been a province for powerful directors such as the aforementioned Ford and Hawks, and also Anthony Mann, Budd Boetticher, and Sam Peckinpah (Kitses 11). Thus, in considering a form as richly diverse as the western, one must also take into account the unique contributions of the genre's most celebrated auteurs, including Clint Eastwood.

In schematizing the western's classic thematic conflicts, Jim Kitses's mapping of such oppositional forces as wilderness-civilization, individual-community, freedom-restriction, nature-culture and garden-desert is highly useful (Kitses 11). But, as *High Noon* illustrates and Thomas Schatz reminds us, the notion of genre should be seen as dynamic rather than static. Thus, while we can theorize the attributes of the classical western, we also need to take account of what Schatz calls generic evolution, the process by which a genre's basic assumptions are loosened for reexamination and rearticulation (Schatz 36–41).

In the western, the results of this evolutionary process have taken several forms. In one, the genre is deconstructed with parodistic mayhem as in Mel Brooks's delirious send-up, *Blazing Saddles* (1974), the highest grossing (monetary, that is) Western up to that time. In the second, the mannerist approach, the classical form is stripped to its stylistic essentials and, in the process, severed from the ideological moorings that had anchored the genre during its primitive and classical periods. Under the heightened aesthetic concerns of the mannerists, we find the spaghetti westerns of Sergio Leone, most prominently, *A Fistful of Dollars* (1964), which made Clint Eastwood a star as The Man with No Name. Significantly, *A Fistful of Dollars* was an Italian–Spanish–West German coproduction, directed by an Italian, who based his script on *Yojimbo* (1961), the acclaimed Japanese samurai film by Akira Kurosawa, who, in turn, had been inspired by the westerns of John Ford. What, one might ask, are the implications of the internationalization of a quintessentially American genre rooted so deeply in American history?

Whether parodistic or mannerist, both postclassical approaches, by subverting and therefore calling attention to the genre's classical conventions, rely on high levels of self-reflexivity. Here, the genre's basics are deconstructed, held up for reexamination and critique, and reconfigured in ways that have become increasingly self-conscious and self-evident to both filmmakers and audiences. Thus, we share in the "inside jokes" of Brooks's *Blazing Saddles*, and appreciate Leone's evocative minimalism, his boiling down of *A Fistful of Dollars* to the genre's bare bones, because we are conversant in the classical Western's bedrock grammar and syntax.

The cross-cultural influences mentioned in regard to *A Fistful of Dollars* also suggest the fluid interplay of generic conventions not only across history, but also across international boundaries. In the postmodern theorizing of critics probing the scale and implications of today's transnational hypermediated culture, *A Fistful of Dollars* exemplifies the construct of an ever-expanding universe of media-propagated signifiers circulating endlessly with little if any reference, historical or otherwise, to their original sources. Thus "freed," the thematic and iconic signifiers of the classical western have been increasingly sliced and diced into ahistorical postmodern melanges in which the genre's classical conventions, while superficially alluded to, have been largely ignored, or perverted, and thus turned upside down. The result in the 1990s, is a markedly uneven crop of idiosyncratic films that in many instances have, arguably, pushed the parameters of the classical western to the breaking point.

Turning to the task of surveying some of the more notable 1990s westerns, several questions might be kept in mind: Is a western a western just because it includes a gunfight at noon, men on horseback, tumbling tumbleweeds, or a temporal backdrop situated sometime between the end of the American Civil War and the turn-of-the-century? If the answer is "no," even provisionally so, then, can we honestly say that the western remains a viable genre? In 1990, Kevin Costner successfully revived the tradition of the big-budget, blockbuster western with *Dances with Wolves*, which won Oscars for Best Picture and Costner's debut as a director. A box-office as well as critical hit, the film takes a quasi-revisionist position by presenting an idealized West that never was. It tells the story of John Dunbar (Costner), a Union Army lieutenant assigned to the Army's westernmost command in the Dakotas. Finding the post deserted, Dunbar resolves to stay to explore the virgin paradise. Soon, the officer is confronted by a band of Sioux. Taking measure of one another, and, in the process, reducing the inherent mistrust between them, Dunbar, warrior Wind in His Hair (Rodney A. Grant), and shaman Kicking Bird (Graham Greene) arrive at a truce based on mutual curiosity.

In the words of Roger Ebert, *Dances with Wolves* is a "what if" movie (Ebert, *Dances* 189). Indeed, it is a nostalgic fantasy with a contemporary liberal spin that succeeds in helping Dunbar, and through Dunbar, the audience, come to a greater appreciation of Native Americans and their unique culture. Costner also deserves credit for using Native American actors, letting them speak their own language, and presenting a vision of them as fully dimensional beings rather than as the clichéd blood-thirsty warriors of Westerns past. Interestingly, in Ebert's review, the critic points up the film's main contradiction. In history, Ebert reminds us, contacts with Native Americans like those of Dunbar hardly, if ever, took place. "The dominant American culture was nearsighted, incurious and racist, and saw the Indians as a race of ignorant, thieving savages, fit to be shot on sight" (Ebert, *Dances* 189). Therefore, and in spite of Costner's good intentions, the film's rose-colored revisionism, the erasure of the genocidal forces let loose by Manifest Destiny, rings false. For white Americans, *Dances with Wolves* seemed to function as a no-pain, feel-good rite of belated atonement, however belated or hollow. Still, if the film helped raise lasting mainstream concerns for the plight of contemporary Native Americans, well and good. Yet that, too, is debatable.

The other western blockbuster of the 1990s is Clint Eastwood's *Unforgiven* (1992). Instead of "what if" revisionism, Eastwood seems to be offering, in what many hailed as "the last great western," a critique of his own western persona. It is a reflexive self-examination told as a tale of an over-the-hill gunfighter and, with it, a probe into the genre containing that gunfighter's bloody past. Like John Ford's last westerns, Eastwood's vision is dark. In contrast to the Edenic imagery of *Dances with Wolves,* in *Unforgiven,* we confront a universe whose primal elements are dust, grime, sweat, mud, and rain. These visual indexes help underscore the film's bleak themes. Indeed, in *Unforgiven,* Eastwood has not come to praise the western, but to deconstruct and deglamorize its myths. Exemplifying the self-referential aspect of today's postmodern sensibility, Eastwood's mannerist endgame puts the mirror up to his career as a western icon.

The story of the seen-better-days gunfighter looking to bury his past is an oft-told tale. In fact, it is a virtual western subgenre. Henry King's *The Gunfighter* (1950), Fred Zinnemann's *High Noon* (1952), and Don Siegel's *The Shootist* (1976) are among *Unforgiven's* worthy antecedents. In Eastwood's hugely lauded box-office smash, which won Oscars for Best Director and Best Picture, Eastwood plays Will Munny, an ex-gunfighter who has hung up his pistols and corked his jug to placate a new wife. When the film opens, eleven years have passed since Munny put his guns down. He is now a celibate widower raising two children, a hog farmer eking out a marginal existence on the Kansas plains. Having fallen off the wagon in despair over his wife's death, he is a pitiable character. A chance to change his miserable circumstances comes with an offer to join a bounty hunt. Munny's dilemma—and opportunity—arises when a brash would-be gunfighter (Jaimz Woolvett), recruits the once legendary gunslinger to help bring down a cowboy lowlife who took a knife to a prostitute's face in Big Whiskey, Wyoming.

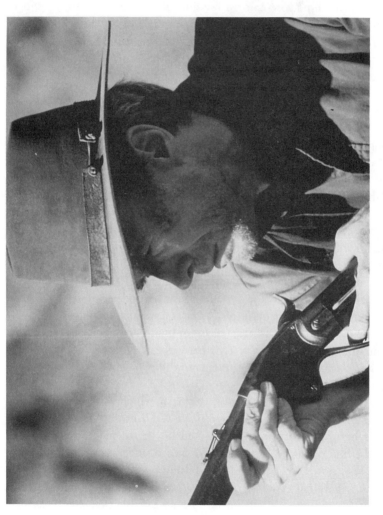

FIGURE 13.1. Clint Eastwood as the symbol of Western integrity and independence in his own film, *Unforgiven*. Courtesy: Jerry Ohlinger Archive.

To strap on his gun or not, that is the question for Munny. For the spectator, the question is whether or not to invest emotionally in Munny's predicament. As to the latter, the audience is left little choice. This is, after all, a Clint Eastwood film. Indeed, Eastwood's extrafilmic legacy looms everywhere, within, between, and beyond the frames. Then, there is Munny's character and his murderous background. In an opening scroll, Munny is described by his mother-in-law as "a man of notoriously vicious and intemperate disposition." Munny himself talks with regret about "the sins of my youth." Still, given his good-faith effort at reform and the fact that he is a father, we cannot help but empathize with his dreary plight. Furthermore, Eastwood's direction makes clear that we are supposed to feel the angst of a reformed man driven by desperate circumstances to again face down the demons of his past.

Munny, along with African American sidekick Ned Logan (Morgan Freeman), makes his reluctant decision and off they go with the Kid to the eventual showdown. Along the way, we see Munny and Ned struggle to regain a semblance of their former fighting forms in scenes played with a comic touch. However, in the end, as the motley trio confronts fascist Sheriff Little Bill Daggett (Gene Hackman) as well as its quarry, a sense of futility italicized by the chilling rain-drenched night pervades all. Eastwood has laid bear his heart of darkness. "It's a helluva thing killing a man," Munny says, "to take away all he's got and all he's going to have." Killing, the film says, is just plain hard.

For many, Eastwood's film is a meditation on the moral ambiguity of violence. On this point, it is useful to recall critic Robert Warshow who described the paradigmatic westerner as a gentleman whose code of honor prohibits him from drawing his gun first (Warshow 657). Due to his scrupulosity in killing, the westerner's just kill can be savored by audiences since any guilt by association has been absolved by the mechanics of the genre that have endorsed the hero's violence. In contrast, Eastwood's wayward westerner, with little remorse, blows his often helpless enemies away. In the words of Richard Alleva, "Eastwood has turned [Warshow's] 'gentleman' into a monster" (Alleva 21). In a mannerist style at times reminiscent of Sergio Leone's spaghetti westerns, Eastwood's deflation of the westerner is complete. This is a westerner without a code. *Unforgiven*, then, just might stand as the western's last will and testament, and, therefore, the western that killed off the genre.

Unforgiven, as mentioned, relies on intertextual connections to Eastwood's previous westerns and the western itself for much of its impact.

Although given a name, Eastwood's "William Munny" is an aging version of "The Man with No Name," a tie to his 1960s collaborations with Sergio Leone. The film's final act also echoes William Wellman's *The Ox-Bow Incident* (1943), one of Eastwood's favorite films. In the latter case, Eastwood's tip-of-the-hat to Wellman is more properly a homage, rather that the kind of ironically postmodern reference that in today's culture has more to do with playing on the stylistics of the fashionably hip than alluding appreciatively, and sincerely, to the genre's landmark works.

The western, like all genres, has been a highly malleable form responsive to the social and career politics of Hollywood as well as to the topical concerns of the day. Combined with the sneering pop cultural deconstruction of establishment values and icons that started in the 1960s, it is hardly surprising that the western has been pushed into so many different and even strange directions. One of these, is the "Brat Pack" western. As exemplified in Christopher Cain's *Young Guns*, which although released in 1988 is treated here because of its impact on 1990s westerns, the Brat Pack approach is more about style than substance. Indeed, its cast of young Hollywood hunks (Emilio Estevez, Kiefer Sutherland, Lou Diamond Phillips, Charlie Sheen, and Dermot Mulroney) is aptly described by Janet Maslin as being "less like a real movie than an extended photo opportunity for its trendy young stars" (Maslin C18). In yet another retelling of Billy the Kid's early days, *Young Guns* opts for adventure with high-jinks rather than historical accuracy. So while offering Brat Pack fans a chance to see idols preening about in western garb, the film, due to a lack of any serious thematic concern, can hardly be ranked as a contribution to the genre.

Still, the Brat Pack formula, reflecting the increasingly youth-oriented demographics of the American movie audience, proved it had economic clout. As a result, audiences were treated to Geoff Murphy's *Young Guns II* (1990), which borrowed its framing device of an aged geezer relating a "true" but unbelievable tale from Arthur Penn's *Little Big Man* (1970). Here, the geezer (a heavily made-up Emilio Estevez) purports to be Billy the Kid. Borrowing from Penn's *Bonnie and Clyde* (1967), *Young Guns II* has the image-aware Billy poring over newspaper clippings chronicling his rise to fame. Here, the film seems to be saying that its aimless antihero is in part motivated by publicity. Unfortunately, James Fusco's script and Murphy's direction are as aimless as the film's protagonist. While there are standard western elements such as a night in a whorehouse, the final shootout falls flat. Like its predecessor, by capitalizing almost exclusively on the drawing power of its postadolescent heartthrobs, the film winds up being not much more than kids playing with guns.

A more probative look into the past is Walter Hill's *Geronimo: An American Legend* (1993). Although covering familiar ground, Hill, perhaps picking up on Costner's sympathetic John Dunbar, gives us Army Indian scouts Al Sieber (Robert Duvall) and Charles Gatewood (Jason Patric), who actually attempt to understand their foe. Even their commander, Brig. Gen. George Crook (Gene Hackman), acquires a grudging respect for the Apache chief. Although featuring a nuanced performance by Cherokee actor Wes Studi in the title role, the film, like *Dances with Wolves*, is told from an exclusively white perspective. In fact, Geronimo is narrated by Lt. Britton Davis (Matt Damon), a recent West Point graduate, whom Roger Ebert perceptively describes as "a witness from the future, seeing how those who understood the situation, like Gatewood, were ignored and reviled because they did not fit in easily with the current sentiments in Washington" (Ebert, *Geronimo* 306). Thus, Studi's Geronimo is underused, serving mainly as a catalyst for revealing the film's white eyes.

Another exhumation of a Western legend is contained in George P. Cosmatos's *Tombstone* (1993). Featuring an "A" cast headed by Kurt Russell (Wyatt Earp), Val Kilmer (Doc Holliday), Sam Elliott (Virgil Earp), Bill Paxton (Morgan Earp), and, for nostalgic reflexivity, Charlton Heston (Henry Hooker), *Tombstone* is a highly stylized but lightweight affair borrowing from Sam Peckinpah and Sergio Leone. The film's lack of focus may stem from its checkered production history. *Tombstone* was to have been writer Kevin Jarre's directorial debut. After a month of shooting, however, Jarre was fired and replaced by action director George Cosmatos. As a result, what might have been a poignant study of classic western types, given Jarre's sensitive script for *Glory*, turns out to be a superficially entertaining but forgettable popcorn feature with Cosmatos's penchant for gratuitous violence much in display.

A more serious take on the same subject is Lawrence Kasdan's *Wyatt Earp* (1994). Here, the principals are played by Kevin Costner (Wyatt Earp), Dennis Quaid (Doc Holliday), and Gene Hackman (Nicholas Earp). Although directed by Lawrence Kasdan, who scored big in the genre with *Silverado* (1985), the Earp biopic lacks *Silverado's* adroit blend of comedy and western lore. Other liabilities are its three-hour running time and its insistence in telling all of Earp's story. The basic problem is that, as seen in this film, Earp's life is just not that interesting. Indeed, he died in 1929, almost a half century after the shootout at the O.K. Corral. In a business where timing is often everything, Kasdan's film also suffered by being released only six months after *Tombstone*. In spite of its loftier ambitions, in general, audiences found *Tombstone* entertaining and *Wyatt Earp* pretentious.

Historically, the western has been a virtually exclusive male-dominated domain. In the 1990s, in response to society's just demands for gender equality, roles for western women expanded. Or, so it seemed. Indeed, in Jonathan Kaplan's *Bad Girls* (1994) and Sam Raimi's *The Quick and the Dead* (1995), we find two westerns with women at the top of the bill. However, upon closer examination, these films offer little in the way of breaking new ground. Like the Brat Pack films, *Bad Girls* and *The Quick and the Dead* are commercially motivated knockouts obviously designed to appeal to women via the novelty of converting glamour gals into take-charge gunfighters. Kaplan's *Bad Girls* is patterned in large part after *Thelma & Louise* (1991), Ridley Scott's influential film that proved there was a market for female-driven projects other than romantic comedies and melodramas. Kaplan was not the original director on the project, but rather took over after a grittier, more feminist approach had been tried by original director Tamra Davis, and then vetoed by the producers. From all accounts, Davis's original film might well have ranked favorably with *Unforgiven*, but Kaplan's revisionist version is both sexist and infantile. With the completed *Bad Girls*, instead of two heroines, we get double that number. Starring four intelligent young actresses, Madeleine Stowe, Mary Stuart Masterson, Andie MacDowell, and Drew Barrymore, the film's principals, like Thelma and Louise, are on the lam because a man pressing his attentions too forcefully has been, well, sort of accidentally shot dead. That, regrettably, is the only point in common with Scott's provocative 1991 film. Sadly, the fine cast of *Bad Girls* is wasted in an unbelievably bad film that asks us to believe that four prostitutes could suddenly ride, shoot, and deploy explosives with an aplomb worthy of Sam Peckinpah's *The Wild Bunch* (1969). Compounding the mess is the foursome's fashion-model good looks. These beauties of the bordello stand in stark contrast to the authentically disheveled and put-upon prostitutes of Eastwood's *Unforgiven*. As more than one wag noted, *Bad Girls* was like *Young Guns* in drag.

More interesting, but still problematic, is Raimi's *The Quick and the Dead* (1995). Intended as a western vanity for actress Sharon Stone looking to recapture the sizzle of Adrian Lyne's *Fatal Attraction* (1987), the film is based on a simple premise: a scraggly lot of gunfighters converges in the town of Redemption to vie in a round-robin shoot-out in which only the victor will remain standing. During the tournament run by Herod (Gene Hackman), the town's evil despot, it is *High Noon* over and over again as contestants fall by the wayside one by one. Although the plot includes a whiff of sexual tension between the Stone and Hackman characters, and a young gun-toting Kid (Leonardo DiCaprio) purportedly Herod's son, these are mere diversions to the relentless windup to the tournament's climax. Stylistically, director Raimi takes a mannerist approach derived from Sergio Leone. Indeed, Stone's character, Ellen, is the gender reversal of Eastwood's Man with No Name. Stone, however, is no Eastwood, and her leaden parody falls flat. The film is partly redeemed by Hackman's inspired villainy and Raimi's stark compositions, flashy editing, and such novel setups as a shot in which we look down Main Street through a hole in a man's head. *The Quick and the Dead* is an often entertaining film. But, like so many westerns of the 1990s, its minimalist plot and stress on attitude and style come at the expense of any real concern with the classical western's thematics, whether conventional or revisionist.

In Mario Van Peebles's *Posse* (1993), we find a West populated with African American cowboys, good guys, and bad guys. We are introduced to the "posse" of the title, a band of Spanish-American War veterans, as they head off for Freemanville, the black township where the group's leader Jessie Lee (Van Peebles) grew up, now under siege by neighboring white racists. As Roger Ebert points out, the saga of black cowboys is a story that needs to be told (Ebert, *Posse* 3C). Van Peebles, however, loses control of his story in self-indulgent displays of cinematic hipness. As the film wobbles between parody and seriousness, and brings in such overworked references as Van Peebles's Man with No Name–inflected protagonist, the disappointment builds. The confusion extends to the casting. Along with such accomplished veterans as Woody Strode, one of only a few blacks to appear in studio-era westerns, Van Peebles includes amateurs like Tone Loc and Big Daddy Kane, rappers brought in to presumably boost teen interest. What might have been an important film winds up being a style-obsessed vanity piece, indeed, a hip-hop western.

Far more satisfying was Richard Donner's *Maverick* (1994), a well-received action-comedy western, at once a homage to the 1950s TV western, and a full-blown spoof of the genre in the manner of Brooks's *Blazing Saddles*. With winning performances by Mel Gibson, Jodie Foster, and James Garner (TV's Maverick), it is a stars-just-want-to-have-fun affair shot from an appropriately frothy script by William Goldman, who penned George Roy Hill's wry *Butch Cassidy and the Sundance Kid* (1969). Though not a western per se, Ron Underwood's *City Slickers* (1991) nonetheless deserves mention for its invocation of a mythic West as a benchmark against which to measure modern life. With its dude ranch, its borrowing of the musical theme from John Sturges's *The Magnificent Seven* (1960), and its inclusion of a crusty old westerner, Curly (Jack Palance), the film succeeds in providing its city slickers (Billy Crystal, Daniel Stern, and Bruno Kirby) with comedic adventures that, in the end, teach them something profound about themselves and life.

Given what we have seen of the 1990s, will the western somehow find a way out of its current postmodern status as a body of free-floating signifiers usable only in parodistic or mannerist or star-vanity ventures? Was *Unforgiven* the last deconstructive nail driven into the wooden coffin of the classical western? While predicting the future is always risky, there is reason to think that, yes, the classical western is dead. First and foremost, the mythic status of the western has understandably crumbled as the doctrine of Manifest Destiny has increasingly come to be understood as a part of America's imperialistic and, indeed, colonial past. The times, then, have bypassed both Manifest Destiny and the western. Also, attempts to revise the western in order to reposition Native Americans, minorities, and women seem viable only as cathartic "what if" fantasies. What, then, is left? Well, exactly, what we have seen in the 1990s. With the ideological gravity of the classical western now demolished, what remains is a grab bag of exhausted and watered down themes, high-fashion stylistics, and, not to be discounted, a nostalgia for an imagined past in which myth and fact are inextricably intertwined. And while westerns of the sorts chronicled here will undoubtedly continue to be made, the western as a means of transmitting epic and unifying tales of the American experience has passed.

WORKS CITED

Alleva, Richard. "Clint's Dark Vision." *Commonweal* (October 9, 1992): 21–22.

Ebert, Roger. "Dances with Wolves." *Roger Ebert's Video Companion: 1998 Edition.* Kansas City: Andrews McMeel, 1997. 189–90.

———. "*Geronimo: An American Legend.*" *Roger Ebert's Video Companion: 1998 Edition.* Kansas City: Andrews McMeel, 1997. 306–7.

————. Review of *Posse*. *The Chicago Sun-Times*. (May 14, 1993): 3C.

Fenin, George N., and William K. Everson. *The Western: From Silents to the Seventies*. New York: Grossman, 1973. 239–40.

Fielding, Raymond. *The American Newsreel, 1911–1967*. Norman: Oklahoma University Press, 1972.

Jacobs, Lewis. *The Rise of the American Film*. 1939; rpt. New York: Teachers College, Columbia University, 1968.

Kitses, Jim. *Horizons West: Anthony Mann, Budd Boetticher, Sam Peckinpah: Studies of Authorship within the Western*. Bloomington: Indiana University Press, 1969.

Maslin, Janet, "Charmin' Billy." *The New York Times* (August 12, 1988): C18.

Schatz, Thomas. "Generic Evolution: Patterns of Increasing Self-Consciousness." *Hollywood Genres: Formulas, Filmmaking, and the Studio System*. New York: Random House, 1981. 36–41.

Warshow, Robert. "Movie Chronicle: The Westerner." 1954, rpt. *Film Theory and Criticism: Introductory Readings*. 5th ed. Ed. Leo Braudy and Marshal Cohen. New York. Oxford University Press, 1998. 654–67.

CHAPTER FOURTEEN

◉

Hanging on a Star: The Resurrection of the Romance Film in the 1990s

CATHERINE L. PRESTON

Although it seems straightforward and obvious, the romance genre is a difficult category to describe or define. A list of the top thirty romance films searched on the *Internet Movie Database* for the week ending September 18, 1998, included Ivan Reitman's *Six Days, Seven Nights* (1998), Peter Howitt's *Sliding Doors* (1998), and James L. Brooks's *As Good As It Gets* (1997). It also included such science-fiction adventures as Jonathan Frakes's *Star Trek: Insurrection* (1998), Robert Zemeckis's *Contact* (1997), and Paul Verhoeven's *Starship Troopers* (1997). What this indicates is that the romance film is often grouped with many other kinds of films. This chapter posits a general definition of the romance film and examines to what extent it may be beneficial to delimit the number of films considered as romance based on a similarity of signs, and to utilize a genre approach in the study of this particular kind of film.

I begin with a very general definition of romance as that film in which the development of love between the two main characters is the primary narrative thread, the main story line. In Hollywood films, these characters are without exception heterosexual. In some of the films I consider, the romance vies for primary place with another plot, such as thriller or mystery, as in Mick Jackson's *The Bodyguard* (1992), or Steven Kloves's *Flesh and Bone* (1993). Following Tom Ryall, I begin with such a general notion in order to see how romance films can be considered a genre or perhaps a subgenre (336). No intellectually precise formulation is possible through which the variances of any large body of films can be explained (Hayward 164). But it may be useful to attempt to move in that direction depending on the research question that is asked of the material. For example, if the question is of a historical nature, a genre approach could answer how the representation of love between men and women has changed over the last sixty years. Similarly, if the study of romance films as genre is a step along the way to conducting a reception study, the researcher would want to know what the range of narratives are and the range of formulas (codes and conventions) for representing those narratives. This chapter will consider the extent to which codes and conventions utilized in romance films constitute a structure recognizable across films. Future researchers may wish to pursue the extent to which audiences recognize and respond to such a structure or what it is about romance films themselves that is appealing and how audiences interpret them.

Why is romance not usually considered a specific genre by film scholars when it clearly is by those who market films, review films, construct popular encyclopedias such as *Cinemania* and *Internet Movie Database*, and especially by film audiences? Romance films often seem to be hybrids, a melange of different, already recognized and theorized genres. As other film scholars have noted, most if not all films include a narrative thread involving romantic tension of some sort (Bordwell, Staiger, and Thompson 16–17). In addition, the romance film, typically aimed at women and debased in popular media as "chick flicks," is often viewed by the academic establishment as not worthy of scholarly investigation. These particular films fall into the bottom tier of popular culture, an area of scholarly attention already suffering under the perception of its object as "low" culture.

Tom Ryall has written that the process of reading a film requires a background context, particular reference points against which the actual film acquires sense and meaning (*Genre and Hollywood* 337). This may be considered the generic system, which is constructed through a range of discourses: the form of the film, its iconography, situational conventions, stock of characters, critical and journalistic discourse in various media, marketing, publicity activities, as well as a memory of previous films. I would add that the environment in which films are produced and circulate is a specific historical, social, cultural, political, and economic moment and that the film is understood by audiences within that environment. In other words, there are periods in history in which the social environment "favors" the production of romance films. They are considered workable vehicles for framing contemporary discourse about culture and social issues.

There has been a steady rise over the last fourteen years in the production of what are referred to in popular reference sources as Hollywood "romance" films. Between 1960 and 1969 there were an average of 7 romances released a year. In the 1970s that figure went down to 5 per year. In 1980 the production of romances began to rise and between 1984 and 1989 an average of 20 were released each year. Between 1990 and 1996, the annual average rose to 26, peaking at 40 in 1991. Hollywood has not approached this level of romance films since the 1950s when there was a yearly average of 13 released over the course of the decade (*Internet Movie Database, Cinemania*).

What can explain this rise in the production of romance films? In this chapter I focus on an analysis of a small sample of films, but consider possible explanations for this rise in view of what kind of messages the films themselves propose about relations between the sexes in the 1990s, and what basic changes in society might contribute to this upswing in the representation of love and marriage. The collection of films chosen for consideration in this chapter were based to an extent on popularity, but I also considered one unpopular film for the purpose of comparison. The films were viewed and analyzed in terms of the conventions that they shared; plot devices such as how the film ends; whether the couple are represented as having sex during the time of the film's plot; whether they have confidants; and how the realization of "true" love is visualized on screen. The films were grouped according to very large narrative distinctions for the purposes of analysis: romantic comedy, screwball comedy, drama, and the hybrid.

The screwball comedy has been defined as a film in which one or both of the lead characters, and perhaps others, engage in situations staged as physical slapstick comedy in the pursuit of their disparate goals and through a comedy of errors, arrive at "true" love by the end of the film (Harvey). Along the way they may make fools of themselves and usually disparage each other but all is forgiven by the end. Three of the films in the group considered here can be called screwball comedies: Lawrence Kasdan's *French Kiss* (1995), Griffin Dunne's *Addicted to Love* (1997), and

P. J. Hogan's *My Best Friend's Wedding* (1997). In none of these is there as much physical humor as one would find in the screwball comedies of the 1930s and 1940s. It is significant that Meg Ryan is in two of these. In fact, she has distinguished herself by appearing in many romantic comedies and screwball comedies. These particular kinds of films have become vehicles for her, and she functions as a vehicle for this type of film as well. This is an example of the intertextuality of films in general, and specifically one way the industry encourages a genre approach by critics and the audience through the use of the star system. Although the films that she stars in all share some common comedic iconographic motifs associated specifically with her body and mannerisms, it is not the case that these films are all screwball comedy since the narratives vary considerably. She is in five of the romances I deal with in this chapter, only two of them screwball comedies and one a romantic drama. This generic reliance on star personas works so well that the early romantic drama she appeared in did not do well at the box office. Kevin Kline plays opposite Ryan in *French Kiss*. Kline is another star who has appeared in several comedies and a few screwball comedies. The pairing of these two for this film was a clear indication to the audience of what to expect in terms of both slapstick comedy and romance. Julia Roberts, who stars in *My Best Friend's Wedding*, also starred in other romantic comedies—Garry Marshall's *Pretty Woman* (1990) and Charles Shyer's *I Love Trouble* (1994). But it is in *My Best Friend's Wedding* that she exhibits the greatest range as a comic actress. What the three of these films share besides the slapstick comedy is that the main female character, and in the case of *Addicted to Love*, also the male character, has been spurned in love and decides to try to win back the lost love. This is not a convention of 1930s or 1940s romances but it may be an innovation of romance films of the 1980s and 1990s.

French Kiss begins with Kate (Ryan) and Charley (Tim Hutton) engaged to be married. Charley goes to Paris and falls in love with another woman. Kate, who is terrified of flying, nonetheless flies over the Atlantic to win him back. Luc (Kline), the son of a winegrower in France who lost his inheritance in a poker game with his brother, has stolen a necklace, which he hides in Kate's bag on the flight over to Paris. Kate's bags get stolen upon arrival at the hotel and Luc's need to find the necklace in order to buy an old grape orchard motivates him to help her win Charley back. During the ensuing events they realize they love each other.

Like *French Kiss*, *Addicted to Love* involves the narrative device of a spurned lover who pursues the lost object of affection, yet in this case there are a pair of them, male as well as female. In this film only one of the spurned, Sam, who is played by Matthew Broderick, wants to get the loved one back. Maggie (Ryan) wants only revenge on the man who left her. The two characters are brought together in an abandoned warehouse across from the couple's apartment where they have come in order to spy on their lost loves. It becomes clear to Sam that his girlfriend, Linda, is not going to break up with Maggie's boyfriend, Anton, and the two set out to plot the demise of that relationship. They succeed after several comedic exploits in which the physical humor is primarily at the expense of Anton, but then they discover that they love each other instead. The film's theme is spoken by Anton (Tchéky Karyo) to Sam as he explains why he left Maggie (and which Maggie hears in the abandoned building across the street). He says "You can't choose who you love" and he loves Linda, Sam's former girlfriend. This is offered as simple wisdom in the film, as if it is the beginning and end of love's responsibility. It is also the key line by which Sam realizes he loves Maggie and not Linda.

The narrative of *My Best Friend's Wedding* involves a professional woman who, upon being told by her close male friend Michael that he is getting married, begins a campaign to win him back. Because Michael's character is so one-dimensional and sexist it is not difficult to read this film as a story about Julianne's journey to self-discovery through self-delusion. She comes to the realization at the end of the film that Michael doesn't love her and that is for the best. The screwball comedies have much in common with the romantic comedies, the primary difference being the physical humor and the futile chase after lost lovers.

There is one other device I analyze as a convention of romantic comedies that is missing in two of the screwball comedies but present in *My Best Friend's Wedding*, and that is the character of the confidant. This someone with whom the main character shares his or her inner feelings is usually a friend, family member, or employer, although in some cases it can be a complete stranger. This person's function in the story is to act as a sounding board for the main character and to communicate to the audience something of the nature of the emotional transformation taking place as he or she considers the prospect of falling in love. The convention does not exist in *French Kiss* or *Addicted to Love*. In *French Kiss* the characters are on their own, one in a foreign country and the other a fugitive from the law. The initial weight of the emotional transformation is treated similarly to romantic dramas in which emotional change is represented through a combination of acting and cinematic techniques such as lingering close-ups. Luc, tries to put his hand into Kate's bag and is kissed by a sleeping Kate. Her head rests on her bag and she is evidently dreaming about kissing Charley. Luc responds strongly by kissing Kate back in close-up. He is confused by his response, and in a medium-close shot he sits back and stares at her with a troubled expression on his face. The next morning Kate is transformed as well and her actions in pursuing Charley take on a half-hearted effort. In this, she is transformed in a similar manner to the female lead in Jean Vigo's *L'Atalante* (1934). Kate is not certain of the motivation for her change of feeling and does not immediately locate Luc as the source of that change having been asleep when they kissed. Luc attempts to ignore the feeling until the end of the film.

In *Addicted to Love*, Sam and Maggie treat each other as unwilling confidants in the first quarter of the film when discussing their former lovers. When that changes we are meant to read the transformation in two events. The first is when Maggie's grandmother has dinner with them and, assuming they are a couple, tells them to kiss while she takes their picture, three times. They do and the third time the kiss is longer and more passionate, confusing and embarrassing both of them. The second and clinching event is experienced separately. For Sam, it occurs after Anton and Linda have broken up. Sam is talking to Anton and says that he loves Maggie (not Linda), thinking it an odd slip of the tongue. For Maggie it occurs when she is watching Anton tell Sam that people cannot choose who they want to love. She feels sorry for Anton and forgives him finally, setting her free to love Sam.

My Best Friend's Wedding is entirely built around another convention of all romantic comedy, including the screwball comedy, which focuses on the idea that one of the characters is engaged to the wrong person. Conventionally, one of the characters realizes that he or she loves someone else more than the person with whom he or she has been involved. In this film, however, this device is played backward. Julianne (Julia Roberts) will not admit she and Michael (Dermot Mulroney) are not right for each other. The confidant in this case, Julianne's gay friend, George (Rupert Everett), spends most of his time listening to her go on about how she is going to win Michael back and then telling her to give it up, Michael does not love her. The visualization of the moment in which Julianne realizes this comes when she goes looking for Kimmy (Cameron Díaz), Michael's betrothed, and finds her in the woman's bathroom at the ballpark. Julianne tries to make things "right" and convince Kimmy that Michael loves her. In doing this Julianne has to verbalize what George has been telling her all along, that Kimmy "won" and she "lost." Saying that allows her to go on with her life. In other romances, the representation of the realization of love is one of the major turning points of the film. Though here it is the realization of an absence of love, it is a major turning point. Typically in this genre the most romantic scene appears at the end of the film, and this film follows suit. However, the romantic moment is parodied by having it take place between George and Julianne. *My Best Friend's Wedding* can be seen as an antiromance in its reversing of many of the conventions that romantic comedies have in common, and I have included it for that purpose.

Each of the following films considered as romantic comedy share the utilization of a confidant but do not have the aspect of physical humor evident in screwball comedies. Beyond this difference there are conventions shared between these two groups that make them more similar than different, such as the marriage of the two leads at the end of the film, the absence of sex before recognition of true love (with three significant exceptions), and the visualization of the moment of transformation. Shumway (382) makes the point that one reason for the increase in romances that imply or end in marriage during the 1930s and 1940s was an upsurge in divorces that occurred in the broader society at that time. It is unlikely that that motivated the increase in romance films beginning in the mid-1980s since the divorce rate had been going up steadily for the previous two decades leveling off around 50 percent in the early 1980s. It is more likely that the political ascendancy of the Republican right and the "New Traditionalists" with "family values" explain this reassertion of marriage, at least in the romantic comedy.

Romantic comedies of the 1970s and early 1980s often ended with the characters getting married but they usually had sex along the way. This is not the case with romantic comedies of the 1990s. This may partially be explained by the AIDS epidemic but since only one of the romantic comedies involving sex, *Pretty Woman*, introduces the practice of safe sex, and that in the situation of sex with a whore, it is as likely explained by the desire for a PG rating in a market environment increasingly hostile to sex outside of marriage. In the other two romantic comedies in which sex before marriage takes place it is represented by the characters as a drastic mistake, not because they did not practice safe sex but because they acted on impulse.

Rob Reiner's *When Harry Met Sally* (1989) is a romance that carries several reassuring messages for those concerned about the high rate of divorce. The film involves two people who get to know each other right after college and continue to cross paths over the next several years as they meet and break up with other people. The film constitutes a running dialogue about the state of sex, love, and marriage in the late twentieth century. The narrative of the film is interspersed with interviews with older couples, framed as documentary, in which they speak to the camera and tell us, the audience, how they met and fell in love. They all appear to be of retirement age, and the majority of them met young and have been together ever since. The narrative itself concerns Harry and Sally and the trials and tribulations they go through before they realize they want to get married and spend the rest of their lives together. They become friends along the way and that is offered as one way to insure the longevity of "true" love. They each have close friends of the same sex in whom they confide, and through these conversations we glimpse their internal emotional struggle with letting themselves trust the other person and the process of falling in love. The last interview of the film is Harry and Sally, after they are married, telling us how they met and fell in love. It is a narrative device that constructs a particular image of marriage as a lifelong commitment.

The exception to this convention within the group of films I viewed was *Pretty Woman*. This film is about Edward (Richard Gere), a one-dimensional New York business man who ruthlessly takes over companies and Vivian (Julia Roberts), a lower-class hooker from Georgia. This is the only romance that makes class difference part of the plot. He hires her to accompany him for the week he is in Los Angeles on business. While he acculturates her to the behavior of the upper class and their pasttimes of eating at expensive restaurants and going to the opera, she teaches him how to relax and encourages him not to be ruthless in business deals. Also qualifying as a romantic comedy according to the notion I began with, the couple in this film have sex every night of the week, which the film's plot covers. This is justified by the fact that Vivian's occupation is a whore. Nevertheless, the film shares the other conventions of romantic comedies: after a series of misunderstandings the ending of the film infers that they get married, they both have confidants through which their emotional transformation is traced, there is the visualization of transformation occurring during the third night in which, for the first time, they kiss each other on the mouth during sex.

The visualization of the moment of transformation sometimes occurs to both characters at the same time and place as in *Pretty Woman*, but most often it occurs separately. Nora Ephron's *Sleepless in Seattle* (1993) is a film in which the two leads do not meet until the last scene of the film although they have seen each other from a distance and communicated through intermediaries. Sam (Tom Hanks) is an architect whose wife died. Sam's small son wants him to date and literally broadcasts that point on an evening radio talk show. Annie (Ryan) hears the show and begins to notice signs and coincidences between them that lead her to a change of heart, to believe that love is magic and fateful and people can know when they are "meant" for each other, just like her mother told her. Sam, who already believes in that kind of love, does not believe that he will meet anyone like that again. But he is led by his son to finally meet Annie and they both realize that they were "meant" for each other. The scene in which both of them become willing to surrender to this possibility, though they have not yet met, occurs in a series of alternating shots. We see each of them separately sitting on their respective benches, each facing a body of water, in separate cities, contemplating the water, the sky, themselves while the soundtrack plays slow orchestration made up primarily of strings. This contemplation is a convention of Hollywood romance film in general. In this film it is a sign to the audience that their meeting, love, and marriage is inevitable because they are, first of all linked by editing, and at this point in the narrative, linked as willing to believe in the magic of love. This film conforms to the conventions of no sex before "true" love. Annie is engaged to Walter (Bill Pullman) and they live together. But we never see them have sex. He is feminized, his health compromised by severe allergies, so we read him as not the "true" love interest almost from the beginning of the film. Other shared conventions include the assumption of marriage at the end of the film, and the presence of confidants with whom the main characters share their emotional uncertainties and changes.

As mentioned earlier, another convention that most romantic-comedy narratives share is the necessary shedding of the "wrong" person. Most often this person is engaged to the main character. Sometimes this shedding is worked out as in *Sleepless in Seattle*; Annie comes to realize that Walter is not right for her and finally tells him so. Sometimes the realization that the main character comes to regarding the current object of affection is a slow process, as in *Addicted to Love*, *French Kiss*, and *My Best Friend's Wedding*. In Jon Turteltaub's *While You Were Sleeping* (1995) though, this convention operates as merely a device against which the true romance is then played out. *While You Were Sleeping* involves Lucy (San-

FIGURE 14.1. Bill Pullman and Sandra Bullock in Jon Turteltaub's *While You Were Sleeping*. Courtesy: Jerry Ohlinger Archive.

dra Bullock) a mass-transit token-booth operator who saves Peter (Peter Gallagher), a man she has been attracted to but has never met, when on Christmas Day he is mugged and thrown on the tracks at her station. Seeing her at the hospital, while he is in a coma, his family assumes she is his fiancée. When she eventually falls in love with his brother, Jack (Bill Pullman) she is caught between telling the truth and losing their love, or marrying the brother she doesn't love. She confides in her employer several times, letting us know she is torn, and confides in the family friend who overhears her telling Peter, still in a coma, the truth. The narrative makes use of this convention of the need to quit the last love in order to realize the true love, and much of the comedy surrounds the fact that she never loved Peter, that fictions are sometimes harder to break than the real thing. Other than this simple twist, the rest of the narrative conforms to those conventions of the genre. She and Jack get married at the end of the film, there is no sex during the plot, and there is the use of confidants to let the viewer in on the internal workings of the main characters.

Another film that uses most of the conventions of the romantic comedy but twists them slightly is *As Good As It Gets*. Melvin (Jack Nicholson), a neurotic, rude, bigoted, antisocial man, becomes attracted to Carol (Helen Hunt), the waitress at a restaurant where he eats breakfast. He is absolutely at a loss as to what to do about it. She also finds him attractive but thinks he is too mean and rude to waste time on. Melvin's gay neighbor, Simon (Greg Kinnear) gets beaten up and hospitalized and as a last resort asks Melvin's help. Slowly Melvin is drawn out of himself, makes changes in his behavior and progresses toward a relationship with Carol. The twist in conventions is that both Carol and Melvin use Simon as a confidant, and Simon is as important in Melvin's development as Carol. In addition, Melvin and Carol agree to date at the end of the film, not marry, though that possibility is not closed off. Similar to other romantic comedies there is no sex during the film, though there is talk of it in a very straightforward manner. This film and *My Best Friend's Wedding* each utilize some of the conventions of romance films, but twist them in ways that nearly make them parodies of romance. The effort needed to engage with the socially accepted romantic paradigm of repartee, love, and marriage is shown in each of these films to be almost totally self-consuming. This is not the positive way it is depicted in the other romance films, but negatively, as if to engage with romance on the conventional terms offered is dangerous to some characters.

The conventions of the romantic drama are different than those of the romantic comedy although the narrative line remains the same. In other words, although the devices through which the characters are defined and through which the action is played out differ, the primary narrative line remains the development and recognition of love between the two hetero- sexual main characters. The conventions differ and contrast with those of the romantic comedy in terms of the four following aspects: greater repre- sentation of sex; greater display of the female body and sometimes the male body; endings that do not indicate marriage between the lovers; and much less use of confidants who act as mediators between the viewer and the inner emotional life of the main characters. The absence of the convention of a confidant serves to emphasize the insularity of the couple in the romance dramas as opposed to romantic comedies. It is an intriguing difference in narrative devices indicating some interesting assumptions about intimacy. The message seems to assume that where there is sexuality within a story of dramatic weight, the function of friends or a community in the couple's life is lessened. No doubt, the needs of the genre come into play as well. It is difficult to sustain a dynamic comedy through the interactions of only two people.

Clint Eastwood's *Bridges of Madison County* (1995) has often been described as the quintessential mid-1990s romantic drama. It is about two middle-age people, Francesca (Meryl Streep) a farmer's wife and Robert (Clint Eastwood) an itinerant photojournalist, who meet while Francesca's family is away at a state fair. They have an affair, fall in love, and at the end of the week he asks her to go with him. She packs her bags but then decides to stay with her family, a decision that is justified by the needs of her family but also serves to retain the fantasy of the affair.

One of the conventions of the romantic drama that works in lieu of the confidant is the musical soundtrack. To be sure, the soundtrack is just as important to the romantic comedy as to the romantic drama, as it is to all films today, acting as a merchandising link as well as constructing the mood and meaning of the film. In the romantic drama, however, it plays an additional role as interpreter of the emotional tenor of the moment. The jazz music chosen by Eastwood, who also directed the film, is a mood setter for the romantic scenes, but there is orchestration that occurs dur- ing the dramatic highlights as well. This is evident when the main char- acters discuss what has been happening between them the past week; when she says that she cannot go with him; and at the end when her chil- dren throw her cremated ashes off Rosemond Bridge the music is pre- dominantly strings, stereotypically dramatic and sad, and meant to focus the scene on the emotions of the characters.

Another convention of the romantic drama that contrasts with the romantic comedy is that closure does not hold out the possibility of marriage at the end of the film. In none of the films considered here does the couple get married at the end of the film. In *Bridges of Madison County* Francesca remains married to her husband and Robert goes off to live the rest of his life alone. Similarly, in only two of the romantic dramas I consider here does the couple begin or continue dating when the film ends. In Michael Hoffman's *One Fine Day* (1996), though there is no sex during the film, the possibility is there by the end when the two main characters resolve their differences and fall asleep next to each other on the couch while their children watch television in the other room. Melanie (Michelle Pfeiffer), an architect, and Jack (George Clooney), a journalist, are late getting their children to the class field trip, miss the boat, (literally), and are stuck taking care of the kids all day. Melanie blames Jack and makes him responsible for child care part of the day. They strike a deal by which they take turns caring for both children while the other gets work done. The message of the film involves the necessity of partnership in a era when (married or not) both people in a relationship have careers, and possibly kids, and the question becomes how to get everyone's needs met.

The ending in Jon Avnet's *Up Close and Personal* (1996) evidences another option for romantic dramas—the death of the male lead (and occasionally the female lead in some contemporary feature films). *Up Close and Personal* is about Tally Atwater (Michelle Pfeiffer), an inexperienced, young broadcast journalist who is taken under the wing of a seasoned reporter, Warren Justice (Robert Redford) and trained to be one of the best news anchorwomen in the country. Along the way they fall in love. Sex and marriage are depicted, but Warren is killed covering a story in Central America. This ending is similar to that of Jerry Zucker's *Ghost* (1990), although the death of the husband happens early in that film.

A significant difference between the romantic comedy and the romantic drama involves the assumption of a particular audience for each type of film. In romantic comedies there is very little emphasis on display of the female star's body or the male star's body. With the exception of *Pretty Woman* and *My Best Friend's Wedding*, the female body is not displayed through clothing or behavior. The fact that there is such a focus in those two films says more about the perception of Julia Roberts as a star and the expectation that through display of her body it may be possible to bring a higher percentage of men into the theater. The depiction of sex becomes another opportunity to display the female body and generally the women who are chosen for leading roles in romantic dramas are women who have bodies that are construed as sexual. The exception to this in the films considered in this chapter is *Flesh and Bone*, starring Meg Ryan in the female lead. Though sex is depicted in the film, the focus is not on her body, as it is on Meryl Streep's in *Bridges of Madison County*, or Michelle Pfeiffer's in *One Fine Day* or *Up Close and Personal.*

The *Bodyguard* and *Flesh and Bone* can thus be considered as romantic hybrids. Both are romantic dramas and also thrillers. They are examples of what Todd Gitlin (64) has called "the recombinant form"; constructed from multiple genre traditions in order to appeal to a larger audience. *The Bodyguard* is about a former secret service man, Frank Farmer, (Kevin Costner) hired to guard superstar and singer, Rachel Marron (Whitney Houston) whose life has been threatened. This is a case similar to nearly all of the other films dealt with in this piece in which intertextuality provided by the star personae constructs the film as much as the narrative. Both stars are essentially "displayed doing 'their thing', action hero and singer, with narrative clearly subordinated to spectacle" (Phillips 146). It is established that they are attracted to each other though Costner plays his character very flat and for the most part expressionless. Early in the film they have sex after she asks him out on a date, and the next morning he says he can not sleep with clients, that to do so compromises his ability to protect them. She gets very angry and a sexual tension persists throughout the rest of the film, while the story line deals with trying to find and stop the madman. Near the end they become friends again and the camera constructs shots typical to most genres of falling in love—they look longingly at each other and they stare off into the distance in solitary moments. He is able to save her life when the madman tries to shoot her but they part company at the end of the film, still in love with each other but following the separate demands of their careers.

Flesh and Bone is a much darker film, about Arlis Sweeney (Dennis Quaid), another fairly expressionless character, who befriends and falls in love with Kay Davies (Meg Ryan), only to find out that she is the sole survivor of a family that his father shot and killed in a robbery thirty years before. Arlis was instrumental in the robbery and when his father shows up to finish off the last member of the family, Arlis protects her from the truth by killing his father. Though he still loves her and she him, his guilt prevents him from staying and he leaves her in a motel in a small Texas town without an explanation. Similar to the other romantic dramas, the main characters do have sex with each other and there are no confidants to let the audience in on the emotional changes they go through. That is done through acting, camera work, and the presence of props, as well as dialogue with the two criminal characters. Of course, in the romantic comedies there are individual shots of each character in contemplation of the object of love or the prospect of true love. However, romantic dramas tend to utilize them more often and to devote more screen time to such shots. The difficulty in casting Meg Ryan in this role in a romantic drama lies in the lingering of the camera on her face in which we see mannerisms similar to those in her romantic comedies. Not only does this kind of film make use of the same stars but it seems more difficult for stars from the comedies to cross over to romantic dramas than for stars who have been dramatic leads to cross over to comedy. Both Richard Gere and Robert Redford played dramatic leads before romantic comedy. It does not necessarily correspond with the acting range of the star. Meg Ryan did receive very good reviews for her role in the later melodrama, Luis Mandoki's *When a Man Loves a Woman* (1994).

Genres must be talked about in terms of the structures that sustain them, not those that fix them. The structures and conventions I have generally outlined in this chapter each deserve fuller treatment and consideration through an analysis of a larger group of films. There are some interesting similarities among films when comedies and dramas are considered separately. There are shared conventions between these groups of films, such as the convention for visualizing the moment of love realized, but the differences between the comedies and the dramas outweigh the similarities. These differences seem to be primarily in terms of the use of confidants, the presence or absence of sex, and whether or not the ending is resolved in marriage. This lends credence to the idea that the romance film might be seen more profitably as subcategories of two major genres, the comedy and the melodrama (Williams 121).

Romantic comedies use the narrative device of one person engaged to or involved with the wrong person, and the plot revolves around recognizing the right person and getting rid of the wrong person. Women typically have nonprofessional or low-paying jobs and want very much to be married whereas men do not. Romance in these films is characterized as an event out of ordinary life. It is treated as a magical, spontaneous, event that takes an enormous amount of energy to resolve. Dramatic romance does not use that device but approaches romance and love as something that *happens to* people in the midst of their going about their lives. This normalizes the idea of romance but also treats its occurrence as magical and spontaneous. It is posed as a natural event rather than a necessary event, but one that requires little effort on the part of those to whom it is happening. The women may have professional jobs but do not give them up for the man.

There are, of course, multiple influences at play in the cultural and political field. But certainly among them is the rise of Reaganism and the Republican right, touting family values and an individualistic mentality. What some have referred to as a "New Traditionalist" agenda is essentially a return to the idealized values of the 1950s in which the gender roles are clearly defined, mother stays home if she has the option, and abortion is rarely available and often illegal. It would seem from this small group of films that the romantic comedy is the more conservative of the two in its representation of women.

When the group is taken as a whole, what stands out is the combination of star power with the notion of genre that I began with. Each of the films exhibits, more or less, twists and reversals of the shared conventions and represents the way in which films play with conventions, provide innovations, while utilizing many of the codes found in the majority of films of this narrative type. Each of the films contained at least one very well known star who had appeared in romances, whether comic or dramatic, during the 1980s, with the exception of *While You Were Sleeping*. This indicates that what characterizes the genre as much as shared conventions is its interaction with and dependence on the star system.

This chapter began with a general notion of what constitutes a romance film. The analysis of a small sample of films conforming to that very general notion rendered similarities at the level of filmic conventions and also revealed the extent to which the romance films utilize the spectacle of stars in conjunction with these conventions. These results must be more fully developed in future studies in order to understand the specific workings of romance films in conjunction with the audience, the industry, and the social, political, and economic environment that contains them both.

WORKS CITED

Bordwell, David, Janet Staiger, and Kristen Thompson. *The Classical Hollywood Cinema: Film Style and Mode of Production to 1960.* New York: Columbia University Press, 1985.

Cinemania Database. Microsoft, 1997.

Gitlin, Todd. *Inside Prime Time.* New York: Pantheon, 1983.

Harvey, James. *Romantic Comedy in Hollywood.* 1987. New York: Da Capo Press, 1998.

Hayward, Susan. *Key Concepts in Cinema Studies.* New York: Routledge, 1996.

Internet Movie Database. September 18, 1998. Online.

Phillips, Patrick. "Genre, Star and Autuer: An Approach to Hollywood." *An Introduction to Film Studies.* Ed. Jill Nelmes. New York: Routledge, 1996. 121–63.

Ryall, Tom. "Genre and Hollywood." *The Oxford Guide to Film Studies.* Ed. John Hill and Pamela Church Gibson. Oxford: Oxford University Press, 1998. 327–41.

———. "The Notion of Genre." *Screen* 11.2 (1970): 22–32.

Shumway, David R. "Screwball Comedies: Constructing Romance, Mystifying Marriage." *Film Genre Reader II.* Ed. Barry Keith Grant. 1st ed. Austin: University of Texas Press, 1995. 381–401.

Williams, Alan. "Is a Radical Genre Criticism Possible?" *Quarterly Review of Film Studies* 9.2 (Spring 1984): 121–25.

NOTES ON
CONTRIBUTORS

◼

Heather Addison is a Ph.D. candidate in Film Studies at the University of Kansas. With the support of a fellowship from the university, she is currently at work on her dissertation, "Hollywood and the 'Reducing' Craze of the 1920s."

Chuck Berg is Professor of Film and Associate Chair of the Department of Theatre and Film at the University of Kansas. His work has appeared in a variety of journals, including *Cinema Journal, The University Film and Video Association Journal, The Journal of Popular Film,* and elsewhere. He is the author of the critical study *Investigation of the Motives for the Use of Music with the American Silent Film.*

Tom Conley is Professor of Romance Languages at Harvard University. His most recent book is *The Self-Made Map: Cartographic Writing in Early Modern France* (1996).

David Desser is Professor of Cinema Studies at the University of Illinois, Urbana-Champaign, where he has been teaching since 1981. A former editor of *Cinema Journal,* he has published numerous books on Japanese cinema and has coedited an anthology on Hong Kong cinema forthcoming from Cambridge University Press.

Wheeler Winston Dixon is the Chair of the Film Studies Program at the University of Nebraska, Lincoln. His most recent books are *Disaster and Memory* (1999) and *The Second Century of Cinema* (2000).

Marc Miller is assistant copy chief at *Business Week* magazine. A member of the Drama Desk and Outer Critics Circle, he writes regularly on theater for *In Theater* and *Stagebill* magazines, as well as *The New York Times'* New York Today Website. He was a theater critic for *Stages* magazine and a film critic for *County Lines* magazine.

Catherine L. Preston is Assistant Professor in the Department of Theater and Film at the University of Kansas. She teaches introductory courses in film and visual studies, contemporary film theory, and ethnicity and gender in visual culture. Her research focuses on the intersection of class, race, gender, and sexuality in the reception of film, television, and other visual media.

Stephen Prince is Associate Professor of Communication Studies at Virginia Tech. His books include *Savage Cinema: Sam Peckinpah and the Rise of Ultraviolent Movies* and *Movies and Meaning: An Introduction to Film.*

Mark A. Reid is Professor of English and African Diasporic Studies at the University of Florida, Gainesville. He is the author of *Redefining Black Film* (University of California Press, 1993) and *PostNegritude Visual and Literary Culture* (SUNY, 1997), editor of *Spike Lee's Do the Right Thing* (Cambridge University Press, 1997) and coeditor of Le Cinema Noir Americain (CinemAction, 1988).

David Sanjek (Ph.D. Washington Univ. 1985) is the Director of the BMI Archives; his essays on numerous cinema topics have appeared in *Cinema Journal, Cinéaste, Spectator, Post Script, Literature/Film Quarterly,* and *Film Criticism.*

John C. Tibbetts is an Assistant Professor of Theater and Film at the University of Kansas. His latest books are *The Encyclopedia of Novels into Film* (coedited with James M. Welsh, 1998) and *Dvorak in America* (1993).

James M. Welsh is perhaps best known as the founding editor of *Literature/Film Quarterly* and the founding president of the Literature/Film Association. His most recent books are *The Encyclopedia of Novels into Film* (1998) and *The Cinema of Tony Richardson: Essays and Interviews* (1999), both coedited with John C. Tibbetts. His essays have appeared in *Sight & Sound, Film Comment, American Film, Films in Review, The Historical Journal of Film, Radio and Television.*

Ron Wilson is a lecturer in the Department of Theatre and Film at the University of Kansas.

INDEX